KENT

COUNTY CRICKET CLUB

Classics

KENT

COUNTY CRICKET CLUB

DAVID ROBERTSON, HOWARD MILTON
& DEREK CARLAW

TEMPUS

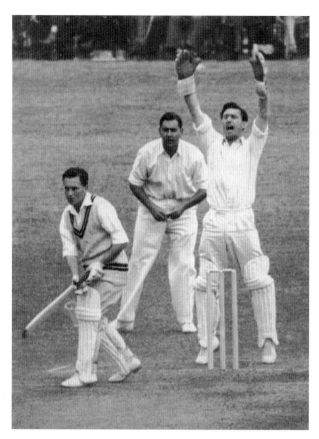

Front Cover:
Kent *v.* Hampshire at Canterbury, 1996. Dean Headley is joined by David Fulton and Martin McCague to celebrate his third hat-trick of the season. [Anthony Roberts]

Back Cover:
St Lawrence Cricket Ground, Canterbury – scene of many memorable matches since 1847. The famous tree blew down in a gale in January 2005.

Frontispiece:
Colin Cowdrey leaves the field at Maidstone in 1973 immediately after reaching his hundredth hundred.

Left:
Derek Ufton (on the right, in action with Colin Cowdrey), Kent 1949-1962, president of Kent County Cricket Club 2001-2002.

First published 2006

Tempus Publishing Limited
The Mill, Brimscombe Port,
Stroud, Gloucestershire, GL5 2QG
www.tempus-publishing.com

British Library Cataloguing in Publication Data.
A catalogue record for this book is available from the British Library.

ISBN 0 7524 3785 2

Typesetting and origination by Tempus Publishing Limited.
Printed in Great Britain.

FOREWORD

BY DEREK UFTON

In the sixty years since the end of the Second World War the game of cricket has suffered somewhat with the pace of present-day living and the accusation of lack of excitement.

Hopefully the 2005 Ashes series will have dispelled these misguided thoughts, for nothing could have been more compelling and exciting than those five tense, closely fought Test matches between England and Australia.

What better time, then, for these three Gentlemen of Kent to take us back through time, remind us of our heritage and treat us to the delights of over 160 years of Kent cricket?

Just reading through the titles of their fifty classic matches will have your nerve ends tingling in anticipation and you will not be disappointed. The great names of the past are there on every page and not only will the memories of these players come flooding back but the very mention of our out grounds of long ago will conjure up the happy days that we who have supported Kent cricket through the years will recall with joy.

May I, on behalf of all lovers of Kent cricket, thank David Robertson, Howard Milton and Derek Carlaw for this, their own classic, for their hard work and dedication that has produced a gem of a book that will give us much happiness and that, I am sure, will have us all deliberating on our own choice of Kent's fifty classic matches.

ACKNOWLEDGEMENTS

A number of individuals have helped us in the preparation and production of this book. Notably we would like to thank Derek Ufton, for so long associated with Kent as a player, administrator and president, for kindly agreeing to write the foreword. We are similarly grateful to Tempus Publishing for their guidance. Access to the Kent County Cricket Club archives in respect of the photographs, scorebooks and other items was of critical importance. Our thanks to the club in this regard. The numerous authors whose books were consulted are acknowledged in the bibliography, while Kent references on the Cricket Archive website were extensively used. Photographs are an important feature of this book and we thank John Turner and Anthony Roberts for the use of some of their excellent work and to David Frith and the *Gloucestershire Echo* for the items in their collections. If we have inadvertently used any copyright material we apologise unreservedly.

PREFACE

If a dozen cricket enthusiasts were chosen at random and asked to define a 'classic' cricket match – or even a 'memorable' one – the probability is that there would be a dozen different answers. With this in mind, when we came to select our fifty matches for this book we concluded that choice was essentially subjective and there would be little point in our attempting to justify or explain at length. With over 3,000 first-class games to choose from it would be a minor miracle if anyone agreed with all, or even most, of our chosen matches.

Naturally, many of the games featured are those in which the result was in doubt until the last over, or even last ball. Because nail-biting finishes are relatively commonplace in limited-overs games we decided to confine our selections to first-class cricket to avoid the risk of overkill. A match can, however, be a 'classic' even where the likely result has been obvious after the first day; 'Laker's Match' in 1956 is a perfect example. Several such are among our selections.

Contests in which David slays Goliath will be among many people's favourites. We have included matches in which a Kentish David has triumphed over a Yorkshire or Surrey Goliath but one-sided encounters can also be memorable and we have chosen one in which a Goliath with a white horse on his cap trampled all over an unfortunate Northamptonshire David.

Cricket is of course a team game but virtually all of our choices feature outstanding individual performances with bat and/or ball. At least two of us might fairly be described as fanatical supporters of Kent cricket but, with what we hope friends and acquaintances will consider admirable impartiality, we have included matches, admittedly not many, in which the star performer was playing for the opposition. In a small number of instances, a brilliant innings or spell of bowling has not led ultimately to what is now called a 'positive result' but here we have taken the view, often after some argument, that the performance has of itself made the game a classic.

For obvious reasons, for matches prior to 1946 we have had to rely on contemporary writings. Fortunately, so much has been written about cricket that, even in the case of matches played more than 150 years ago, it is possible – with a bit of research – to build up a reasonably accurate picture of events. Since 1946, it is disconcertingly indicative of advancing years to find that at least one of us was present on at least one day or at worst knows somebody who was.

For at least some of our readers, this book will, we hope, revive happy memories of the recent past as well as helping to preserve the memory of great players of earlier days.

BIBLIOGRAPHY

Among numerous sources of information, the following publications were of particular value:

C.W. Alcock, *Famous Cricketers and Cricket Grounds*, 1895.
Leslie Ames, *Close of Play*, 1953.
Anon., *The Doings of the Fourth Australian Team in England*, 1884.
John Arlott (ed.), *The Middle Ages of Cricket*, 1949.
R.L. Arrowsmith, *Kent: A History of County Cricket*. 1971.
Philip Bailey & others, *Who's Who of Cricketers*, Second Edition, 1994.
Peter Barnsley, *The Tenth Wicket Record*, 1987.
Brian Bearshaw, *From the Stretford End: The Official History of Lancashire County Cricket Club*, 1990.
W. Methven Brownlee, *W.G. Grace*, 1887.
Neville Cardus, *The Summer Game*, 1929.
James D. Coldham, *Lord Harris*, 1983.
James D. Coldham, *Northamptonshire Cricket: A History*, 1959.
Matthew Engel & Andrew Radd, *The History of Northamptonshire County Cricket*, 1992.
John Evans & others, *Images of Kent Cricket: The County Club in the Twentieth Century*, 2000.
David Frith, *The Golden Age of Cricket 1890-1914*, 1978.
C.B. Fry, *The Book of Cricket: A Gallery of Famous Players*, 1899.
Alfred Gover, *The Long Run: An Autobiography*, 1991.
W.G. Grace, *Cricket*, 1891.
Lord Harris, *A Few Short Runs*, 1921.
Lord Harris & F.S. Ashley-Cooper, *Kent Cricket Matches 1719-1880*, 1929.
Lord Harris & others, *The History of Kent County Cricket Club* (with appendices A-D) 1907, Appendices E-J, 1907-2003.
J.W. 'Jack' Hearne, *Wheelwrights to Wickets: The Story of the Cricketing Hearnes*, 1996.
Alan Hill, *Les Ames*, 1990.
Errol Holmes, *Flannelled Foolishness: A Cricketing Chronicle*, 1957.
David Lemmon, *Percy Chapman: A Biography*, 1985.
David Lemmon, *Essex County Cricket Club: The Official History*, 1988.
David Lemmon, *'Tich' Freeman and the Decline of the Leg-break Bowler*, 1982.
David Lemmon, *The History of Surrey County Cricket Club*, 1989.
David Lemmon, *The History of Worcestershire County Cricket Club*, 1989.
Howard Milton, *Cricket Grounds of Kent*, 1992.
Howard Milton, *Kent Cricketers 1834-1983*, 1984.
Howard Milton, *Kent Cricket Records 1815-1993*, 1994.
Patrick Morrah, *Alfred Mynn and the Cricketers of his Time*, 1963.
Grahame Parker, *Gloucestershire Road*, 1983.
Ian Peebles, *Straight from the Shoulder: Throwing – its History and the Cure*, 1968.
Ian Peebles, *Woolley: The Pride of Kent*, 1969.
Clive Porter, *Kent Cricket Champions 1906*, 2000.
David Robertson & others, *Kent County Cricket Club: 100 Greats*, 2005.
Christopher Scoble, *Colin Blythe: Lament for a Legend*, 2005.
Peter Sharpham, *The 1899 Australians in England*, 1997.

Grenville Simons, *Lillywhite's Legacy: A History of the Cheltenham Festival*, 2004.
John Wallace, *Sussex County Cricket Club: Fifty of the Finest Matches*, 2003.
Richard Walsh, *All Over in a Day*, 1993.
J.R. Webster, *The Chronicle of WG*, 1998.
E.M. Wellings, *Vintage Cricketers*, 1983.
Frank Woolley, *The King of Games*, 1936.
R.E.S. Wyatt. *Three Straight Sticks*, 1951.

Relevant issues of the following annuals, periodicals, newspapers and other continuing works were also of value: *Association of Cricket Statisticians and Historians Important/First-Class Cricket Matches*; *Bell's Life*; *Cricket: a Weekly Record of the Game*; *The Cricketer [International]*; *The Cricket Field*; *Cricket Scores and Biographies of Celebrated Cricketers*; *The Daily Telegraph*; *The Guardian*; *James Lillywhite's Cricketers' Annual*; *Kent County Cricket Club 'Blue Book'/Annual/Yearbook*; *Kent Messenger*; *Kentish Gazette*; *The Times*; *Wisden Cricketers' Almanack*.

STATISTICAL NOTES

Throughout the text of this publication * indicates not out or unfinished partnership.

In the scorecards the following apply:
* = Captain
† = Wicketkeeper
Second innings batting order is indicated when different from the first innings by the figures in brackets.
Unless stated in the bowling analysis, the overs in the matches concerned consisted of 6 balls.

THE 50 CLASSIC MATCHES

1839	v. England	Town Malling (West Malling)
1847	v. England	Canterbury
1876	v. MCC	Canterbury
1883	v. Lancashire	Old Trafford, Manchester
1884	v. Australians	Canterbury
1888	v. Sussex	Tonbridge
1889	v. Nottinghamshire	Foxgrove Road, Beckenham
1895	v. Gloucestershire	Gravesend
1899	v. Australians	Canterbury
1899	v. Yorkshire	Tonbridge
1906	v. Lancashire	Canterbury

1907	*v.* Northamptonshire	Northampton
1909	*v.* Worcestershire	Stourbridge
1910	*v.* Gloucestershire	College Ground, Cheltenham
1911	*v.* Surrey	The Oval
1913	*v.* Warwickshire	Tonbridge
1922	*v.* Nottinghamshire	Dover
1922	*v.* Sussex	Hove
1926	*v.* Lancashire	Dover
1927	*v.* Lancashire	Maidstone
1932	*v.* Warwickshire	Folkestone
1933	*v.* Yorkshire	Dover
1934	*v.* Essex	Brentwood
1934	*v.* Surrey	Blackheath
1935	*v.* Surrey	The Oval
1937	*v.* Gloucestershire	Dover
1938	*v.* Essex	Castle Park, Colchester
1946	*v.* Hampshire	Canterbury
1947	*v.* Middlesex	Lord's
1950	*v.* Middlesex	Canterbury
1955	*v.* Surrey	The Oval
1960	*v.* Worcestershire	Tunbridge Wells
1964	*v.* Yorkshire	Bradford
1967	*v.* Yorkshire	Canterbury
1970	*v.* Nottinghamshire	Folkestone
1973	*v.* Surrey	Maidstone
1975	*v.* Australians	Canterbury
1977	*v.* Warwickshire	Edgbaston, Birmingham
1978	*v.* Middlesex	Canterbury
1984	*v.* Sussex	Hastings
1987	*v.* Middlesex	Lord's
1991	*v.* Middlesex	Canterbury
1993	*v.* Glamorgan	Canterbury
1995	*v.* Glamorgan	Tunbridge Wells
1996	*v.* Somerset	Canterbury
1996	*v.* Hampshire	Canterbury
2001	*v.* Leicestershire	Grace Road, Leicester
2003	*v.* Nottinghamshire	Maidstone
2004	*v.* Worcestershire	Canterbury
2005	*v.* Surrey	Guildford

KENT v. ENGLAND

Date: 19-21 August 1839   **Location:** Town Malling (West Malling)

By the time Queen Victoria had settled on her throne, Kent, with their 'five mighty cricketers' Felix, Wenman, Hillyer, Fuller Pilch and Alfred Mynn, were the dominant force in English cricket and would remain so for more than a decade. In 1836 Thomas Selby, a prominent citizen of Town Malling, who had been largely instrumental in persuading Pilch to settle in the town, was also the driving force behind the formation of a Kent County Cricket Club. Short lived and in no way representative, this was arguably the first properly constituted Kent CCC. Presumably as part of the deal with Pilch, a Kent v. England match was staged for his benefit, the beginning of a series of matches that would last – although not at Town Malling – for ten years.

The Town Malling ground covered only 3 acres (1.2 hectares), which, when filled with the carriages of the upper classes and the farm wagons and hop carts of lesser humanity, brought problems with crowd control. With sublime disregard for the welfare of their paying customers, the management revived an eighteenth-century practice by employing a man with a whip as 'ring keeper'.

In contrast with some of the later England sides, England at Town Malling was fully representative. If there was no all-rounder in the class of Kent's mighty Alfred Mynn, Charles Taylor was the best amateur batsman in England and Edward Grimston was not far behind him, while Nottinghamshire's Joe Guy was probably second only to Pilch among the professionals. Lillywhite was acknowledged as the finest bowler in the country and it was a moot point whether Mynn or Sam Redgate was the most feared among fast bowlers. As wicketkeeper, Tom Box was the only rival to Kent's Ned Wenman.

England were 'managed' by the autocratic Lord Frederick Beauclerk. In his day Beauclerk was the country's finest all-rounder but as manager he was a pest. When Kent batted he frequently went on the field to speak to the bowlers and dictated most of the bowling changes. Kent too had a handicap; they were without Felix (aka Nicholas Wanostrocht).

When rain ended play on the first day Kent were 55 for 4. Next morning Pilch and Wenman produced the best batting of the match, Wenman playing almost exclusively off the back foot while Pilch indulged in his favourite front-foot drives, colloquially known as 'Pilch's pokes'. The *Maidstone Journal* enthused,

'Whether the balls came fast or slow, creeping grounders or regular flings, Pilch and Wenman knew exactly how to take them.' Kent had no tail. For reasons that have not survived, Tom Adams, who usually opened for Kent, batted number eleven but once Pilch was caught at 110 the remaining 5 wickets managed only another 35.

At stumps England were 114 for 5, a total due almost entirely to a partnership between Guy and Grimston. Against the pace of Mynn, digging the ball in from round the wicket and slanting the ball across the batsman, backed by the accurate medium pace of 'Topper' Hillyer, the rest struggled. Three of Mynn's victims were caught at slip; three behind the wicket.

Kent fared no better. After Stearman and Clifford had added 30, a collapse began when Redgate replaced Cobbett. In one of the most famous overs in cricket's history, the first ball bowled Stearman, whereupon the bowler drank a glass of his favourite tipple, brandy. His second ball removed Mynn's off bail. This called for another brandy. The third ball narrowly missed Pilch's off stump, the fourth demolished the wicket and Redgate demolished another brandy. Lillywhite joined in to get Clifford

Tall, strong and trained on beef and beer, Alfred Mynn was a formidable fast bowler on the rough wickets of his day.

Kent won the toss and elected to bat Umpires: J. Bayley and B. Good

KENT	1ST INNINGS		2ND INNINGS	
W.R. Hillyer	st Box b Lillywhite	9	(9) b Lillywhite	0
W. Stearman	c Guy b Lillywhite	12	(1) b Redgate	15
W.P. Mynn	c Cobbett b Lillywhite	10	(8) c & b Lillywhite	1
A. Mynn	b Lillywhite	11	(3) b Redgate	0
F. Pilch	c Ponsonby b Lillywhite	35	(4) b Redgate	0
*†E.G. Wenman	c Box b Lillywhite	37	(5) b Lillywhite	8
C.G. Whittaker	b Cobbett	1	(11) not out	0
R. Mills	c Box b Cobbett	9	(6) b Lillywhite	12
W. Dorrinton	b Lillywhite	0	(10) b Redgate	0
W. Clifford	not out	0	(2) lbw b Lillywhite	18
T.M. Adams	c & b Cobbett	10	(7) b Redgate	6
Extras	(B 3, NB 4, W 4)	11	(B 2, W 2)	4
TOTAL	(all out)	145	(all out)	64

FOW: 1-?, 2-?, 3-?, 4-?, 5-110, 6-?, 7-?, 8-?, 9-?   1-30, 2-30, 3-30, 4-?, 5-?,6-?, 7-?, 8-?, 9-?

Bowling (4 balls per over)

	O	M	R	W
Lillywhite	44	20	57	7
Cobbett	28.2	12	50	3
Redgate	19	8	24	0
Taylor	2	0	9	0
Garrat	2	0	5	0

	O	M	R	W
Lillywhite	21	11	33	5
Cobbett	5	1	9	0
Redgate	15.2	6	22	5

ENGLAND	1ST INNINGS		2ND INNINGS	
W. Garrat	b A. Mynn	5	(3) c Dorrinton b Hillyer	3
J. Guy	c Wenman b A. Mynn	30	(4) run out	10
Hon. E.H. Grimston	c Wenman b A. Mynn	46	(7) c Wenman b Hillyer	0
T. Sewell	c Hillyer b A. Mynn	4	(5) b A. Mynn	1
J. Cobbett	c Hillyer b A. Mynn	10	(8) b A. Mynn	5
G. Jarvis	b Hillyer	9	(10) b A. Mynn	7
†T. Box	c Wenman b Hillyer	3	(2) c Stearman b Hillyer	12
C.G. Taylor	c Hillyer b A. Mynn	1	(1) b Hillyer	3
Hon. F.G.B. Ponsonby	run out	1	(6) run out	2
S. Redgate	b A. Mynn	5	(9) not out	20
F.W. Lillywhite	not out	0	b Hillyer	0
Extras	(B 12, W 4)	16	(B 12, W 2)	14
TOTAL	(all out)	130	(all out)	77

FOW: 1-?, 2-?, 3-?, 4-111, 5-?, 6-?, 7-?, 8-?, 9-?   1-?, 2-8. 3-28, 4-34, 5-?, 6-?, 7-38, 8-?, 9-76

Bowling (4 balls per over)

	O	M	R	W
A. Mynn	36.3	16	50	7
Hillyer	18	6	30	2
Whittaker	7	3	12	0
Mills	8	0	17	0
Adams	19	10	21	0

	O	M	R	W
A. Mynn	27	11	37	3
Hillyer	26.2	9	40	5

Kent won by 2 runs

lbw and, although Kent managed to prolong the innings, only Richard Mills achieved double figures. Redgate and Lillywhite shared the wickets. Whether Redgate took another two brandies history does not say.

Needing only 80, England were immediately in trouble against Mynn and Hillyer. Of the recognized batsmen only Box and Guy reached double figures and it was not until Redgate came in at 38 for 7 that an England win looked a possibility. He hit 5 threes and lifted a ball over the scorer's booth for four, but Mynn bowled Cobbett and Jarvis and the score was 76 for 9 when Lillywhite came to the wicket. An enthusiast offered Hillyer £5 if he took a wicket in his next over. Redgate took a single from the first ball. The second narrowly missed Lillywhite's wicket; the third bowled him to give Kent a 2-run victory.

With odds fluctuating one punter reputedly lost £1,500. Pilch had a good benefit but with timing calculated to delight the most unscrupulous modern agent, he revealed he had received an offer from Sussex too good to refuse. Wealthy Kent supporters dug deep and he stayed.

Sadly, 1839 was the high point of Sam Redgate's career. He had given up cricket by 1846 and died in 1851. People blamed the foreign brandy. Mynn was three years older and a lot heavier but he trained on English beef and beer and played until 1859.

KENT v. ENGLAND

Date: 2-4 August 1847 **Location:** Canterbury

Kent had played England in the opening game of the first Canterbury Cricket Week in 1842 on the now-vanished Beverley Ground in Sturry Road. Now England again provided the opposition for the inaugural match at St Lawrence. The Beverley Club had moved there earlier in the year, taking groundsman/manager Fuller Pilch with them. Kent had already beaten England twice at Lord's that season, leaving the overall record since 1834 standing at 14 wins to Kent, 12 to England with 1 draw.

The week was becoming a highlight of the sporting calendar, although this year there was the distraction of a General Election. The *Kentish Gazette* dwelt on 'Kent's famed beauties promenading or reclining in their carriages – the moustached militaire, the commanding figures and noble mien of the representatives of Kent's ancient houses' contrasted with 'the honest bluff countenances of the more staidly attired yeoman'. But seemingly not all men of Kent (or possibly Kentish men) approved. *The Times* noted that, although 'many visitors from distant counties and likewise from London', were present 'it was the subject of almost general comment that scarcely a family or resident of the city "graced" the ground with their presence.'

The St Lawrence ground was different in 1847. The playing area was smaller with no permanent buildings and a ditch running across part of it. Interestingly, if there was a tree within the playing area, nobody seems to have mentioned it. In other respects the scene was much the same. Corporate hospitality was unknown but, to quote the *Kentish Gazette* again, there were 'Marquees and pavilions, and refreshment booths erected in different parts of the ground, forming a ring fence, the Union Jack and the Royal Standard gaily floating in the breeze'.

England began with few indications of impending collapse. Jemmy Dean played steadily as was usual and William Nicholson scored five with a 'glorious hit round to long leg' but once the opening pair were parted the innings subsided apart from stubborn resistance by William Clarke, better known as cricket's first great entrepreneur and chief surviving exponent of underarm bowling. The damage was done not by

the still potent pace of Alfred Mynn but by the more subtle skills of 'Topper' Hillyer. With his arm usually below the statutory shoulder level, he bowled accurate medium pace with a deceptive flight, always liable to persuade batsmen to play forward to balls shorter than they looked. Four batsmen fell to catches by the predatory Felix at point; Kynaston was caught and bowled. For good measure 'Topper' added a blinding catch at slip to dispose of Johnny Wisden.

Adams and William Mynn, Alfred's nephew, gave Kent a sound start against a formidable England attack and when Adams was dismissed on 32, Lyttelton Bayley, younger brother of the better-known Emilius, contributed 18 in 'excellent and free style'. By the time these two and Martingell had succumbed to the wiles of Lillywhite and Clarke, Kent were already in the lead and with Fuller Pilch and Felix now together, the game swung towards the home side. Both gave chances but, in what *The Times* called 'a beautiful illustration of the science of cricket' they added 75 before both falling at the same total. Kent were 157 for 6 when stumps were drawn at 7.30 p.m.

With his accuracy and deceptive flight, 'Topper' Hillyer was the perfect foil to Mynn's intimidating pace.

England won the toss and elected to bat   Umpires: J. Bayley and W. Caldecourt

ENGLAND	1ST INNINGS		2ND INNINGS	
W. Nicholson	c Felix b Hillyer	11	c Felix b Mynn	21
J. Dean	c Felix b Hillyer	13	(10) b Hillyer	4
†T. Box	b Hillyer	0	c Felix b Adams	19
J. Guy	c Felix b Hillyer	1	b Martingell	17
G. Parr	b Mynn	9	c Martingell b Hillyer	16
T. Sewell	st Dorrinton b Hillyer	0	(7) run out	0
W. Clarke	not out	20	(2) c Fagge b Hillyer	16
H.W. Fellows	b Mynn	2	(9) c Felix b Mynn	5
R. Kynaston	c & b Hillyer	0	(6) b Hillyer	39
J. Wisden	c Hillyer b Mynn	1	(8) st Dorrinton b Hillyer	8
F.W. Lillywhite	c Felix b Hillyer	3	not out	1
Extras	(B 3, W 4)	7	(B 5, W 3)	8
TOTAL	(all out)	67	(all out)	154

FOW: 1-23, 2-23, 3-28, 4-31, 5-37, 6-37, 7-40, 8-44, 9-?   1-43, 2-43, 3-73, 4-94, 5-114, 6-124, 7-140, 8-145, 9-149

Bowling (4 balls per over)

	O	M	R	W
Mynn	22	?	?	3
Hillyer	21.3	?	?	7

	O	M	R	W
Mynn	29	?	?	2
Hillyer	36.2	?	?	5
Martingell	13	?	?	1
Adams	5	?	?	1

KENT	1ST INNINGS		2ND INNINGS	
T.M. Adams	c Wisden b Lillywhite	19	b Lillywhite	11
W. Pilch	b Lillywhite	22	b Lillywhite	2
L.H. Bayley	b Clarke	18	(9) not out	0
W. Martingell	c Sewell b Clarke	7	(3) b Wisden	11
F. Pilch	c Dean b Lillywhite	40	b Lillywhite	1
N. Felix	b Wisden	24	(7) c & b Wisden	0
A. Mynn	not out	12	(8) not out	16
†W. Dorrinton	b Lillywhite	11	(6) c & b Wisden	0
E. Martin	b Wisden	1	(4) c Dean b Wisden	11
J.F. Fagge	b Wisden	0		
W.R. Hillyer	b Wisden	4		
Extras	(B 6, W 7)	13	(B 1)	1
TOTAL	(all out)	171	(for 7 wickets)	53

FOW: 1-32, 2-46, 3-60, 4-68, 5-143, 6-143, 7-166, 8-167, 9-167   1-?, 2-16, 3-?, 4-30, 5-30, 6-30, 7-41

Bowling (4 balls per over)

	O	M	R	W
Lillywhite	37	?	?	4
Wisden	13	?	?	4
Clarke	19	?	?	2
Dean	6	?	?	0
Fellows	7	?	?	0

	O	M	R	W
Lillywhite	15	?	?	3
Wisden	12	?	?	4
Clarke	2	?	?	0

Kent won by 3 wickets

Next morning Wisden's fast bowling cleaned up the tail, leaving Mynn stranded without a partner. England devoted the rest of the day to compiling 154. Nicholson and Clarke gave their side encouragement with an opening stand of 43 but both were dismissed at the same total and, although Box, Guy and Parr all got started, none managed to reach twenty. Tom Sewell, often good for runs in a crisis, was run out before he had scored.

Within a few years George Parr would be the most famous batsman in the country but at the time he might fairly be described as Hillyer's 'rabbit'. At this stage of his career he had played 33 innings in first-class cricket and Hillyer had claimed his wicket 15 times. Top scorer for England was Roger Kynaston, subsequently secretary of the MCC. A batsman of unusual technique, he stood with his legs 'as far away from the wicket as possible'. Hillyer finished with 12 wickets in the match and Felix held three more catches at point to bring his total in the match to seven.

Facing a modest target of 51, Kent had to fight hard on the last day on a worn wicket against the tight control and infinite variations of Lillywhite and the pace of the 5ft 4½in Wisden. There were signs of panic, the fourth, fifth and six wickets falling for no runs, but a few stout blows from the mighty Mynn secured a hat-trick of wins against England, an outcome only slightly marred by defeat for the Gentlemen of Kent at the hands of the Gentlemen of England in the second game of the week.

KENT v. MCC

Date: 10-12 August 1876   **Location:** Canterbury

The second match of the 1876 Canterbury Week began on Thursday, Ladies Day, under a hot sun 'tempered by a westerly breeze' with a crowd estimated by the *Kentish Herald* at 7,000. *The Sportsman* referred to spectators 'six and seven deep' 'on the upper side of the ground under the famous tree'. The first game of the week, Kent and Gloucestershire v. England, had produced 1,132 runs (W.G. Grace 9 and 91) for the loss of only 33 wickets and with Grace appearing again in ideal batting conditions, another run feast was likely. Nobody, however, could have expected what followed. MCC were all amateurs; Kent played only two professionals, George Hearne and wicketkeeper Edward Henty.

Kent won the toss and began at noon against a moderate MCC attack. Grace had taken 98 wickets in the season but of the rest only Cottrell and Lucas had bowled in a first-class match that year and could claim only 1 wicket between them. Kent were in control from the first over and at the close were 453 for 10 (Hearne 51*), the innings dominated by their captain Lord Harris. Seventh out for 154 including 24 fours, *Bell's Life* called it 'a brilliant display' during which he cut W.G. 'time and again.' In the course of his fourth-wicket partnership of 118 with Bill Yardley the ball was, according to the local press, hit 'over the tent, into the cornfield and over the boundary lines'. Widely considered second only to W.G. as the best batsman in England, Yardley frequently backed himself for half a crown to outscore the champion and, judged purely on the first innings, on this occasion he won. In rather less festive mode than the amateurs, the twenty-year-old Hearne, in registering his first fifty for the county, was at the wicket while 169 runs were scored.

On Friday morning the Kent innings lasted only another 7 overs and the MCC commenced batting at 12.25 p.m. On a placid wicket with a lightning-fast outfield, Grace was well caught by Hearne at mid-on from the quick left-arm Henry Thomson, playing his first game for Kent, and only Leonard Howell, whose chief claim to fame was as an FA Cup winner with the Wanderers, settled in. By 4.55 p.m. the MCC were following on. The main damage was done by James Fellowes, a Captain in the Royal Engineers (right-arm fast), and Hearne (left-arm fast-medium).

In his *Cricket*, Grace – or more precisely his ghost – writes, 'Everyone believed the match was now a hopeless thing for the old club and I was extremely anxious to get off that night so that I might reach

Clifton next day and have a quiet Sunday's rest before meeting Nottinghamshire on the Monday. It was no use playing carefully so I made up my mind to hit.' With some effect. When stumps were drawn at 6.45 p.m. he was 133*, his fifth century of the season, scored in 110 minutes in what *The Daily Telegraph* thought 'the most astonishing free and brilliant hitting ever seen'. One hundred of his runs came in fours, at least three of which would have been sixes under present laws.

Next day Grace, possibly still thinking about railway timetables, at first appeared 'nervous and fidgety', a mood not aided by a broken bat and a replacement 'too small for his hands' until rectified by improvisation using an old glove bound with twine. Although less inclined to extravagant risk, Grace was quickly back to normal and at lunch, taken at 2 p.m., the score was 364 for 4 (Grace 225*). He was now nearing his personal highest, 268 at The Oval in 1871, as well as the then highest in first-class cricket, William Ward's 278 in 1820. Just before 4 p.m. Percy Crutchley was caught having contributed 84 to a

Aged twenty-eight, W.G. was at his peak. Following his record-breaking 344 at Canterbury his next two innings were 177 v. Nottinghamshire at Clifton and 318* v. Yorkshire at Cheltenham.

Kent won the toss and elected to bat   Umpires: T. Hearne and E. Willsher (Twelve a side)

KENT	1ST INNINGS	
V.K. Shaw	b Clarke	17
C.A. Absolom	b Grace	10
W.B. Pattisson	c & b Clarke	20
W. Yardley	b Meares	47
*Lord Harris	c Meares b Crutchley	154
F. Penn	run out	0
F.A. Mackinnon	c & b Grace	23
G.G. Hearne	not out	57
H.S. Thomson	c Clarke b Grace	27
W. Foord-Kelcey	b Grace	31
J. Fellowes	c Hone-Goldney b Crutchley	32
†E. Henty	b Meares	19
Extras	(B 28, LB 4, W 4)	36
TOTAL	(all out)	473

FOW: 1-10, 2-41, 3-59, 4-177, 5-183, 6-256, 7-304, 8-357, 9-399, 10-436

Bowling (4 balls per over)

	O	M	R	W
Grace	77	32	116	4
Meares	32.2	9	85	2
Clarke	20	8	50	2
Cottrell	19	4	49	0
Lucas	6	0	19	0
Hone-Goldney	9	1	30	0
Tennant	6	2	20	0
Crutchley	24	6	68	2
Bird	2	2	0	0

MCC	1ST INNINGS		2ND INNINGS	
W.G. Grace	c Hearne b Thomson	17	(2) c Shaw b Harris	344
A.P. Lucas	b Absolom	0	(1) c Thomson b Hearne	7
†G. Bird	c Henty b Fellowes	4	b Foord-Kelcey	13
J. Turner	c Absolom b Fellowes	15	(7) b Harris	15
C.F.C. Clarke	c Absolom b Fellowes	19	(8) c Hearne b Harris	12
L.S. Howell	b Foord-Kelcey	34	(5) c Shaw b Thomson	30
C.E. Cottrell	b Fellowes	17	(9) c Thomson b Harris	10
W.H. Hay	b Hearne	12		
G.H. Hone-Goldney	b Fellowes	0	(10) not out	0
G.B. Meares	c & b Hearne	14	(11) not out	0
H.N. Tennant	st Henty b Hearne	3	(4) c Penn b Absolom	12
P.E. Crutchley	not out	0	(6) c Pattisson b Absolom	84
Extras	(B 3, LB 1, W 5)	9	(B 14, LB 11, W 5)	30
TOTAL	(all out)	144	(for 9 wickets)	557

FOW: 1-3, 2-17, 3-32, 4-59, 5-66, 6-112, 7-117, 8-117, 9-138, 10-141 1-7, 2-59, 3-125, 4-203, 5-430, 6-506, 7-547, 8-552, 9-557

Bowling (4 balls per over)

	O	M	R	W
Absolom	32	15	43	1
Thomson	7	3	14	1
Fellowes	41	22	49	5
Foord-Kelcey	17	9	24	1
Hearne	4.1	4	0	3
Penn	4	2	5	0

	O	M	R	W
Absolom	39	12	105	2
Hearne	35	9	91	1
Foord-Kelcey	40	11	84	1
Fellowes	28	6	63	0
Harris	19	6	59	4
Thomson	20	5	52	1
Shaw	4	2	14	0
Penn	7	0	25	0
Yardley	8	0	27	0
Henty	2	0	7	0

Match Drawn

partnership of 227 in a little under 195 minutes and at 4.20 p.m. Grace took his score to 279. Play was here interrupted for 'champagne and seltzer from the officers' tent'.

Suitably fortified, Grace continued to punish tired bowling, pressing on past the landmark 300 until at 5.35 p.m. and 546 for 7 he was caught low down at mid-off, at which the successful bowler gave an undignified but wholly understandable leap for joy. He batted for six hours twenty minutes and hit 51 fours. In the words of *The Times*, 'Never was a more striking exhibition of endurance against exhaustion manifested.' Kent used ten bowlers including wicketkeeper Henty. In a sense they used eleven as the ambidextrous Yardley bowled left-arm until Grace hit him into the adjacent cornfield when he switched to his right.

At Clifton two days later on 14 August Grace hit 177 against Nottinghamshire and on 17-18 August made 318* against Yorkshire at Cheltenham. His 344 remained the highest in first-class cricket until 1895.

KENT v. LANCASHIRE

Date: 4-6 June 1883   **Location:** Old Trafford, Manchester

Throughout his life Lord Harris was at the forefront of moves to eliminate throwing from the game. When, in 1864, bowlers were officially permitted to raise their arms above the shoulder, the change not only gave them greater freedom, it also spawned a rash of suspect actions. When the Australians arrived in 1878 they found half a dozen or more they thought doubtful. Many in England shared their views, Lord Harris prominent among them and, with umpires unwilling to act, rumblings of discontent continued through the early 1880s.

To many the biggest offender was Lancashire's Nottinghamshire-born fast bowler Jack Crossland. The most successful pace bowler in England, he seems to have been capable of bowling fairly but his extra fast ball was judged by many – even by some Lancastrians – a blatant throw. According to some accounts, he tended to use it sparingly if he thought he was being closely watched – at Lord's for example. At the time spotting a throw was the responsibility of the umpire at the bowler's end and it was alleged that, when about to bowl his faster ball, Crossland sometimes deliberately overstepped the crease on the preceding ball in order to divert the umpire's attention from the next. His action had generated considerable ill feeling. In 1882 it was reported that the Australian tourists intended to object if he was picked for England and when he took 11 for 79 against Surrey at The Oval there were 'groans and hisses from all parts of the ground' accompanied by cries of 'well thrown' and 'take him off.' Lancashire had two other bowlers with doubtful actions, Alec Watson (off-spin) and George Nash (slow left-arm) and Middlesex declined to play them at all in 1883. Lord Harris's views were common knowledge and, as he was also one of the best batsmen in England against fast bowling, large crowds flocked to Old Trafford for his confrontation with Crossland.

Opening the innings, Harris batted, according to *Wisden*, in 'brilliant style', adding 166 for the third wicket with Richard Jones and reaching his highest score of the season before falling to a catch at mid-on. As much at ease with Crossland as with any of the other six bowlers tried, he batted for 205 minutes and hit 15 fours, mainly drives and cuts. Kent continued to progress until the previously innocuous Crossland was reintroduced to the attack. Immediately he bowled Jones, who had scored a career-best 83, and Leslie Wilson without addition to the total and the remaining 5 wickets fell for 25 runs. Crossland had taken 6 wickets at a personal cost of 16. At close of play Lancashire were 30 for 1 (Hornby 25*, Roper 4*).

In 1883 the follow-on was compulsory if the arrears were 80 or more. By close of play on day two Lancashire had duly followed on and were 235 for 9 in their second innings. Their captain 'Monkey' Hornby played superbly – 88 out of 148 in the first innings, 96 out of 169 in the second – but of the rest only Crossland, with vigorous use of the long handle, passed 40 and defeat seemed inevitable. For Kent, Stanley Christopherson, a fast bowler with an impeccable action, took 6 for 39 on debut.

On the final morning Lancashire added only another 3, leaving Kent what seemed a modest target of

136, but by now the pitch was badly worn and Kent disintegrated against Barlow and Watson. There was no need for Crossland's pace. Only the captain and Thornton achieved double figures to give Lancashire an unexpected victory.

The compulsory follow-on had been Kent's downfall but, although the deficit was raised to 120 in 1894, the optional follow-on was not introduced until 1900.

Lancashire in the 1880s. Jack Crossland is second from the left in the back row. Other suspects Nash and Watson are respectively first and fifth in the same row.

Kent won the toss and elected to bat   Umpires: W. Rigley and J. Rowbotham

KENT	1ST INNINGS		2ND INNINGS	
*Lord Harris	c Crossland b Barlow	118	c Pilling b Barlow	19
E. O'Shaughnessy	c Hornby b Barlow	4	st Pilling b Watson	5
G.G. Hearne	c Massey b Nash	26	c Pilling b Barlow	0
R.S. Jones	b Crossland	83	c & b Barlow	2
R.T. Thornton	c & b Watson	24	not out	18
L. Wilson	b Crossland	0	c & b Watson	0
A.C. Gibson	not out	5	(8) c Barlow b Watson	0
S. Christopherson	b Crossland	4	(7) c Steel b Watson	6
J. Wootton	b Crossland	0	b Barlow	0
†J. Pentecost	b Crossland	0	c Crossland b Barlow	0
F. Lipscomb	c Robinson b Crossland	2	c & b Barlow	0
Extras	(B 28, LB 5)	33	(B 10, LB 5)	15
TOTAL	(all out)	309	(all out)	65

FOW: 1-7, 2-65, 3-231, 4-286, 5-286, 6-286, 7-291, 8-293, 9-293   1-13, 2-16, 3-32, 4-43, 5-44, 6-46, 7-62, 8-65, 9-65

Bowling (4 balls per over)

	O	M	R	W
Barlow	64	15	74	2
Crossland	39.2	16	82	6
Watson	58	30	58	1
Nash	23	7	33	1
Briggs	3	0	8	0
Hornby	1	0	6	0
Robinson	5	1	15	0

	O	M	R	W
Barlow	32	17	32	6
Watson	31	22	18	4

LANCASHIRE	1ST INNINGS		2ND INNINGS	
*A.N. Hornby	c Thornton b Christopherson	88	c Harris b Hearne	96
R.G. Barlow	b Lipscomb	6	b Wootton	14
E. Roper	c & b Wootton	22	c Thornton b Lipscomb	23
H.B. Steel	b Wootton	0	b Lipscomb	37
W. Robinson	c O'Shaughnessy b Christopherson	37	c Wootton b Hearne	5
J. Briggs	c Pentecost b Christopherson	15	b Lipscomb	1
W.M. Massey	b Christopherson	5	run out	1
A. Watson	c Hearne b Wootton	3	b Lipscomb	0
J. Crossland	not out	7	c Wootton b Christopherson	43
G. Nash	c Thornton b Christopherson	1	not out	6
†R. Pilling	b Christopherson	10	c Christopherson b Wootton	3
Extras	(B 11, LB 3, W 4)	18	(B 5, LB 1)	6
TOTAL	(all out)	206	(all out)	238

FOW: 1-12, 2-94, 3-104, 4-142, 5-172, 6-183, 7-186, 8-186, 9-198   1-28, 2-82, 3-169. 4-176, 5-177, 6-178, 7-182, 8-186, 9-235

Bowling (4 balls per over)

	O	M	R	W
Lipscomb	19	4	49	1
Hearne	22	10	30	0
Wootton	27	6	50	3
Christopherson	18.1	6	37	6
Harris	5	0	22	0

	O	M	R	W
Lipscomb	28	8	61	4
Hearne	23	10	39	2
Wootton	27.3	8	70	2
Harris	2	0	20	0
Christopherson	20	6	42	1

Lancashire won by 70 runs

This was not the end of the Harris/Crossland saga. In the return at Gravesend, Crossland had the Kent captain caught at cover but only after he had hit 50. In 1884 at Old Trafford Harris was hit repeatedly by Crossland while scoring 53 but the fast bowler did not take his wicket. Harris was invited to play for England at Manchester but Crossland was also in the twelve and he declined. By 1885 Gloucestershire and Nottinghamshire had also refused to play Lancashire but Harris was viewed as the power behind the objections and there were scenes of wild jubilation at Old Trafford when Crossland bowled him third ball for 0. The bowler was successful again in the second innings, albeit less dramatically, via a catch at mid-on when Harris had scored 33. Letters were exchanged between the two clubs and the upshot was that Kent (in effect Lord Harris) declined to play the return at Tonbridge, offering to have wickets pitched to enable Lancashire to claim the match. Eventually an impasse was avoided when Crossland was found to have broken his qualification by living in his native county. Normal relations were resumed in 1886 but controversies over dubious actions have recurred at intervals ever since. Recent recourse to science and technology seems, if anything, to have exacerbated the problem.

KENT v. AUSTRALIANS

Date: 4-6 August 1884   **Location:** Canterbury

The Australians began the first match of Canterbury Week in the aftermath of an unpleasant game at The Oval where the crowd had been irked by the tourists' insistence on taking lunch when within 11 of victory with 9 wickets standing. The visitors were probably glad to get away to the more relaxed ambience of St Lawrence but even so *The Times'* correspondent at Canterbury noted, somewhat ambiguously, that 'No enthusiasm was shown, although spectators were orderly and appreciative.'

In the Kentish camp, Lord Harris's decision to include twenty-one-year-old Alec Hearne, youngest of the three brothers, was not well received. Although successful for the second XI, Hearne had done little in his four first-team appearances and besides, to play unknown pros in Cricket Week was simply not done. The week was still, in the eyes of many, primarily for amateurs. Harris, on the other hand, reasoned, correctly as it proved, that the novelty of Hearne's quickish leg-breaks might puzzle the tourists.

The visitors had the best of the first day, finishing only 33 behind Kent's modest 169 with 6 wickets in hand. After hitting fifty in the first half-hour, Kent found scoring difficult against accurate bowling – Spofforth began with 19 overs for 3 runs and 2 wickets – and their last 5 wickets fell to Palmer and Giffen for 17. For Kent, Mackinnon and George Hearne batted responsibly while future Bishop of Melanesia Cecil Wilson, profiting from a missed return catch to Palmer, played his shots.

Australia began with their two big hitters, George Bonnor and Percy McDonnell. Bonnor fell almost immediately, bowled leg stump by Jim Wootton's arm ball but, joined by Australia's leading batsman, captain Billy Murdoch, McDonnell began to display the firm-footed straight driving for which he was famous. Together the pair added 50 in half an hour and when Murdoch was out, followed shortly afterwards by Giffen, both caught at mid-off, McDonnell continued to drive everything within reach while his new partner Alec Bannerman defended. When 67 had been added Bannerman was run out and play ended for the day. McDonnell, 80*, had hit 7 fours.

Next day McDonnell was caught at point trying to cut Alec Hearne's third ball and the remaining 5 wickets fell for 41 runs, all but one to young Hearne who, in the morning session, took 5 for 19 in 53

balls. Wicketkeeper 'Bishop' Kemp stood back to pace bowlers Christopherson and Lipscomb and conceded no byes. In contrast, there were 20 in the Kent innings. Murdoch, deputising for the great Blackham who had injured a finger, persisted in standing up. He had started his career behind the stumps but by now his best keeping days were behind him and he would probably have been better standing back, at least to Spofforth.

Kent opened their second innings with Mackinnon and Kemp, an exuberant batsman with a penchant for short singles. No batsman was entirely at ease with Palmer, who aimed mainly at leg stump and turned the ball both ways, but 14 came from the first 2 overs. After Kemp was bowled with the score at 42, 3 more wickets fell for 35 and at lunch Kent were 87 for 4. After lunch only 2 more had been scored when Palmer bowled Wilson, bringing Frank Hearne to join his captain for the highest partnership of the match. When Hearne lifted a drive to mid-on, 80 runs had been added and with the remaining 4 wickets contributing 44, the game was now tilted in favour of the home side. Lord Harris was ninth

Alec Hearne took 5 for 36 and 2 for 30 against the Australians in only his fifth first-team appearance. When he retired in 1906 he had more runs and more wickets to his credit than any other Kent cricketer.

Kent won the toss and elected to bat   Umpires: F.H. Farrands and J. West

KENT	1ST INNINGS		2ND INNINGS	
F.A. Mackinnon	c Palmer b Spofforth	28	b Palmer	29
F. Hearne	c Palmer b Spofforth	7	(7) c Bannerman b Boyle	45
G.G. Hearne	b Palmer	27	b Spofforth	6
*Lord Harris	b Spofforth	2	b Palmer	60
W.H. Patterson	b Giffen	19	c Spofforth b Palmer	3
C. Wilson	hit wicket b Giffen	37	b Palmer	3
†M.C. Kemp	not out	11	(2) b Palmer	21
S. Christopherson	b Palmer	1	c Bonnor b Midwinter	14
J. Wootton	b Palmer	0	b Palmer	8
A. Hearne	c Bonnor b Giffen	5	b Palmer	2
F. Lipscomb	b Palmer	4	not out	0
Extras	(B 20, LB 8)	28	(B 15, LB 7)	22
TOTAL	(all out)	169	(all out)	213

FOW: 1-21, 2-58, 3-64, 4-94, 5-122, 6-152, 7-153, 8-153, 9-164   1-42, 2-67, 3-71, 4-75, 5-89, 6-169, 7-186, 8-205, 9-212

Bowling (4 balls per over)

	O	M	R	W
Spofforth	39	23	45	3
Midwinter	12	3	28	0
Palmer	38.3	20	52	4
Giffen	12	6	16	3

	O	M	R	W
Giffen	18	6	43	0
Palmer	36.2	14	74	7
Spofforth	16	3	39	1
Boyle	10	3	22	1
Midwinter	14	7	13	1

AUSTRALIANS	1ST INNINGS		2ND INNINGS	
P.S. McDonnell	c F. Hearne b A. Hearne	80	b Lipscomb	19
G.J. Bonnor	b Wootton	5	c Patterson b A. Hearne	9
*W.L. Murdoch	c Harris b Wootton	24	c Harris b A. Hearne	4
G. Giffen	c G.G. Hearne b Wootton	5	c Kemp b Lipscomb	0
A.C. Bannerman	run out	18	not out	35
H.J.H. Scott	c Harris b A. Hearne	19	c Harris b Christopherson	32
W.E. Midwinter	b Wootton	12	b Wootton	8
†J.McC. Blackham	st Kemp b A. Hearne	6	b Wootton	0
G.E. Palmer	c F. Hearne b A. Hearne	0	b Christopherson	2
F.R. Spofforth	c Kemp b A. Hearne	0	c & b Christopherson	4
H.F. Boyle	not out	4	b Wootton	0
Extras	(LB 4)	4	(B 4, LB 2)	6
TOTAL	(all out)	177	(all out)	109

FOW: 1-6, 2-61, 3-69, 4-136, 5-136, 6-155, 7-166, 8-168, 9-168   1-15, 2-28, 3-36, 4-41, 5-74, 6-83, 7-85, 8-92, 9-102

Bowling (4 balls per over)

	O	M	R	W
Lipscomb	16	1	41	0
Wootton	36	12	72	4
Christopherson	14	4	24	0
A. Hearne	21.1	10	36	5

	O	M	R	W
Lipscomb	13	2	40	2
A. Hearne	16	9	30	2
Wootton	22.3	13	21	3
Christopherson	19	15	12	3

Kent won by 96 runs

out and Kent had scored their runs – which included another 15 byes – in 265 minutes.

The Australians started badly against tight bowling, losing Bonnor from a mishit drive to long-off, Murdoch caught at mid-off, McDonnell bowled and Giffen caught behind with only 41 runs on the board. Scott hit 3 fours in a partnership of 33 with the obdurate Bannerman but, at close of play, Australia were 83 for 6 (Bannerman 17*), still 122 in arrears with the wicket showing signs of wear.

Fifty minutes were enough on the final day. Lipscomb was late and for the first twenty minutes Spofforth, who had not yet batted, fielded in his place. Bannerman seemed untroubled and remained undefeated but nobody ever looked like staying with him. As captain and Kent's top scorer, Lord Harris was carried in triumph round the ground and, although the crowd was 'not particularly large' according to The Times, a spontaneous collection raised £80 to be divided among the four professionals.

This was the 1884 tourists' only defeat at the hands of a county. The 1882 side were unbeaten by any county and Kent thus became the first county to beat the Australians since Nottinghamshire in 1880.

The Kent team in this match were remarkable for their longevity. In 1932, forty-eight years later, they were all still alive.

KENT v. SUSSEX

Date: 2-3 August 1888   **Location:** Tonbridge

1888 was a season twenty-first-century bowlers can only dream about. Frequent rain was interspersed with spells of wind and sunshine so that, with pitches uncovered, genuine 'sticky' wickets abounded. As a bonus, hours spent listening to the patter of rain on pavilion roofs meant that, for once, the normally overworked professional bowlers were not tired out by August. Of the twenty-one bowlers taking 50 or more wickets, thirteen did so for under 15 runs apiece. Two bowlers took over 200 wickets, three others over 150. Only three batsmen averaged over 30.

Rain had fallen in Tonbridge almost incessantly for a day and a half prior to the start of Kent's match against Sussex at Tonbridge but the morning of the match was bright and sunny and, with a drying wind, play began at 3.40 p.m. As usual in August, both sides were able to call on most of their talented amateurs, Kent fielding seven, Sussex five. At this stage of the season Kent had won 3 county matches – including a victory over Sussex at Hove – drawn 1 and lost 2; Sussex had won 0, drawn 2 and lost 5 but had the consolation of having beaten the Australians.

The Sussex captain, Aubrey Smith of future Hollywood fame, won the toss and decided to bat. Making the most of conditions before the effect of the roller had worn off, the left-hander Francis Gresson hit out but nobody else reached double figures and the innings was over in about ninety minutes. Fred 'Nutty' Martin and Walter Wright bowled unchanged, as they would many times in the future. Both left-arm medium, Martin's stock ball turned away from the bat, varied by an arm ball, a well-disguised slower delivery and a genuine out-swinger. Wright relied primarily on his in-swinger but in the right conditions he could also gain sharp movement off the pitch.

Faring no better against the accuracy of Jesse Hide (right-arm fast-medium) and brother Arthur (left-arm medium), Kent lost their first 3 wickets for 4 runs and at close of play were 33 for 5 (Fox 6* Marchant 6*). The second morning was bright but the wicket still favoured the bowlers. Much was expected of

Marchant, who often succeeded on slow wickets, but he was bowled after a few lofted drives and it was not until Alec Hearne came in at 56 for 8 that the game swung in Kent's favour. While Walter Wright defended, Hearne began to show some of the skill that would eventually elevate him to one of his county's most successful opening batsmen. Together they added a priceless 31 and, with last man Martin contributing some lusty blows, the home side finished with a lead of 52. Wright batted seventy-five minutes for his 8*.

The Sussex openers began aggressively, hitting a rapid 34, but once again the roller brought only temporary improvement and the innings followed a pattern broadly similar to the first, apart from a few characteristic drives from Brann and stubborn resistance from Humphreys. Wright was handicapped by a strain, but the Sussex batsmen found Alec Hearne, with his off-spinners and occasional leg-breaks, every bit as troublesome.

Although the wicket was becoming more difficult,

Unfairly best remembered for dropping a vital catch in a Test match, Fred Tate's 5 wickets for 1 run in 16 balls narrowly failed to give Sussex an improbable victory.

Sussex won the toss and elected to bat   Umpires: H. Jupp and G. Panter

SUSSEX	1ST INNINGS		2ND INNINGS	
F.H. Gresson	c Wilson b Wright	22	b A. Hearne	18
W. Quaife	c Marchant b Martin	4	b Martin	10
G. Brann	c & b Martin	0	c Wilson b A. Hearne	10
W. Newham	b Wright	0	b A. Hearne	9
J.M. Cotterill	c Wright b Martin	5	c G.G. Hearne b A. Hearne	3
J.B. Hide	b Wright	3	(10) b Martin	1
W.A. Humphreys	b Martin	5	(6) b A. Hearne	11
*C.A. Smith	b Wright	1	(7) c Fox b Martin	8
A.B. Hide	c Marchant b Martin	2	(8) b A. Hearne	7
F.W. Tate	not out	0	(9)c G.G. Hearne b Martin	7
†H. Phillips	st Kemp b Martin	1	not out	0
Extras	(B 6, LB 2)	8	(B 9, LB 3)	12
TOTAL	(all out)	51	(all out)	96

FOW: 1-11, 2-12, 3-?, 4-?, 5-28, 6-43, 7-44, 8-47, 9-?   1-34, 2-45, 3-47, 4-51, 5-68, 6-81, 7-81, 8-94, 9-96

Bowling (4 balls per over)

	O	M	R	W
Martin	24.2	11	27	6
Wright	24	15	16	4

	O	M	R	W
Martin	35	20	23	4
Wright	6	0	14	0
A. Hearne	29.2	11	47	6

KENT	1ST INNINGS		2ND INNINGS	
W. Rashleigh	b J.B. Hide	0	c Newham b A.B. Hide	12
J.N. Tonge	c A.B. Hide b J.B. Hide	0	c Humphreys b A.B. Hide	2
*W.H. Patterson	b J.B. Hide	4	c Tate b A.B. Hide	7
C.J.M. Fox	c A.B. Hide b J.B. Hide	10	b Tate	11
L. Wilson	lbw b A.B. Hide	12	c Tate b A.B. Hide	0
G.G. Hearne	lbw b J.B. Hide	1	b Tate	7
F. Marchant	b A.B. Hide	13	b Tate	0
W.S. Wright	not out	8	b Tate	1
†M.C. Kemp	run out	7	not out	0
A. Hearne	b A.B. Hide	28	b Tate	0
F. Martin	b J.B. Hide	10	not out	2
Extras	(B 9, LB 1)	10	(B 3)	3
TOTAL	(all out)	103	(for 9 wickets)	45

FOW: 1-0, 2-1, 3-4, 4-19, 5-20, 6-47, 7-49, 8-56, 9-99   1-3, 2-18, 3-30, 4-31, 5-41, 6-41, 7-42, 8-43, 9-43

Bowling (4 balls per over)

	O	M	R	W
A.B. Hide	42	24	46	3
J.B. Hide	37.2	21	33	6
Smith	7	5	5	0
Tate	13	7	9	0

	O	M	R	W
A.B. Hide	26.1	14	21	4
J.B. Hide	22	14	20	0
Tate	4	3	1	5

Kent won by 1 wicket

with only 45 needed a Kent victory seemed certain. Rashleigh played a few strokes but soon fell to Arthur Hide, who also dismissed Tonge, Patterson, rated among the best in England on a bad wicket, and Leslie Wilson. At 41 for 4 the result still seemed a formality but Smith replaced Jesse Hide with Fred Tate. Twenty-two years old at the time, Tate was playing only his twelfth match for the county and his medium-pace off-spinners (or possibly off-cutters) had so far earned him 16 wickets at 24.81.

George Hearne, who batted patiently for 7, failed to score from Tate's first 3 balls and was bowled by the fourth. Marchant succumbed to the final ball of Tate's second over, another wicket maiden, Fox and Alec Hearne fell to the second and fourth balls of his third, still without conceding a run. Meanwhile, 2 runs had come from Arthur Hide at the other end, leaving 2 to win.

The second ball of Tate's fourth over accounted for Wright, bringing last man Martin to join Kemp, a notoriously eccentric runner but 'a rare man at a pinch' according to *Cricket*. Warned by his captain to look out for Tate's yorker – and possibly Kemp's running – Martin played his second ball straight to Jesse Hide at cover. Not even considering a run, Martin looked up to see Kemp halfway down the wicket. Fortunately Jesse threw to the wrong end. An almost equally risky run off Arthur Hide gave Kent the victory. Martin had match figures of 10-50 to go with his 2 crucial runs, but the honours went to Tate who stood the match on its head by taking 5 wickets (all bowled, mostly yorkers) for one run. In the scorebook his bowling reads: ...W, ..W., .W.W, .W.1.

KENT v. NOTTINGHAMSHIRE

Date: 29-30 August 1889   **Location:** Foxgrove Road, Beckenham

The Nottinghamshire team arrived at Beckenham for the last game of the season needing only a draw to become champions ahead of Lancashire and Surrey, both of whom had completed their programme. The portents were all in their favour. Under their new captain John Dixon they had started with 10 successive victories, 9 by an innings and, although their form had slumped during a wet August, they had lost only once. Kent had a respectable 6 wins to their credit, including a double over Yorkshire, but they had gone down by an innings and 43 runs at Trent Bridge. Seven of the visitors had played for England against Australia; in the home side only Lord Harris had experience at that level but Fred 'Nutty' Martin would do so with outstanding success the following year.

The picturesque Beckenham ground was still a relatively new venue for Kent. Some considered it too small – *The Times* suggested boundaries should only count three – and, although this was only the fourth county game played there, *Wisden* commented that the wicket 'never had a very good reputation for wearing well'. In the previous year, after Surrey had totalled 142, 30 wickets had fallen for 223 runs. And in Martin and Wright Kent had one of the most destructive bowling combinations in the country on worn or drying pitches.

Dixon won the toss and chose to bat on a pitch soft after an unusually heavy overnight dew, and at lunch Nottinghamshire were 61 for 3. Dixon departed to a catch at slip; Shrewsbury, generally considered second only to Grace on a turning wicket, was brilliantly caught one-handed by Wright at mid-off; and Barnes was bowled leg stump. Cautious but looking safe, Gunn made full use of his long reach, batting two-and-a-quarter hours, adding 37 with Flowers until both fell at the same total. With the wicket becoming more difficult as it dried, by 4.45 p.m. the remaining 5 wickets had tumbled for only 41. No batsman had been at ease with Martin but Wright, who had begun his career at Trent Bridge, was oddly ineffective and 5 wickets fell to the accurate but not usually deadly medium pace of Charles Fox, a useful all-rounder who scored large numbers of runs for the Crystal Palace Club. The avuncular-looking, luxuriantly moustached Fox was a genuine amateur who played the game for pleasure. Against Sussex at Hove in 1891, he was 0* at lunch but left the ground and arrived back too late to resume his innings, excusing himself with the immortal words 'I was lunching with a widow.'

Opening for Kent, Lord Harris played on with the score at 27 but Patterson picked up runs with cuts, pushes and his trademark strokes off his legs and at the close the home side were 44 for 1 (Patterson 23*, George Hearne 8*).

Next morning was bright but again there had been heavy dew and the wicket was showing ominous signs of wear. Patterson was missed behind the wicket off the first ball of the day and bowled 5 runs later, Marchant's attempt to hit his way out of trouble ended in a lobbed catch to mid-off and within an hour Kent were 73 for 7. Attewell looked unplayable but wicketkeeper 'Bishop' Kemp squeezed an invaluable 45 runs out of the tail, mixing orthodox drives with the short singles for which he was famous – even notorious. Nottinghamshire's second innings started disastrously with Shrewsbury out, uncharacteristically caught at slip from a leg-side shot, without a run on the board and Dixon mishitting to cover, but Gunn and Barnes played steadily and at lunch Notts were 24 for 2, 40 runs ahead.

Following Wright's lack of success in the first innings, Fox had opened the bowling with Martin but the ex-Notts man had come into the attack shortly before lunch and immediately on the restart the Martin/ Wright combination began to click. Barnes succumbed to Martin's arm ball, Flowers was bowled by a shooter, Gunn caught at mid-off and in what Wisden described as 'the most remarkable cricket of the season' Notts lost 8 wickets in fifty minutes for just 11 runs, including two brilliant stumpings by Kemp.

KENT v. NOTTINGHAMSHIRE

Nottinghamshire won the toss and elected to bat Umpires: C.K. Pullin and J. Street

NOTTINGHAMSHIRE 1ST INNINGS

*J.A. Dixon	c A. Hearne b Martin	2
A. Shrewsbury	c Wright b Martin	12
W. Gunn	c Kemp b Martin	40
W. Barnes	b Barton	12
W. Flowers	b Fox	26
W.H. Scotton	c G.G. Hearne b Fox	10
W. Attewell	b Fox	8
H.B. Daft	lbw b Martin	2
F.J. Shacklock	b Fox	0
H. Richardson	b Fox	13
†M. Sherwin	not out	7
Extras	(B 1, LB 1)	2
TOTAL	(all out)	134

2ND INNINGS

(2) c Marchant b Martin		2
(1) c A. Hearne b Martin		0
c Fox b Martin		17
b Martin		8
b Wright		0
b Martin		4
(8) b Wright		1
(7) st Kemp b Martin		0
st Kemp b Martin		3
b Wright		0
not out		0
		0
(all out)		35

FOW: 1-4, 2-25, 3-57, 4-94, 5-94, 6-99, 7-112, 8-112, 9-125

1-0, 2-7, 3-24, 4-25, 5-27, 6-29, 7-30, 8-34, 9-35

Bowling (5 balls per over)

	O	M	R	W
Martin	55	30	50	4
Wright	24	12	26	0
Fox	34.2	16	43	5
Barton	4	0	13	1

	O	M	R	W
Martin	22.1	15	18	7
Fox	9	6	10	0
Wright	13	8	7	3

KENT 1ST INNINGS

*Lord Harris	b Shacklock	13
W.H. Patterson	b Richardson	28
G.G. Hearne	b Attewell	16
F. Marchant	c Flowers b Attewell	9
C.J.M. Fox	b Attewell	2
A. Hearne	c Barnes b Attewell	1
F. Hearne	b Attewell	4
V.A. Barton	b Shacklock	7
†M.C. Kemp	not out	28
F. Martin	c Scotton b Flowers	9
W. S. Wright	b Attewell	1
Extras		0
TOTAL	(all out)	118

2ND INNINGS

(2) b Attewell		10
(1) c Shrewsbury b Attewell		0
not out		14
b Attewell		0
b Flowers		1
lbw b Flowers		0
c Shrewsbury b Attewell		9
not out		12
(B 7)		7
(for 6 wickets)		53

FOW: 1-27, 2-53, 3-66, 4-68, 5-69, 6-70, 7-73, 8-101, 9-117

1-0, 2-11, 3-11, 4-15, 5-16, 6-25

Bowling (5 balls per over)

	O	M	R	W
Attewell	32.3	10	53	6
Richardson	30	17	36	1
Shacklock	11	5	16	2
Barnes	1	0	6	0
Flowers	2	0	7	1

	O	M	R	W
Attewell	25	21	7	4
Flowers	18	10	30	2
Richardson	7	4	9	0

Kent won by 4 wickets

Although Kent needed only 52, expert opinion favoured the visitors despite their lack of a left-arm spinner on a wicket that cried out for one. Patterson, the most dependable batsman in the conditions, was caught at point before a run had been scored and Harris was bowled after half an hour with the total only 11. While the left-handed George Hearne, concentrating on defence, to some extent negated the off-spin of Attewell and Flowers, Marchant, Fox and Alec Hearne all fell at the other end for the addition of only 5 runs. A few bold strokes from Frank Hearne persuaded Dixon, probably mistakenly with hindsight, to bring on the medium-pace Richardson in place of Flowers but when Frank was caught at point, 27 were still needed with 4 wickets standing.

Victor Barton, who now joined George Hearne, was in his first season, playing as a professional while still serving with the Royal Artillery at Woolwich. Thanks to a fumble by wicketkeeper Sherwin, he narrowly escaped a run out before he had scored but subsequently played with the aplomb of a veteran.

Sporting two of the finest moustaches on the county circuit, Fred 'Nutty' Martin (*opposite*) and Charles Fox (*right*) played key roles in ensuring that Nottinghamshire gained only a one-third share of the championship.

In company with the phlegmatic, hugely experienced Hearne, Barton saw the total to 49 for 6 when an off-drive for four by the left-hander settled the match and the destination of the championship. Hearne's 14* in 105 minutes was as valuable an innings as any he played during his long career for the county. The result meant that for the first and only time, the championship ended in a triple tie.

This was Frank Hearne's last match for Kent before emigrating to South Africa. At lunch on the last day the Kent president Francis Mackinnon presented him with the proceeds of a collection, £144 9s 10d. He was reported to have moved to a warmer climate for health reasons. If so, the cure worked; he coached Western Province, played for South Africa, toured England with a South African team in 1894 and died at 91.

This was also Lord Harris's last game before taking up his appointment as Governor of Bombay (now Mumbai). At the time he believed, wrongly as it turned out, that it would be his last appearance for the county. He made his final appearance in 1911.

Nobody liked the triple tie and at a meeting of the county secretaries in December 1889 it was decided to operate a formally recognised County Championship with a points system, in which losses would be deducted from wins and draws ignored. Previously the decision had been largely in the hands of the cricketing press.

KENT v. GLOUCESTERSHIRE

Date: 23-25 May 1895   **Location:** Gravesend

Kent saw county cricket on the Bat and Ball Ground in Gravesend over a period of 122 years, playing 142 matches. It was claimed that the ground was the smallest in the world to host first-class cricket and certainly a lightning-fast outfield aided quick scoring. Of all the matches played there this was the most famous, albeit the result was not one Kent wanted or expected, particularly after the first day's play.

1895 was W.G. Grace's *annus mirabilis*. By the time he reached Gravesend, the now forty-six-year-old had scored 499 runs towards becoming the first batsman to score a thousand runs by the end of May. As always, interest in seeing the great cricketer was high and 6,000 spectators were squeezed into the small ground to witness his first match there since 1875.

Kent won the toss and batted. Gloucestershire were weak in bowling with both J.J. Ferris and C.L. Townsend absent and William Murch, having missed the train, not able to appear before 5.30 p.m. The day belonged to the Kent all-rounder Alec Hearne. Opening the innings, he was the mainstay of a close-of-play total of 451 for 7. After a careful start, he hit with great freedom, latterly scoring at 50 runs an hour and offering only one chance on 109. His 155, his highest score to date for Kent, included 21 fours and his main support came from the amateur Gerry Weigall, with whom he added 173 in two hours. The idiosyncratic Weigall, a useful if admittedly not great batsman, was to be part of the Kent cricket scene for many years as coach, raconteur and presence.

Day two belonged to Grace. The Kent innings was soon completed for the addition of 19 runs. Between a little after noon until 6.30 p.m., W.G. put together an innings of 210* out of a total of 355 for 7. The bowling was not bad and the fielding was reported as being 'thoroughly good'. Bowlers of the quality of Fred Martin, Jack Mason and Alec Hearne required some care in technique. But, after spending two hours over his first fifty, Grace settled down to a more vigorous game, adding 160 in the next three-and-a-quarter hours. The level of his fitness – he now weighed untold stone – is borne witness by the fact that his completed innings included over 100 singles. Five men were out for 166, but with S.A.P. Kitcat adding 156, the Kent total was in striking distance.

With the first innings yet to be completed, the odds were on a draw when the teams entered the final day. Indeed, so certain were Gloucestershire of this that they released Murch to return to the West of England to play in a one-day game. Grace took his score to 257 before mistiming a ball from Alec Hearne to long-on. Last out, he batted through an innings of seven hours and thirty-five minutes scoring 24 fours. It was to remain the highest first-class score on the Bat and Ball Ground.

Events now took an unexpected turn. The wicket remained hard and true yet, despite Gloucestershire being a bowler short, the Kent innings totally collapsed. Grace had somewhat surprisingly passed the ball to medium-pace bowler John Painter, who incredibly had not bowled for the county for a couple of years. In an hour-and-a-quarter, Kent tumbled to 53 for 9, 7 wickets to Painter. Only Alec Hearne, who carried his bat, again offered any resistance and with Martin made a spirited attempt to check the slide and use up valuable time towards the approaching close. Together they added 23 in forty minutes. But the inevitable end came at 5 p.m. with Painter finishing with 7 for 25.

W.G. Grace – photographed on the Gravesend ground in 1913. [David Frith]

Kent won the toss and elected to bat   Umpires: W.B. Clarke and R.A. Thoms

KENT	1ST INNINGS		2ND INNINGS	
*F. Marchant	b Grace	38	c & b Painter	4
A. Hearne	c Board b Kitcat	155	not out	22
J.W. Easby	c Thomas b Roberts	28	b Roberts	17
G.J.V. Weigall	b Painter	74	b Painter	1
G.G. Hearne	b Murch	49	b Painter	6
J.R. Mason	c Board b Roberts	21	c Bracher b Painter	5
G.C. Hubbard	c & b Grace	36	c Board b Painter	4
P. Northcote	not out	27	b Roberts	0
†C.H. Hunter	c Board b Murch	6	c Board b Painter	4
W.S. Wright	b Roberts	5	b Painter	0
F. Martin	b Murch	7	b Roberts	12
Extras	(B 17, LB 2, NB 5)	24	(LB 1)	1
TOTAL	(all out)	470	(all out)	76

FOW: 1-43, 2-77, 3-250, 4-346, 5-?,6-413, 7-?, 8-?, 9-?

1-6, 2-26, 3-?, 4-?, 5-?, 6-?, 7-?, 8-?, 9-53

Bowling (5 balls per over)

	O	M	R	W
Roberts	58	23	131	3
Grace	43	13	115	2
Wrathall	12	3	36	0
Sewell	10	2	48	0
Kitcat	9	1	40	1
Francis	2	0	11	0
Painter	6	3	14	1
Murch	26.3	8	51	3

	O	M	R	W
Roberts	29	12	50	3
Painter	28	15	25	7

GLOUCESTERSHIRE	1ST INNINGS		2ND INNINGS	
*W.G. Grace	c Hubbard b A. Hearne	257	not out	73
H. Wrathall	b A. Hearne	13	c sub b A. Hearne	2
C.J. Francis	c Hunter b Martin	8		
C.O.H. Sewell	st Hunter b Hubbard	14		
J.R. Painter	c A. Hearne b Mason	40	(3) not out	31
W.H. Murch	c Hubbard b G.G. Hearne	0		
S.A.P. Kitcat	b Martin	52		
E.L. Thomas	b A. Hearne	6		
F.C. Bracher	b A. Hearne	16		
†J.H. Board	c Mason b Northcote	17		
F.G. Roberts	not out	8		
Extras	(B 6, LB 4, W 2)	12		0
TOTAL	(all out)	443	(for 1 wicket)	106

FOW: 1-32, 2-?, 3-77, 4-165, 5-166, 6-312, 7-?, 8-379, 9-412   1-15

Bowling (5 balls per over)

	O	M	R	W
Martin	63	23	96	2
A. Hearne	56.3	15	93	4
Wright	23	6	67	0
Mason	30	9	54	1
Hubbard	6	0	25	1
G.G. Hearne	23	10	41	1
Northcote	15	1	47	1
Easby	3	1	8	0

	O	M	R	W
Martin	8	2	29	0
A. Hearne	11	2	38	1
Wright	2.2	0	15	0
Mason	2	0	9	0
G.G. Hearne	4	1	15	0

Gloucestershire won by 9 wickets

Gloucestershire were left an hour-and-a quarter to score 104, not an easy task. But again Grace took the lead, completely mastering the Kent bowling, scoring 73* and finishing the match with fifteen minutes to spare. He had been on the field of play for every ball bowled in the game. He sprinted to the pavilion to avoid the engulfing spectators and was cheered all the way along the street to his hotel.

For Kent this was a bitter defeat. Never before had a side scored as many as 470 and lost, let alone as comprehensively as by 9 wickets. They would not again suffer the indignity of making such a score and losing until 1997. It was the first match of a depressing season when, plagued by injuries and unavailability of players, they slumped to the bottom of the championship table for the first time since the competition had been formally organised in 1890. They did not repeat this ignominy until exactly 100 years later. Grace, of course, completed a thousand runs by the end of May, no mean effort since he did not score a first-class run before 9 May.

KENT v. AUSTRALIANS

Date: 6-8 August 1899   **Location:** Canterbury

The 1899 Australian team was the first to undertake a full programme of five Test matches – albeit each of only three days' duration – and also the first to wear the green and gold colours. By August, with 1 win and 3 draws in the Test matches and 13 wins, 7 draws and 2 defeats in their other fixtures, they looked set to become the most successful touring side ever. If the bowling was not quite as dominant as in the Spofforth era, in Hugh Trumble and 'Mary Ann' Noble they had two of the all-time greats, and Ernie Jones was one of the fastest of his day. As for the batting, there was almost no tail. Only Howell, Jones and reserve wicketkeeper Johns had not hit a first-class hundred.

In front of a crowd said by *Wisden* to be 'the biggest ever seen on the St Lawrence ground', Joe Darling won the toss, breaking a sequence of seven successive wrong calls. With 61 on the board, Jack Worrall was out to a spectacular running catch by Burnup at long-on, which brought in the man everyone wanted to see, Victor Trumper. Last choice for the tour, a magnificent century in the Lord's Test match and a triple century at Hove had quickly established him as the most exciting batsman of the day. Now he demonstrated his artistry, hitting 50 (out of 61) in forty-five minutes, but departed unexpectedly to a catch behind the wicket from the very occasional medium-pace of Arthur Du Boulay. At lunch the total was 127 for 2.

Belying the reputed depth of their batting, the tourists' remaining 8 wickets added a mere 100 runs, the last four falling at the cost of 3 singles. Seven wickets fell to catches at slip or behind the stumps. Apart from Trumper, none of the Australians was at ease with Bradley's pace and lift but the success of Burnup came as a surprise. Brought on as fifth change, his rarely used outswingers earned him 3 wickets in 4 overs. At close of play Kent were 29 for 0, Burnup 8*, Stewart (twice missed) 21*.

Next day Burnup and Stewart took the score to 53 when the former fell to another slip catch. Stewart, scoring almost entirely with wristy off-drives and cuts, added a further 59 with Alec Hearne before he too edged to slip. Six runs later Hearne, who batted fifty minutes for his 20, left to another slip catch and with 4 more wickets following cheaply – including Mason, Patterson and Weigall, all caught at slip – Kent lunched at a depressing 151 for 7. After the interval Australian dominance continued, only briefly interrupted by a ninth-wicket partnership of 31 between Du Boulay and 'Punter' Humphreys. The innings lasted only 165 minutes, Charles McLeod (7 for 87) producing his best figures for the tour.

After his first innings success, Burnup opened the bowling with Bradley and, apart from one over, they bowled unchanged. Six runs came in the first twenty minutes when Burnup claimed his first victim, Noble to the seemingly inevitable slip catch, and the innings rapidly declined to 58 for 8. Laver and Jones hit out briefly but Kent were left needing only 138. Seven Australian wickets fell to catches, three at slip, one behind the wicket, two at point and one a superb diving effort by Day running in from deep third man but, well as Kent bowled and fielded, the collapse was – and remains – inexplicable. Burnup, who at one time

Haldane Campbell Stewart was a talented musician as well as a fine attacking batsman. Top scorer in Kent's first innings, he steered them through a crisis in the second to give Kent victory.

Australians won the toss and elected to bat   Umpires: W. Hearn and J. Lillywhite

AUSTRALIANS	1ST INNINGS		2ND INNINGS	
J. Worrall	c Burnup b Hearne	36	c Hearne b Burnup	10
M.A. Noble	c Huish b Bradley	49	c Mason b Burnup	1
V.T. Trumper	c Huish b Du Boulay	50	c Mason b Bradley	13
S.E. Gregory	b Mason	3	c Bradley b Burnup	8
*C.J. Darling	c Hearne b Bradley	16	b Bradley	4
F.A. Iredale	c Hearne b Burnup	37	c Huish b Burnup	0
†J.J. Kelly	c Bradley b Burnup	26	b Burnup	1
F.J. Laver	c Huish b Bradley	1	c Bradley b Mason	20
C.E. McLeod	c Mason b Burnup	0	b Bradley	0
E. Jones	c Huish b Bradley	1	c Day b Bradley	29
W.P. Howell	not out	0	not out	0
Extras	(B 7, LB 1)	8	(B 6, LB 1, W 1)	8
TOTAL	(all out)	227	(all out)	94

FOW: 1-61, 2-127, 3-138, 4-159, 5-164, 6-224, 7-225, 8-226, 9-227   1-6, 2-28, 3-34, 4-40, 5-40, 6-40, 7-43, 8-58, 9-86

Bowling (5 balls per over)

	O	M	R	W
Bradley	23.1	10	39	4
Mason	21	7	55	1
Hearne	20	6	30	1
Humphreys	15	5	42	0
Patterson	5	2	13	0
Du Boulay	10	4	33	1
Burnup	4	1	7	3

	O	M	R	W
Bradley	22.3	11	42	4
Burnup	21	9	44	5
Mason	1	1	0	1

KENT	1ST INNINGS		2ND INNINGS	
C.J. Burnup	c Howell b McLeod	25	(4) c Noble b McLeod	24
H.C. Stewart	c Howell b McLeod	71	(9) not out	15
A. Hearne	c Kelly b Howell	20	(5) c Kelly b Howell	17
S.H. Day	b Howell	4	(6) c Kelly b McLeod	5
W.H. Patterson	c Worrall b McLeod	7	(7) c Howell b McLeod	2
*J.R. Mason	c Howell b McLeod	0	(8) b Howell	6
A.H. Du Boulay	c Noble b McLeod	33	(3) b Jones	27
G.J.V. Weigall	c Howell b McLeod	0	(10) not out	12
†F.H. Huish	c Worrall b McLeod	11	(1) lbw b Noble	13
E. Humphreys	b Noble	13		
W.M. Bradley	not out	0	(2) b Noble	11
Extras		0	(B 6, LB 3)	9
TOTAL	(all out)	184	(for 8 wickets)	141

FOW: 1-53, 2-112, 3-118, 4-121, 5-122, 6-135, 7-135, 8-153, 9-184   1-17, 2-44, 3-64, 4-97, 5-105, 6-107, 7-114, 8-114

Bowling (5 balls per over)

	O	M	R	W
Jones	24	8	52	0
Howell	20	5	45	2
McLeod	36	9	87	7
Noble	0.2	0	0	1

	O	M	R	W
Jones	15	5	29	1
Howell	22	8	36	2
McLeod	19	7	41	3
Noble	12	4	26	2

Kent won by 2 wickets

bowled six successive maidens, never again achieved anything comparable with the ball. With time for only one over, Kent sent in Huish and Bradley as dual nightwatchmen. At the close, Kent were 0 for 0.

The makeshift openers put on 17 when Bradley, who considered himself 'the worst batsman in England' was bowled after a rare excursion into double figures. Du Boulay, who for unspecified reasons 'had to leave early' came in at number three and, although clearly not relishing the pace of Jones, added 27 with Huish and 20 with Burnup before succumbing to the fast bowler. Burnup was batting with his usual aplomb but his exit to a catch at point triggered a mini-collapse and, despite several missed catches, lunch came with the game poised at 107 for 6.

Crisis came immediately after lunch with the loss of Mason and Patterson for the addition of only 7 runs, which brought together Stewart and Weigall. The latter was missed at the wicket before he had scored but both were highly experienced and opted to play strokes. With the scores level, Stewart was missed at point off the next ball but a cut for four gave Kent victory, their fifth against the Australians. The tourists suffered no further defeats and retained the Ashes with a draw in the final Test at The Oval.

KENT v. YORKSHIRE

Date: 21-23 August 1899 **Location:** Tonbridge

Yorkshire were champions in 1898 and, with only one more game to come, took the field at Tonbridge with justified expectation of retaining the title. They had lost one more match than their nearest rivals Surrey but could claim 15 wins to the Southerners' 8. In contrast Kent, in the lower reaches of the table, had won only 3 and lost 8, including an innings defeat at Leeds.

Yorkshire started badly, losing Jackson, Tunnicliffe and Denton for 18, all to the fast-medium bowling of Jack Mason. Frank Mitchell hit a robust fifty and George Hirst (11 fours) hit 60 in seventy-five minutes but overall Yorkshire, on a firm, true wicket, did not bat like champions. Bowling very fast and making the ball lift, Bradley troubled everyone and rounded off the innings with a hat-trick (all bowled), his second of the season. Mitchell played him better than most and had looked set for a century when, at 86 for 4, Mason handed the ball to a tall, young left-arm spinner, a product of the Tonbridge Nursery, now making his debut. His first ball pitched marginally outside leg stump, Mitchell played forward defensively, failed to middle it and played on. This was the first of 2,503 first-class wickets for Colin 'Charlie' Blythe, arguably the finest left-arm spinner of them all.

Yorkshire's greatest strength lay in their out-cricket and Kent too began shakily, with Hearne and Sam Day succumbing to the pace bowling of Ernest Smith, but Cambridge Blues Cuthbert 'Pinky' Burnup and Tom Perkins provided the best batting of the day, hitting their first hundred in ninety minutes. Both exceptionally strong on the back foot, they were relatively at ease with the multi-talented Yorkshire attack that, with Rhodes, Hirst, Wainwright, Haigh and Jackson, had claims to be considered the strongest in England. At the close Kent were 159 for 2 (Burnup 90* Perkins 44*).

One of the most reliable and consistent batsmen of his era, who knew his capabilities and played within them, Burnup had the ability to keep the score moving without taking risks. He was very much a 'modern' batsman, tending to play back and across and scoring a high proportion of his runs off his legs. In contrast, many of his public school/Oxbridge contemporaries played mainly off the front foot, reaching out to the pitch of the ball in what was then considered the 'classical' manner. He had hit a memorable century against the 1896 Australians in his debut year and now he steered Kent towards a winning total, adding 118 with Perkins and 117 in ninety minutes with Rashleigh in what many consider the best innings of his career. He was sixth out having hit 25 fours and batted for 270 minutes.

When they batted again, Bradley's pace once more had the visitors in trouble, inflicting second failures on Tunnicliffe (caught at slip) and Denton (caught behind) both from short balls hitting high on the bat. Stanley Jackson, the best batsman in the side, looked likely to play a substantial innings but he fell to Alec Hearne, whose off-spinners mixed with the occasional leg-break then accounted for most of the middle order and, until Lord Hawke joined Ted Wainwright at 166 for 7, a Kent victory in two days seemed on the cards. At close of play Yorkshire had scored 208 for 7 (Wainwright 57*, Hawke 28*), a lead of 3.

To say a good word about Martin Bladen, 7th Baron Hawke is now deemed politically incorrect but, although hardly one of the game's great intellects and despite a fondness for airing his often reactionary views on cricket and weightier matters,

Rated as one of the best batsmen never to play for England, Cuthbert 'Pinky' Burnup ruined Yorkshire's championship hopes.

Yorkshire won the toss and elected to bat   Umpires: V.A. Titchmarsh and W.A. Woof

YORKSHIRE	1ST INNINGS		2ND INNINGS	
F.S. Jackson	b Mason	1	c Huish b Hearne	33
J. Tunnicliffe	c Hearne b Mason	0	c Hearne b Bradley	5
D. Denton	c Huish b Mason	0	c Huish b Bradley	2
F. Mitchell	b Blythe	53	b Hearne	15
E. Wainwright	c Weigall b Bradley	19	c Stewart b Mason	100
G.H. Hirst	c Burnup b Bradley	60	lbw b Hearne	15
E. Smith	c Mason b Bradley	4	c Stewart b Hearne	21
S. Haigh	not out	15	c Huish b Bradley	18
*Lord Hawke	b Bradley	0	b Hearne	81
W. Rhodes	b Bradley	0	not out	10
†D. Hunter	b Bradley	8	b Blythe	5
Extras	(LB 1, NB 1)	2	(B 11, LB 8, NB 1)	20
TOTAL	(all out)	164	(all out)	325

FOW: 1-1, 2-1, 3-18, 4-66, 5-86, 6-105, 7-144, 8-144, 9-144   1-12, 2-16, 3-56, 4-57, 5-87, 6-109, 7-166, 8-304, 9-310

Bowling (5 balls per over)

	O	M	R	W
Bradley	24.1	6	84	6
Mason	22	11	34	3
Hearne	11	4	19	0
Blythe	4	0	25	1
Burnup	1	1	0	0

	O	M	R	W
Bradley	40	10	125	3
Mason	27	9	49	1
Hearne	34	8	66	5
Burnup	9	2	24	0
Blythe	14.1	2	41	1

KENT	1ST INNINGS		2ND INNINGS	
C.J. Burnup	c & b Smith	171	not out	65
A. Hearne	b Smith	9	b Hirst	22
S.H. Day	c Hunter b Smith	12	st Hunter b Rhodes	15
T.T.N. Perkins	c Hunter b Smith	47	not out	17
*J.R. Mason	b Smith	7		
W. Rashleigh	run out	44		
H.C. Stewart	b Rhodes	21		
G.J.V. Weigall	c Wainwright b Smith	22		
†F.H. Huish	b Rhodes	7		
W.M. Bradley	not out	9		
C. Blythe	c Tunnicliffe b Rhodes	0		
Extras	(B 9, LB 8, NB 1, W 2)	20	(B 5)	5
TOTAL	(all out)	369	(for 2 wickets)	124

FOW: 1-30, 2-48, 3-166, 4-180, 5-297, 6-321, 7-337, 8-359, 9-365   1-42, 2-87

Bowling (5 balls per over)

	O	M	R	W
Rhodes	46.4	19	90	3
Smith	50	11	120	6
Wainwright	10	3	27	0
Hirst	17	4	35	0
Jackson	14	3	46	0
Haigh	11	1	31	0

	O	M	R	W
Rhodes	15	4	27	1
Smith	17.2	4	52	0
Hirst	13	8	23	1
Wainwright	6	3	17	0

Kent won by 8 wickets

he made a huge contribution to Yorkshire cricket. He was certainly no fool as a captain and, although he customarily batted down the order, was a more than competent batsman – especially in a crisis. His partnership with Wainwright produced 138 runs in 135 minutes. Thrice missed, twice by the near-infallible Mason at slip, he hit 1 five (four overthrows) and 12 fours. Wainwright, whose innings *The Times* termed 'a model of care and skill', was ninth out, caught at slip after batting 225 minutes and hitting 12 fours. Blythe had the satisfaction of picking up the last wicket.

Although requiring only 121, the wicket was beginning to crumble and against the spin of Rhodes and Wainwright and the pace of Hirst and Smith it would have been no great shock if Kent had been in trouble. In the event, Burnup and Hearne gave their side a sound start and with the former picking up very much where he left off in the first innings, the runs came with relative ease.

In their final fixture Yorkshire were unable to bowl Sussex out twice on the placid Hove wicket and had to settle for a draw and with it third place behind Middlesex and Surrey. Kent finished eighth.

KENT v. LANCASHIRE

Date: 9-11 August 1906   **Location:** Canterbury

At the start of the most momentous season in their history most of the pundits did not see Kent as potential champions. By Canterbury Week things were beginning to look different. Kent had lost to Yorkshire in their first match of the season and succumbed by 10 wickets at Old Trafford in June but now their record stood won 10, drawn 4, lost 2. They were in a run of five successive wins, the last an innings defeat inflicted on Sussex in the first game of the week.

Coming straight from losing to Yorkshire, Lancashire cannot have gone into the match in the best of spirits. Their attack was weakened by the absence of fast bowler Walter Brearley, who was having one of his periodic disputes with the committee, Australian stock bowler Alex Kermode and veteran all-rounder Willis Cuttell. To cap it all, they were delayed on their journey from Manchester, lost the toss and it was not until 12.25 p.m. that they took the field in front of a record Ladies' Day crowd in excess of 13,000.

With their full cast of amateurs now available, there was no room in the Kent side for the promising Frank Woolley, Jack Hubble, 'Wally' Hardinge, the veteran Alec Hearne or Bill Fairservice among the pros or the highly talented Day brothers among the amateurs. All of these had, to varying degrees, contributed to earlier successes. Seldom before or since can Kent have been blessed with such an abundance of talent.

Dillon fell early to Harry Dean but Burnup, who started uncharacteristically shakily, taking fifty minutes over his first 8 runs, and Seymour batted through to lunch, taken with the score 107 for 1. Shortly after the resumption, MacLaren caught Seymour at slip when the partnership had added exactly 100 (in eighty-five minutes). This brought in Hutchings, who had hit a patch of devastating form and currently averaged 63.30. Ninety-nine runs now came in just seventy minutes, a run spree ended only when both batsmen found themselves at the same end and Burnup sacrificed himself for his in-form partner. He had hit 13 fours in his 94.

Probably the most famous of all cricket paintings. The artist, Albert Chevallier Tayler, cheated slightly. The non-striker, Billy Findlay, did not play in the match.

Kent won the toss and elected to bat   Umpires: A.J. Atfield and V.A. Titchmarsh

KENT	1ST INNINGS	
E.W. Dillon	c Poidevin b Dean	8
C.J. Burnup	run out	94
J. Seymour	c MacLaren b Gregson	50
K.L. Hutchings	c MacLaren b Gregson	176
J.R. Mason	c Dean b Gregson	88
E. Humphreys	b Harry	18
R.N.R. Blaker	c Worsley b Harry	7
*C.H.B. Marsham	c Worsley b Harry	0
†F.H. Huish	c Poidevin b Harry	7
C. Blythe	not out	8
A. Fielder	c Tyldesley b Harry	4
Extras	(B 8, LB 6, NB 5)	19
TOTAL	(all out)	479

FOW: 1-9, 2-109, 3-208, 4-421, 5-440, 6-459, 7-459, 8-466, 9-475

Bowling

	O	M	R	W
Dean	21	6	86	1
Harry	39	7	156	5
Poidevin	10	1	53	0
Gregson	38	3	125	3
Sharp	10	0	40	0

LANCASHIRE	1ST INNINGS		2ND INNINGS	
R.H. Spooner	lbw b Fielder	0	b Blythe	0
J.W.H. Makepeace	c Huish b Blythe	6	b Fielder	9
J.T. Tyldesley	c Seymour b Blythe	19	c Seymour b Fielder	4
L.G.S. Poidevin	c Seymour b Fielder	45	c Seymour b Fielder	0
J. Sharp	run out	25	c Huish b Fielder	32
*A.C. MacLaren	st Huish b Blythe	22	c Mason b Fielder	39
F. Harry	not out	26	c Mason b Fielder	3
A.H. Hornby	b Fielder	6	c Humphreys b Fielder	7
H. Dean	b Blythe	0	b Blythe	1
W.R. Gregson	c Dillon b Blythe	10	c Seymour b Blythe	13
†W. Worsley	b Fielder	2	not out	0
Extras	(B 4, NB 4)	8	(B 4, LB 1, NB 2)	7
TOTAL	(all out)	169	(all out)	115

FOW: 1-0, 2-25, 3-28, 4-67, 5-113, 6-121, 7-143, 8-144, 9-160   1-1, 2-10, 3-11, 4-20, 5-80, 6-84, 7-92, 8-93, 9-111

Bowling

	O	M	R	W
Fielder	22.3	4	81	4
Blythe	23	1	80	5
Humphreys	1	1	0	0

	O	M	R	W
Fielder	16	4	49	7
Blythe	10.4	5	27	3
Mason	7	3	17	0
Humphreys	2	0	15	0

Kent won by an innings and 195 runs

The arrival of Mason to join Hutchings brought complete domination of the Lancashire bowling, with 201 runs scored in 110 minutes. At the close Kent were 403 for 3, (Hutchings 167*, Mason 71*). Hutchings' first fifty came in seventy minutes; his hundred in two hours. *The Times* praised Lancashire's fielding but, possibly overlooking the quality of the batting, thought the bowling 'looked weak'.

Next day, in front of another large crowd of around 8,000, the pair took their partnership to 213 in two hours when Mason was dismissed after hitting 11 fours, the majority off-drives and shots to either side of cover. Hutchings followed 19 runs later. Both were caught off the fast bowling of Bill Gregson, making only his third appearance for the county.

Often compared with the great Victor Trumper, Hutchings was the most exciting English batsman of his day. With exceptionally strong wrists and forearms, he drove and cut with tremendous power and had a particular flair for hitting good-length balls on middle and leg to the boundary between square leg and wide mid-on with a flick of the wrist. His 176 had taken 190 minutes and contained 1 five and 27 fours, and during his innings he completed his thousand runs for the season. He also broke three bats.

KENT V. LANCASHIRE

With declarations only allowed on the last day and conscious of the need to get the visitors batting as soon as possible, the remaining Kent batsmen tried to force the pace, providing an unexpected bonus for hard-working Frank Harry, whose medium pace had yielded figures of 0 for 147 on the previous day.

Against Arthur Fielder and 'Charlie' Blythe Lancashire made the worst possible start, losing Reggie Spooner in the first over, Makepeace (caught at the wicket) and Tyldesley (caught at slip) before the score had reached 30. Kent will have been especially glad to see the end of Johnny Tyldesley. At Old Trafford he had punished the Kent bowlers, albeit minus Blythe, for 295*. There was resistance from the middle order but Sharp, while ambling a third run, was run out by a magnificent throw from the deep by Hutchings and the innings was all over in 165 minutes. Missed at least twice, MacLaren played a few typical strokes, including a lofted off-drive that consigned an elderly spectator to hospital, but the only innings of real substance was played by the amateur Leslie Poidevin, an Australian who had previously appeared for New South Wales.

Interrupted by a break for rain, Lancashire followed on and immediately lost Spooner for a pair, Makepeace bowled by a ball that came back from outside off stump and Tyldesley and Poidevin to slip catches by Seymour, the first a magnificent effort, one-handed at full stretch. Sharp and MacLaren then counterattacked, providing a semblance of respectability by hitting 58 in forty-five minutes. At stumps Lancashire were 78 for 4 (Sharp 30*, MacLaren 28*).

On the last day the remains of the Lancashire batting disintegrated against Fielder and Blythe and it was all over in half an hour. Fielder, with a match return of 11 for 30, emphasised his development as

Close of play. Lord Harris distributes the proceeds of the collection for the professionals.

England's leading fast bowler, the first to exploit the outswinger as his primary attacking weapon, varied by a ball coming back from outside off stump and a good yorker. During the season he captured 172 wickets, including a record all 10 for Players v. Gentlemen.

The championship was now looking a clear possibility and at the close of play Lord Harris made a short speech emphasising 'not only the splendid manner of the actual cricket but the fine spirit in which Kent played. Whether Kent won or lost the championship, the county would appreciate the great skill and the fine nature of the side this year.' He also distributed the proceeds of a collection taken on the ground for the professionals in appreciation of their services during the season – Fielder £30, Huish, Woolley and Blythe £15 each, Humphreys, Alec Hearne, Fairservice and Seymour £12 each, Hardinge and Hubble £6 10s each.

Kent went on to win all five of their remaining county fixtures to gain their first ever championship. Lancashire finished fourth.

The game was immortalised in the Albert Chevallier Tayler painting, commissioned by Kent to celebrate their championship win and destined to become probably the most famous of all cricket pictures. It provides an interesting example of artistic license. The non-striker shown, Billy Findlay, did not appear in the match at Canterbury in 1906 although he had played in the previous year. The reason seems to have been purely practical. The club paid Johnny Tyldesley's expenses for posing but presumably saved money by using Findlay, who had now become secretary of Surrey. Living in London, he would have been cheaper.

KENT v. NORTHAMPTONSHIRE

Date: 30-31 May, 1 June 1907   **Location:** Northampton

At the end of May Kent had hopes of repeating their 1906 triumphs. Northamptonshire, Sussex and Derbyshire had all been beaten by an innings, Somerset by 8 wickets, MCC by 95 runs. Their only defeat, by Lancashire, was by the narrow margin of 6 runs. Although the batting lacked consistency, the bowlers were very much in form. 'Charlie' Blythe had 37 wickets at 11.21, 'Pip' Fielder 49 at 9.20.

Northamptonshire, in their third first-class season, had lost at Catford in their first ever meeting with Kent. Now, in the return, rain restricted play on the first day to three hours in the afternoon, during which Kent scored 212 for 4. Hardinge, twice missed, added 64 for the first wicket with Woolley and 71 for the second with Seymour. At the close Hutchings was 49*, Dillon 9*.

Rain kept everyone inside on the second day but on day three play started on time, although the weather remained gloomy. Seven runs had been added when Hutchings, Dillon and Humphreys, adopting a 'get on or get out' policy, were all dismissed at the same total. The remaining batsmen contributed another 35.

On a pitch slow and soggy but far from the 'sticky' wicket of batsmen's nightmares, Northants commenced to the bowling of Blythe (pavilion end) and Fairservice. From Blythe's fourth ball wicketkeeper-batsman Walter Buswell played forward, missed, lifted his heel and was smartly stumped. The next ball rose to the shoulder of Charles Pool's bat, providing a simple catch for Fielder at point. Billy Kingston stopped the hat-trick and in Blythe's second over scored the first run of the innings.

Mark Cox was stumped in Blythe's third over and George Thompson bowled in his fifth – 3 for 4. Thompson, a talented all-rounder who subsequently played for England, had actually signed forms for Kent in 1898 and taken rooms in Catford in order to qualify when it was discovered that Northants were unwilling to release him. In over number six Blythe had Kingston lbw, captain Eddie Crosse (one of the Crosse & Blackwell family) caught at cover and Billy East, who tried to hit his way to glory, taken by Huish from a skyer – 4 for 7. At this point Blythe's figures were 6-5-1-7.

'Tubby' Vials hit Fairservice for the first boundary of the innings and in Blythe's seventh over Alexander Thompson scored a single. From the next ball Blythe dropped a return catch from Vials and 7 runs came from the remaining 3 balls. Much has been written about this miss, Frank Woolley thirty years later even claiming that Blythe 'could not bowl another ball'. This is obviously untrue and it is hard to see why the drop should have affected his bowling for more than a ball or two. At the mid-point of his career, Blythe had already twice taken 9 wickets in an innings, 8 once and 7 on no fewer than ten occasions, so he was hardly in unfamiliar territory. And runs often accrue when batsmen chance their arms in desperate situations. Vials and Thompson added 20 before Blythe had the latter taken at slip, followed shortly afterwards by Wells, caught at close mid-on. Vials hit Blythe over cover-point's head for four and last man Lancelot

Colin 'Charlie' Blythe, the supreme artist among left-arm spinners. Only two bowlers have equalled his 17 wickets in a day (10-30 and 7-18).

Kent won the toss and elected to bat   Umpires: W. Attewell and C.E. Dench

KENT	1ST INNINGS		
F.E. Woolley	b Driffield		26
H.T.W. Hardinge	c Cox b East		73
J. Seymour	b Wells		37
K.L. Hutchings	b Driffield		52
A.P. Day	c Kingston b East		23
*E.W. Dillon	b East		4
E. Humphreys	c Pool b Driffield		0
†F.H. Huish	not out		19
W.J. Fairservice	b East		9
C. Blythe	c Vials b Driffield		6
A. Fielder	b East		1
Extras	(B 2, LB 1, NB 1)		4
TOTAL	(all out)		254

FOW: 1-64, 2-135, 3-151, 4-204, 5-219, 6-219. 7-219, 8-243, 9-250

Bowling

	O	M	R	W
G.J. Thompson	15	1	76	0
East	33.2	6	77	5
Wells	6	1	34	1
Driffield	22	9	50	4
Cox	5	1	13	0

NORTHAMPTONSHIRE 1ST INNINGS			2ND INNINGS	
†W.A. Buswell	st Huish b Blythe	0	(8) c Woolley b Blythe	7
M. Cox	st Huish b Blythe	0	st Huish b Blythe	12
C.J.T. Pool	c Fielder b Blythe	0	st Huish b Blythe	5
W.H. Kingston	lbw b Blythe	2	lbw b Blythe	0
G.J. Thompson	b Blythe	0	c Hardinge b Blythe	1
W. East	c Huish b Blythe	0	(7) c Huish b Fairservice	0
*E.M. Crosse	c Fairservice b Blythe	0	(9) c Hardinge b Blythe	2
A.R. Thompson	c Seymour b Blythe	10	(6) c Humphreys b Blythe	7
G.A.T. Vials	not out	33	(1) b Fairservice	1
W. Wells	c Humphreys b Blythe	0	b Humphreys	0
L.T. Driffield	b Blythe	12	not out	1
Extras	(B 1, LB 2)	3	(B 3)	3
TOTAL	(all out)	60	(all out)	39

FOW: 1-0, 2-0, 3-1, 4-3, 5-4, 6-4, 7-4, 8-24, 9-26   1-1, 2-12, 3-12, 4-20, 5-20, 6-21, 7-32, 8-35, 9-35

Bowling

	O	M	R	W
Blythe	16	7	30	10
Fairservice	12	5	17	0
Fielder	3	0	10	0

	O	M	R	W
Blythe	15.1	7	18	7
Fairservice	9	3	15	2
Humphreys	6	3	3	1

Kent won by an innings and 155 runs

Driffield joined in, persuading Dillon to bring on Fielder in place of Fairservice, but the two were still there at lunch, taken at 54 for 9, Vials 30*, Driffield 9*.

On resumption, the innings lasted only another 3 overs, Blythe capturing all 10 wickets for the first and only time in his career. In the follow-on Vials, the hero of the first innings, opened with Cox but with the wicket becoming quicker as it dried, boldness was not his friend. An attempt to drive Blythe resulted in a spiralling catch to cover that was dropped by Fairservice, who atoned by bowling him in the next over. Eleven runs later Pool and Kingston fell to successive balls in Blythe's fourth over, followed 3 overs later by George Thompson, caught at long-off, and Cox, stumped. With East falling to Fairservice, Northants were 21 for 6 after 16 overs. Three missed catches, including another caught and bowled chance to Blythe, delayed the end but Wells played on and, in trying to emulate Vials's bold approach, Buswell, Driffield and Alexander Thompson fell to catches. The second innings had lasted 5 balls fewer than the first.

Despite relatively weak opposition, Blythe's 17 for 48 was a sublime display of spin bowling by one of the true masters of the art. Although his figures were subsequently eclipsed by Laker at Old Trafford in 1956, his 17 wickets in a day has only twice been equalled – by Hedley Verity at Leyton in 1933 and by Tom Goddard (against Kent) at Bristol in 1939.

When, in the first innings, Northants were 4 for 7 complete debacle seemed on the cards. It was a short reprieve. Ten days later Gloucestershire dismissed them for 12, thanks mainly to over-adventurous batting. Kent finished eighth.

KENT v. WORCESTERSHIRE

Date: 5-7 July 1909   **Location:** Stourbridge

Kent's hopes of a second championship title had suffered a jolt in mid-June with defeats in Tonbridge Week at the hands of Worcestershire and Lancashire. The latter was by the decisive margin of 312 runs but for the Kentish faithful losing to relative newcomers Worcestershire will have been the harder to stomach. It was only the second since the teams first met in 1900; Kent had won 10.

Times were changing. When Ted Dillon called wrongly and took the field, he was one of only three amateurs in the Kent side. In contrast with 1906, their last championship season, only once throughout 1909 would the 'coloured caps' outnumber the pros.

On a benign wicket in front of a crowd of 3,000, Fred Bowley and Harold Bache successfully negotiated Kent's all-international opening attack and it was not until Fielder returned for his second spell that the breakthrough came. Bowley misjudged a leg glance and was lbw and Bache was bowled shortly afterwards – 89 for 2. Better known as a Cambridge University, Corinthians and West Bromwich Albion

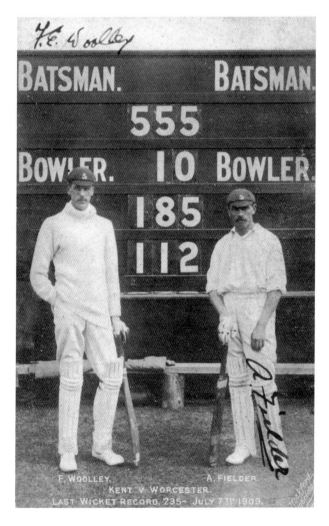

Frank Woolley and Arthur Fielder in front of the scoreboard. Their tenth-wicket partnership of 235 is still the English first-class record.

Worcestershire won the toss and elected to bat Umpires: B.W. Mason and J.E. West

WORCESTERSHIRE	1ST INNINGS		2ND INNINGS	
H.G. Bache	b Fielder	22	b Blythe	10
F.L. Bowley	lbw b Fielder	37	c Huish b Blythe	1
F.A. Pearson	c Huish b Fairservice	161	b Blythe	43
*H.K. Foster	run out	4	c Seymour b Blythe	8
E.G. Arnold	c Seymour b Fairservice	1	b Blythe	12
J.A. Cuffe	b Blythe	57	b Fielder	1
M.K. Foster	c Huish b Fielder	15	c Huish b Fielder	30
W.B. Burns	c Seymour b Woolley	14	c Dillon b Blythe	3
R.E. Turner	c Seymour b Woolley	6	c Hutchings b Blythe	19
W.H. Taylor	not out	13	c Huish b Fielder	5
†G.W. Gaukrodger	b Fairservice	10	not out	8
Extras	(B 5, LB 9, NB 6)	20	(B 10, LB 1, NB 10 W 1)	22
TOTAL	(all out)	360	(all out)	162

FOW: 1-55, 2-66, 3-85, 4-87, 5-209, 6-258, 7-287, 8-303, 9-345   1-3, 2-21, 2-29, 4-57, 5-68, 6-122, 7-122, 8-134, 9-154

Bowling

	O	M	R	W
Fielder	26	4	95	3
Blythe	20	3	67	1
Fairservice	29.5	6	103	3
Woolley	23	5	75	2

	O	M	R	W
Fielder	25	7	67	3
Blythe	24.5	10	44	7
Fairservice	6	1	19	0
Woolley	6	3	10	0

KENT	1ST INNINGS	
*E.W. Dillon	b Burns	0
E. Humphreys	c Burns b Cuffe	37
J. Seymour	b Burns	4
K.L. Hutchings	c Taylor b Cuffe	61
F.E. Woolley	c H.K. Foster b Arnold	185
H.T.W. Hardinge	lbw b Arnold	30
W.J. Fairservice	b Cuffe	1
L.H.W. Troughton	b Taylor	46
†F.H. Huish	b Taylor	23
C. Blythe	c Cuffe b Taylor	0
A. Fielder	not out	112
Extras	(B 34, LB 14, W 8)	56
TOTAL	(all out)	555

FOW: 1-0, 2-4, 3-107, 4-133, 5-181, 6-192, 7-276, 8-320, 9-320

Bowling

	O	M	R	W
Burns	20	1	87	2
Cuffe	50	10	157	3
Pearson	14	0	82	0
Arnold	21	5	61	2
Taylor	20	0	93	3
Turner	3	0	19	0

Kent won by an innings and 33 runs

footballer, Bache was one of four playing in the match (two on each side) destined to die on the Western Front in 1916-17. William Burns, Colin Blythe and Kenneth Hutchings were the others.

Two more wickets fell quickly, skipper Harold Knollys Foster the victim of a direct hit by 'Wally' Hardinge and Ted Arnold caught at slip, but Pearson settled in and, in company with Australian John Cuffe, batted through to lunch, taken at 119 for 4. After lunch the pair attacked the Kent bowling, taking their partnership to 122 when Cuffe, like many before him, fell to Blythe's arm ball. Pearson continued to play superbly, eventually departing caught at the wicket, ninth out for 161. Fairservice claimed the tenth wicket almost on the stroke of time.

'Dick' Pearson batted for 225 minutes and hit 23 fours. Born in Brixton and originally on The Oval staff, Pearson came to Kent for a trial in 1898. He was judged a 'good bat' and 'fair bowler' but nothing came of it. Had he been with a more fashionable county, he might well have played for England.

The second day was overcast and, in front of a disappointingly small crowd, Kent started shakily, losing Dillon in the first over and Seymour in the third, both to Burns, a bowler with a slingy, some thought dubious, action, but rated by many the fastest in England for a few overs. 'Punter' Humphreys was joined by Kenneth Hutchings and, despite a short break for rain, together they saw the hundred up in only ninety-five minutes. When Humphreys was caught at slip the partnership had added 103. Woolley now joined Hutchings but, when he had scored 19, a mistimed pull against Ted Arnold on a wicket enlivened by lunchtime rain resulted in a badly split lip, in his own words 'a fat nose', and a return to the pavilion for rest and repairs.

At 133 Hutchings was caught, having hit 3 sixes, 7 fours and only 3 singles in his 61. Hardinge and Troughton added 48 but when the former was lbw and shortly afterwards Fairservice bowled, Kent, at 192 for 6, still needed 18 to avoid the follow-on. Having had an hour to recover, Woolley resumed his innings and began to play strokes much as he had before his injury, adding 84 with Troughton and 44 with Huish. The latter was bowled at 320 and with Blythe caught at slip from the next ball, Kent found themselves still 40 in arrears with 1 wicket standing, Woolley 94*.

Fielder was no fool with the bat but having only once passed fifty and with a career average for his county of 10.18 – boosted of course by a confirmed number eleven's usual quota of not outs – he hardly seemed the ideal man to stop a hat-trick, still less to help Kent to a first innings lead. He did both. In trying to reach his hundred with a lofted drive off Cuffe, Woolley almost got out without a run added. Turner on

'Dick' Pearson, who very nearly became a Kent player, scored almost forty per cent of Worcestershire's runs.

the long-off boundary got his hands to the ball but could not hold it. The batsmen ran two and Woolley hit the next ball for four to reach his century and for the rest of the day the bowling was completely mastered. While Woolley went through his full repertoire of strokes, Fielder displayed an impeccable defence and unfailing judgement in hitting the bad ball. According to some sources he gave a chance to slip at 13 and was bothered by the pace of Burns, but he actually outscored his partner, 119 runs coming in the last hour. At the close of play, Kent were 439 for 9 (Woolley 136*, Fielder 67*).

On the final day, again watched by a small crowd, the Worcestershire bowlers, particularly Cuffe, bowled tighter after a night's rest but Woolley hit the first ball of the day for four and the batsmen were quickly back in control. Fielder reached his first (and only) first-class hundred and when Woolley cut Arnold straight into the hands of H.K. Foster at point a further 116 runs had been scored in eighty minutes, 235 runs for the partnership. When they reached 231 they passed the previous tenth wicket record of 230 set by R.W. Nicholls and W. Roche for Middlesex v. Kent at Lord's in 1899 (with Fred Huish behind the stumps). Woolley's 185 was his personal highest, scored in 285 minutes with 1 six and 24 fours. Fielder batted 140 minutes and hit 14 fours.

One hundred and ninety-five behind with only a draw to play for, Worcestershire lost Bowley, caught at the wicket from Blythe's third ball, but Bache and Pearson held on and at lunch the score was 21 for 1. Despite heavy rain during the interval, play resumed on time, Blythe bowling Bache in his first over and having Foster caught at short leg shortly afterwards. Arnold lived dangerously but not for long and, when Fielder bowled Cuffe, the total was only 68 for 5. Maurice Foster, brother of the skipper and one of seven Foster brothers to play for the county, then stayed with Pearson long enough to compel a change of bowling until another heavy shower drove the players in and tea was taken. Post tea, the score was taken to 122 but with Blythe and Fielder back in the attack, both batsmen fell at the same total. The tail offered little resistance and Kent won just before 6 p.m.

Whether the rain contributed to Blythe's success and the home team's defeat is unclear. *The Times'* correspondent for one thought it handicapped the bowlers by making the ball slippery. Kent went through the rest of the season unbeaten, winning 8 of their remaining 13 county fixtures and finishing champions for the second time in their history.

The Woolley/Fielder partnership stood as a world tenth-wicket record until Alan Kippax and Halford Hooker put on 307 for New South Wales v. Victoria in Melbourne in 1928/29. It remains the English record.

KENT v. GLOUCESTERSHIRE

Date: 11-12 August 1910   **Location:** College Ground, Cheltenham

Despite a change in the method of deciding the championship – percentage of wins to matches played – Kent's second successive title seldom looked in doubt. At the start of the second of three matches in Cheltenham Week no other county looked likely to match their record of 16 championship wins, all by substantial margins, 6 by an innings. Unexpected defeats at Leicester and Leyton were little more than minor hiccups.

Kent won the toss and commenced batting against a Gloucestershire attack that perhaps relied rather too much on one man. George Dennett was one of the finest left-arm spinners of his day and desperately unlucky to be a contemporary of Blythe and Rhodes. But with Jessop now merely an occasional change bowler, the only substantial support came from Charlie Parker, aided by a variety of amateur medium-pacers of relatively modest attainment. Parker was at the time bowling left-arm fast-medium, but within a decade he would metamorphose into one of the truly great spinners, whose Test career was unfairly blighted by his deep-rooted inability to treat the upper echelons of cricket's hierarchy with the respect they – but not Charlie – thought they deserved.

Parker claimed the first wicket when eighteen-year-old Freddie Knott, in his last year at Tonbridge and playing only his second county match, was caught at the wicket after an opening partnership of 93 in just over an hour. With the arrival of Seymour, Kent began to demonstrate the power and depth of their batting. Seymour hit 90 in seventy-five minutes in a partnership of 140 with Humphreys. Humphreys and Hutchings then added 93 in an hour. With Humphreys leaving after hitting 1 six and 24 fours and Woolley, mercifully perhaps, getting out relatively cheaply, Charles Hooman, in his first (and only) season, and the experienced Mason came together to hit 85 in forty minutes and when Hooman gave Parker his second wicket, Mason and Huish increased the tempo, adding 134 in fifty-five minutes. At the close of play Kent were 607 for 6, scored at 4.9 an over. Mason's 121* contained 1 six and 19 fours.

Dillon declared at the overnight total, leaving Gloucestershire with a mammoth task on a wicket enlivened by overnight rain. They were soon in trouble with the early loss of Langdon, caught at slip from Fielder's out-swinger, and Salter bowled, both without scoring, but wicketkeeper Jack Board, usually reliable in a crisis, and Sewell added 54. Once Douglas Carr had broken the partnership only Jessop, who cut, drove and swept with his customary vigour, looked capable of dealing with the Kent bowling for any length of time.

The main damage was done by Carr, a late developer who had come into first-class cricket in the previous year at the advanced age of thirty-seven. Heavily built and far from athletic in appearance, he had taught himself to bowl the new-fangled googly and had quickly become England's leading exponent of the art, so much so that in his first season he had been capped for England against Australia at The Oval, played twice for Gentlemen v. Players and finished second in the Kent bowling averages. A teacher by profession, he was never able to play a full season but in his four previous matches in 1910 he had picked up 29 wickets at 10.55.

The Cheltenham Festival, 1910. Kent in the field on the final day. [*Gloucestershire Echo*]

KENT v. GLOUCESTERSHIRE

Kent won the toss and elected to bat   Umpires: T.A. Brown and H. Wood

KENT	1ST INNINGS	
F.H. Knott	c Board b Parker	33
E. Humphreys	c Salter b Sewell	162
J. Seymour	c Salter b Dennett	90
K.L. Hutchings	c Salter b Brownlee	57
F.E. Woolley	c F.B. Roberts b Sewell	29
C.V.L. Hooman	c Langdon b Parker	46
*J.R. Mason	not out	121
†F.H. Huish	not out	44
D.W. Carr		
C. Blythe		
A. Fielder		
Extras	(B 17, LB 5, W 3)	25
TOTAL	(for 6 wickets declared)	607

FOW: 1-93, 2-233, 3-326, 4-378, 5-388, 6-473

Bowling

	O	M	R	W
Brownlee	20	1	130	1
Dennett	37	2	149	1
A.W. Roberts	20	4	108	0
Parker	28	8	83	2
F.B. Roberts	8	0	43	0
Sewell	5	0	35	2
Langdon	5	0	34	0

GLOUCESTERSHIRE	1ST INNINGS		2ND INNINGS	
†J.H. Board	b Carr	36	lbw b Carr	19
T. Langdon	c Woolley b Fielder	0	c Mason b Fielder	0
M.G. Salter	b Fielder	0	c Huish b Carr	27
C.O.H. Sewell	c Hooman b Blythe	42	b Carr	62
W.M. Brownlee	st Huish b Carr	16	(8) b Carr	3
F.H. Bateman-Champain	c Hutchings b Blythe	6	c Hooman b Blythe	30
*G.L. Jessop	st Huish b Carr	35	(5) hit wicket b Carr	0
F.B. Roberts	c & b Carr	10	(7) b Carr	33
A.W. Roberts	b Carr	0	c Knott b Blythe	0
C.W.L. Parker	not out	14	not out	8
E.G. Dennett	run out	2	st Huish b Blythe	5
Extras	(B 6, NB 1)	7	(B 6, LB 1, NB 3)	10
TOTAL	(all out)	168	(all out)	197

FOW: 1-1, 2-3, 3-57, 4-83, 5-97, 6-114, 7-128, 8-128, 9-165   1-1, 2-39, 3-65, 4-65, 5-133, 6-176, 7-183, 8-184, 9-184

Bowling

	O	M	R	W
Fielder	11.1	4	36	2
Blythe	14	2	57	2
Carr	15	1	68	5

	O	M	R	W
Fielder	12	2	56	1
Mason	3	0	10	0
Carr	11	0	42	6
Woolley	6	0	31	0
Blythe	10	0	48	3

Kent won by an innings and 242 runs

Following on, Gloucestershire again started badly, losing Langdon caught at slip off Fielder for the second time in the match to complete a pair, and once Carr came into the attack they never looked like taking the game into a third day. Their main hope, Jessop, hit his wicket trying to cut Carr's googly before he had scored. Cyril Sewell played by far the best innings. Born in Pietermaritzburg, Sewell, whose father had played for Middlesex in the 1860s, came to England with the first ever South African tourists and subsequently settled in Gloucestershire. A high-class batsman with a wide range of strokes, he hit eight centuries for his adopted county, captained them for two seasons as well as serving as a hardworking, efficient secretary.

Kent won their next two games and, although beaten in the penultimate fixture at The Oval, duly achieved their second successive championship, their third in all. They finished 22 percentage points ahead of their nearest rivals Surrey. It is indicative of their strength in depth that Woolley, who did the double in 1910, was only called on to bowl 6 overs at Cheltenham. At the end of the season Carr led Kent's bowling averages with 60 wickets at 12.16.

KENT v. SURREY

Date: 21-23 August 1911   **Location:** The Oval

Although they had never gained as much attention from the media as Roses matches, Kent v. Surrey encounters are often every bit as hard-fought. Alone among the Southern counties, Surrey have always had a strong professional backbone and since the present Kent Club was formed in 1870 they had frequently been outgunned by their Southern rivals. In 1911 the record stood Kent won 23, Surrey won 35, 1 tied, 25 drawn but the balance had begun to shift. When the two met at The Oval in 1911 Surrey had not won since 1905. In the same period Kent had won 6, including a 4-wicket victory at Blackheath three weeks earlier. At the time Kent still nursed hopes of a fourth title; Surrey's were by now almost extinct.

The legendary Oval groundsman Sam Apted, now in his last season, was renowned for producing the finest batting wickets in England, but in those long-departed days when pitches were uncovered, rain on The Oval's heavily marled turf could bring on a dramatic character change. On Thursday 21 August it poured steadily and a start was not possible until after 4 p.m. The conditions seemed tailor-made for Blythe (or his pupil Woolley) but Surrey's downfall came through the quickish leg-breaks and googlies of Douglas Carr. At close of play his figures were 8 for 52 and Surrey were 111 for 9 (Strudwick 12*, Smith 9*).

Further rain delayed the start on the second day but when the Surrey last pair got to the wicket at 2.45 p.m. they added what turned out to be a crucial 34. In his benefit match, Strudwick, more competent with the bat than his career figures might indicate, became the first Surrey batsman to pass 20. Four batsmen fell to stumpings. Despite the early loss of Arthur Day, Kent looked tolerably well placed with Humphreys and Woolley together at 68 for 2, but 6 wickets tumbled for 24 runs with Smith capturing 5 in 45 balls. The day ended with Kent 92 for 8 (Prest 9*, Blythe 0*).

Although never picked for England, William Charles Smith was one of the deadliest in the country when

F. HUISH. (KENT)

the ball was turning. Known as 'Razor' because he was reckoned the skinniest on the county circuit, he normally relied on the off-break bowled at near medium-pace, but his armoury also included a ball that, on flat wickets, went straight on with his arm and in the right conditions spun away from the bat 'like a fast leg-break'. Pelham (later Sir Pelham) Warner considered him second only to the great Sydney Barnes on a genuine sticky wicket. Oxford-born, Smith had a trial for Kent in 1898 but settled for The Oval.

On the final morning Blythe became Smith's eighth victim and, although Prest managed to double his score, he fell to the left-arm medium pace of Kirk and the visitors were soon in the field again facing a deficit of 38. Carr dismissed Hobbs and Hayward with 8 runs on the board but Hayes and Ducat took the score to 52 and Surrey looked likely to achieve a comfortable lead when both fell to Frank Woolley at the same total. Brought on in place of Carr in the ninth over, Woolley, making full use of his height, took 7 wickets in 39 balls for 9 runs, dismantling

Fred Huish, never capped for England but one of the outstanding wicketkeepers of his day, achieved a world record 1 catch and 9 stumpings. He is still the career record holder for dismissals for Kent.

Surrey won the toss and elected to bat   Umpires: J. Moss and J.E. West

SURREY	1ST INNINGS		2ND INNINGS	
T.W. Hayward	c Prest b Carr	7	st Huish b Carr	5
J.B. Hobbs	st Huish b Carr	17	c Hutchings b Carr	2
E.G. Hayes	c Blythe b Carr	3	b Woolley	12
A. Ducat	st Huish b Carr	12	c Seymour b Woolley	34
H.S. Bush	st Huish b Carr	12	st Huish b Woolley	0
*M.C. Bird	b Blythe	17	st Huish b Woolley	4
I.P.F. Campbell	lbw b Carr	1	st Huish b Woolley	0
†H. Strudwick	c Hubble b Blythe	25	b Woolley	1
E.C. Kirk	st Huish b Carr	2	st Huish b Blythe	0
J.W. Hitch	lbw b Carr	17	c Huish b Woolley	2
W.C. Smith	not out	20	not out	0
Extras	(B 6, LB 3, NB 3)	12	(LB 2, W 1)	3
TOTAL	(all out)	145	(all out)	63

FOW: 1-19, 2-24, 3-42, 4-45, 5-67, 6-75, 7-75, 8-84, 9-111   1-7, 2-8, 3-52, 4-52, 5-55, 6-59, 7-60, 8-61, 9-63

Bowling

	O	M	R	W
Blythe	25.2	7	66	2
Carr	25	4	67	8

	O	M	R	W
Blythe	13	4	19	1
Carr	7	0	32	2
Woolley	6.3	3	9	7

KENT	1ST INNINGS		2ND INNINGS	
A.P. Day	b Smith	3	c Strudwick b Smith	19
E. Humphreys	c Bird b Smith	30	run out	17
J. Seymour	c Hitch b Kirk	12	c Strudwick b Hayes	10
F.E. Woolley	b Smith	22	st Strudwick b Smith	8
*K.L. Hutchings	c & b Smith	7	b Smith	0
H.E.W. Prest	c Campbell b Kirk	18	c Hayes b Smith	4
J.C. Hubble	c & b Smith	2	c & b Kirk	15
†F.H. Huish	lbw b Smith	4	lbw b Smith	1
D.W. Carr	lbw b Smith	0	not out	12
C. Blythe	st Strudwick b Smith	1	b Kirk	6
A. Fielder	not out	3	c Smith b Kirk	0
Extras	(LB 3, NB 2)	5		0
TOTAL	(all out)	107	(all out)	92

FOW: 1-5, 2-33, 3-68, 4-71. 5-78, 6-82, 7-88, 8-92, 9-96   1-34, 2-37, 3-45, 4-51, 5-57, 6-59, 7-60, 8-82, 9-82

Bowling

	O	M	R	W
Smith	31	16	31	8
Kirk	30.5	9	71	2

	O	M	R	W
Smith	20	10	33	5
Kirk	8.4	1	33	3
Hayes	11	1	26	1

Surrey won by 9 runs

Surrey's strong batting line-up while his mentor Blythe was restricted to 1 wicket at the other end. The undemonstrative, ever-reliable Fred Huish gave outstanding support behind the stumps with 1 catch and 5 stumpings, bringing his total for the match to caught 1, stumped 9, a world record.

Chasing 102, Day and Humphreys added 34 but after the latter was needlessly run out, the effects of the roller wore off and Smith became very nearly unplayable, although the final 2 wickets fell to Kirk. Only Jack Hubble had looked like staying but even so Kent got to within 10 of the target.

Had the method of deciding the championship used in 1910, percentage of wins to matches played, still been in force Kent would have finished champions, but a new system had been introduced. Now there were 5 points for a win, 3 for first innings lead and 1 for a team behind on first innings in a drawn match, the title going to the team with the highest percentage of points gained to points possible. As a result Warwickshire were champions. Surrey had beaten them by an innings in May and had rather the worst of a draw at Edgbaston. Kent, who were runners-up, did not play them at all.

Huish, at the age of forty-one, ended 1911 with 101 dismissals, the first wicketkeeper to achieve three figures in a season.

KENT v. WARWICKSHIRE

Date: 19-21 June 1913   **Location:** Tonbridge

One of the hallmarks of a great team is the ability to turn almost certain defeat into victory, a quality never better illustrated than by Kent over three days in June 1913 at the now sadly defunct Angel Ground, Tonbridge.

In the first meeting between the two counties since 1899, Warwickshire, having won the toss on a firm, true wicket, suffered the early loss of two of their most dangerous batsmen, Jack Parsons and captain Frank Foster, both to the quicker bowlers, for 33. Crowther Charlesworth, using his feet to Blythe and Woolley, and Bill Quaife, giving, according to *The Times*, 'an object lesson of the science of batting' added 50. When they fell to the spinners, there came a robust partnership of 61 between wicketkeeper Charles Baker and Percy Jeeves, followed by another of 63 between William Hands and Sydney Santall. Woolley was the pick of the Kent bowlers but the team's fielding was said by *The Times* to have been 'below its best'. Left with an hour's batting, Kent lost Humphreys, caught at the wicket, Hardinge at short leg and Woolley to the last ball of the day, playing at a wide ball he could easily have left alone. *The Times* describes him as having been caught by Hands 'in the box', which is a touch confusing until realisation dawns that 'the box' was at the time another name for gully. At the close, Kent were 40 for 3 (Seymour 6*).

Warwickshire's 262 was considered a reasonable score but with rain on the second day restricting play to an hour it began to look a winning total once the wicket began to dry. Kent lost 1 wicket and closed at 104 for 4 (Hubble 22*, Dillon 15*).

On the final day, with a pitch drying under a hot sun and little but a draw to hope for, Kent lost their remaining 6 wickets to Foster and Jeeves in forty-five minutes for 28 runs. At 12.20 p.m. Warwickshire started their second innings with what appeared to be a decisive lead of 130. Forty-three minutes and 62 balls later they were all back in the pavilion with the lead a mere 146, all 10 wickets having fallen to the left-arm spin of Blythe and Woolley, described by *Wisden* as 'quite unplayable'. Five wickets fell with the score at 12; Parsons was top scorer with 6.

Despite the Warwickshire debacle, most 'experts' still seem to have felt the odds favoured the

Midlanders. However, with hindsight, it is clear that while the pitch was ideal for Blythe and Woolley, with two other left-armers, Humphreys and Hardinge, in reserve if necessary, Warwickshire, with an attack consisting of Foster, fastish left-arm, Hands and Jeeves, right-arm fast medium and the veteran Syd Santall, who bowled medium-pace off-cutters, and no left-arm spinner, lacked the bowling for the conditions.

Kent lost the important wickets of Humphreys and Seymour before lunch for 16 runs but, after the interval, Woolley took charge. With Hardinge he hit 37 in twenty-five minutes, 20 in twenty minutes with Hubble and finally 54 with Dillon. Forcing the pace with 'dazzling brilliancy' according to *Wisden*, Woolley scored his runs in eighty minutes, the match ending at 3.40 p.m.

It was suggested at the time that the Warwickshire captain made conditions worse by opting for the heavy roller rather than the lighter one chosen by Dillon, and should have entrusted more of the bowling to the

The Tonbridge scoreboard at the close of the Warwickshire second innings: all out for 16.

Warwickshire won the toss and elected to bat Umpires: A.J. Atfield and J. Moss

WARWICKSHIRE	1ST INNINGS			2ND INNINGS	
C. Charlesworth	c Hatfeild b Woolley		47	(3) c Seymour b Blythe	1
J.H. Parsons	b Day		0	(1) st Huish b Woolley	5
*F.R. Foster	b Fielder		13	(5) c Hubble b Blythe	2
W.G. Quaife	c Seymour b Blythe		31	b Blythe	0
†C.S. Baker	c Dillon b Humphreys		59	(2) c Humphreys b Woolley	4
P. Jeeves	b Woolley		30	c Blythe b Woolley	0
G. Curle	b Woolley		1	st Huish b Blythe	0
W.C. Hands	lbw b Blythe		21	b Woolley	0
S. Santall	c Dillon b Woolley		31	c Huish b Woolley	3
L.T.A. Bates	lbw b Woolley		4	not out	0
J.D. Brown	not out		0	st Huish b Blythe	1
Extras	(B 14, LB 9, NB 2)		25		0
TOTAL	(all out)		262	(all out)	16

FOW: 1-2, 2-33, 3-83, 4-118, 5-179, 6-190, 7-192, 8-255, 9-259

1-5, 2-6, 3-6, 4-12, 5-12, 6-12, 7-12, 8-12, 9-15

Bowling

	O	M	R	W
Fielder	21	4	56	1
Day	18	4	61	1
Blythe	22	4	50	2
Woolley	16.5	4	44	5
Humphreys	10	2	26	1

	O	M	R	W
Blythe	5.2	1	8	5
Woolley	5	1	8	5

KENT	1ST INNINGS		2ND INNINGS	
E. Humphreys	c Baker b Jeeves	11	lbw b Santall	1
H.T.W. Hardinge	c Jeeves b Foster	15	b Foster	27
J. Seymour	c Hands b Jeeves	24	c Jeeves b Foster	9
F.E. Woolley	c Hands b Jeeves	8	not out	76
J.C. Hubble	c Bates b Foster	24	b Charlesworth	10
*E.W. Dillon	c Baker b Foster	15	not out	18
A.P. Day	b Foster	0		
C.E. Hatfeild	b Foster	10		
†F.H. Huish	not out	7		
C. Blythe	c Quaife b Jeeves	6		
A. Fielder	b Foster	0		
Extras	(LB 8, W 4)	12	(B 5, LB 1)	6
TOTAL	(all out)	132	(for 4 wickets)	147

FOW: 1-23, 2-27, 3-40, 4-66, 5-104, 6-104, 7-113, 8-116, 9-129

1-1, 2-16, 3-73, 4-93

Bowling

	O	M	R	W
Foster	29	8	62	6
Hands	8	2	14	0
Jeeves	12	5	27	4
Santall	10	5	17	0

	O	M	R	W
Foster	10	1	44	2
Jeeves	7	0	20	0
Santall	11	0	27	1
Hands	3.4	0	27	0
Charlesworth	6	0	23	1

Kent won by 6 wickets

experienced Santall. Possibly, but what is beyond question is that after the first day Kent played superb cricket and above all they had Frank Woolley, who had match figures of 10 for 52 as well as playing a match-winning innings.

According to Woolley's autobiography *King of Games*, Foster, on leaving the field at the end of the Kent first innings, was asked by a spectator if he was enforcing the follow-on and replied 'No fear. We've got you where we want you, we're going in again and you can have fourth innings on that stuff.' Fred Huish overhears and comments prophetically 'I've seen sides out for next to nothing on such a pitch with two left-handers bowling.' A good story except that then, as now, the follow-on figure was 150.

Kent won their fourth championship in eight years, winning 20 games, four more than anyone else, and finishing 11.11 percentage points ahead of their nearest rivals Yorkshire. On a sadder note, Percy Jeeves, like Colin Blythe, was to die on the Western Front. Considered one of the most promising all-rounders in the country, he was killed in 1916 in front of High Wood during the Battle of the Somme. He did, however, achieve immortality of a sort when, during a Gloucestershire *v.* Warwickshire game at Cheltenham, a spectator named Wodehouse chose the name for his most famous creation.

KENT v. NOTTINGHAMSHIRE

Date: 16-18 August 1922   **Location:** Dover

One of the joys of county cricket for the true aficionado is that, now and again, a run-of-the-mill, journeyman player, one unregarded by the sporting press and never likely to catch the selectorial eye, steals the limelight from the headline makers. For one such, George Collins, his 'fierce hour and sweet' came at Dover in 1922.

Heavily built and clumsy looking, George had joined the Kent staff in 1908 but Kent had 'dispensed with his services' in 1913 only to take him back again after the First World War. As a left-handed batsman he was adaptable. When going in early he was tenacious with a strong defence but was generally considered dull. Down the order he could hit hard when necessary but it was pretty unexciting fare for Kent crowds accustomed to watching Frank Woolley. Earlier in the season he had hit his maiden first-class hundred, 108 v. Lancashire at Old Trafford. As a right-arm bowler he took a long bounding run but, to quote the historian R.L. Arrowsmith, 'his comfortable fast-medium was a sad anti-climax'. Capable of bowling long spells with a good outswinger in the right conditions, more often he was required to concentrate on line and length to shut up an end or merely take the shine off for the spinners who formed the cutting edge of the Kent attack. In the field he tried hard but was not really built for it. Although he hardly looked the part, he could also keep wicket.

Kent won the toss and spent the first day totalling 351 against an attack consisting of two past and two future England cricketers. Playing 'flawless cricket' according to *Wisden*, Jack Bryan and 'Wally' Hardinge began with a partnership of 158 and there were useful contributions from most of the middle order, although nobody else settled in to play a long innings. The more aggressive of the openers, Jack Bryan, hit 1 six and 11 fours.

G. COLLINS, KENT.

On the second day rain allowed only thirty minutes' cricket before lunch, play beginning in overcast conditions on what all agreed was a good wicket. Five of the first six in the Nottinghamshire batting order were or would shortly be Test cricketers but Collins was in the form of his life, moving the ball in off the seam, with the wind and damp atmosphere to help his outswinger. Whysall was the first to go, caught from a mishit drive at mid-off, followed immediately by George Gunn who, despite being known as a destroyer of pace bowling, missed a quicker ball that may have kept low. Future England captain Arthur Carr and forty-eight-year-old former England all-rounder John Gunn put on 37, the largest stand of the innings, but both fell to the rampant Collins, Carr bowled and Gunn beautifully caught low down at slip. Garnet Lee fell to another slip catch and Staples was bowled to give George his sixth scalp. Hardstaff and Richmond added 26 for the last wicket but the innings was over by 4 p.m.

Following on, Nottinghamshire made a disastrous start. George Gunn is still famous for his habit of walking down the wicket to the fastest of bowling.

With figures of 6 for 18 and 10 for 65, George Collins had the game of his life.

Kent won the toss and elected to bat   Umpires: B. Brown and G.A. Fuller

KENT	1ST INNINGS	
J.L. Bryan	b Richmond	84
H.T.W. Hardinge	c Oates b Richmond	90
J. Seymour	b Staples	21
F.E. Woolley	b Richmond	31
A.F. Bickmore	lbw b J.R. Gunn	26
G.J. Bryan	b Staples	28
W.H. Ashdown	b Staples	7
G.C. Collins	lbw b Staples	5
†J.C. Hubble	b Barratt	30
*L.H.W. Troughton	b Barratt	15
A.P. Freeman	not out	1
Extras	(LB 10, NB 2, W 1)	13
TOTAL	(all out)	351

FOW: 1-158, 2-190, 3-232, 4-241, 5-288, 6-288, 7-300, 8-315, 9-344

Bowling

	O	M	R	W
Barratt	27.5	5	81	2
Staples	40	11	92	4
Richmond	23	2	87	3
J.R. Gunn	33	7	78	1

NOTTINGHAMSHIRE	1ST INNINGS		2ND INNINGS	
G. Gunn	lbw b Collins	6	b Collins	6
W.W. Whysall	c G.J. Bryan b Collins	4	lbw b Collins	2
J.R. Gunn	c Ashdown b Collins	15	b Collins	4
*A.W. Carr	b Collins	22	c Freeman b Collins	0
J. Hardstaff	not out	18	lbw b Collins	49
W.R.D. Payton	c Woolley b Freeman	2	c Hubble b Collins	42
G.M. Lee	c Woolley b Collins	1	c & b Collins	1
S.J. Staples	b Collins	5	b Collins	19
†T.W. Oates	lbw b Freeman	1	c Ashdown b Collins	8
F. Barratt	b Freeman	11	c Freeman b Collins	19
T.L. Richmond	b Woolley	19	not out	7
Extras	(B 4, LB 10, NB 2)	16	(B 2, LB 1, NB 1, W 1)	5
TOTAL	(all out)	120	(all out)	162

FOW: 1-12, 2-12, 3-49, 4-50, 5-61, 6-62, 7-68, 8-71, 9-94

1-6, 2-12, 3-12, 4-13, 5-96, 6-98, 7-113, 8-130, 9-147

Bowling

	O	M	R	W
Collins	17	6	18	6
Woolley	13.4	2	47	1
Freeman	14	4	21	3
G.J. Bryan	7	0	18	0
	O	M	R	W
Collins	19.3	4	65	10
Ashdown	5	0	8	0
Freeman	20	7	55	0
Woolley	7	2	15	0
G.J. Bryan	3	0	14	0

Kent won by an innings and 69 runs

He did so now to Collins in the first over and was bowled middle stump. In Collins' next over Whysall was lbw and in his third John Gunn was bowled by a ball coming back from outside off stump. Carr, missed behind the wicket from the first ball he received, tried to drive an outswinger and was caught from a skyer at cover-point – Collins had 4 for 14. Hardstaff and Payton then restored some dignity to the proceedings with a hard-driving partnership of 83 but shortly before the close both fell to Collins, Payton caught at the wicket with the score at 96 and Hardstaff lbw 2 runs later. The day closed with the visitors 98 for 6.

The final day was sunny but still breezy and Nottinghamshire's last hopes were blown away when Lee gave Collins a simple caught and bowled. Play lasted only forty-five minutes with Collins finishing with 10 for 65, 16 for 83 in the match. He was the first Kent player to take all ten for the county since Blythe in 1907. There was an awkward moment when last man Fred Barratt gave a chance to Collins at mid-on and he dropped it. Poor George was distraught in case anyone thought he had missed it deliberately. The bowler was Freeman and it did not help that it was Freeman who took a difficult catch at cover to provide George with his tenth.

Against Middlesex in the very next match George began with 5 wides. *The Times* thought him 'quite one of our most extraordinary cricketers; both as a batsman and a bowler he never appears to know quite what he is about to do'. Although he finished with respectable career figures – 6,237 runs (avge 22.35), 378 wickets (avge 23.71) – George never approached such form again.

KENT v. SUSSEX

Date: 30-31 August, 1 September 1922   **Location:** Hove

Alfred 'Tich' Freeman was a late starter. He did not make his first-class debut until he was twenty-six but by 1922, at the age of thirty-four, he was well on the way to establishing himself as one of the country's leading exponents of the leg-break, top-spinner and googly, although he was not yet the phenomenal wicket taker he would ultimately become. When he arrived in Hove for the final county match of the season his haul of wickets stood at 177 at 15.66, his highest to date.

After a delayed start due to persistent rain, future England captain Arthur Gilligan chose to bat on a wet but, according to most accounts, not particularly difficult wicket. Sussex opened aggressively against the bowling of George Collins and Frank Woolley and, after 1 over, which had cost him 6 runs, Collins was replaced by Freeman. Joe Vine and Ted Bowley rapidly took the score to 25 when Freeman had the former caught at slip from a leg-break. Without addition Richard Young, leading scorer for Sussex in 1922, was stumped stretching forward at another. Bowley and Jupp both fell trying to drive, Tommy Cook was deceived by a top-spinner and when further heavy rain brought an early finish after just fifty minutes'

play the home side were 44 for 5 (Roberts 9*, Cox 4*) and Freeman had taken all 5 wickets in 8 overs at a personal cost of 10 runs.

On day two, the state of the wicket prevented play until 2.30 p.m.; by 2.50 p.m. the innings was over. Freeman's first two deliveries accounted for Cox, caught at slip, and Tate, bowled. When Arthur Gilligan was ninth out to another slip catch with the total at 47, Freeman's figures were 9 for 11. In the next over Woolley had wicketkeeper George Street caught, depriving 'Tich' of his chance of all ten.

Sussex began with Maurice Tate, who had recently adopted the fast-medium method that would make him famous, and Ted Bowley, who delivered high-tossed leg-breaks often bowled from a yard behind the crease. Bowley accounted for Jack Bryan in his first over but Gilligan soon switched to a more orthodox attack for the conditions, forty-eight-year-old George Cox, left-arm spin, and Vallance Jupp, an off-spinner capped for England the previous season. The change accounted for Seymour and Woolley with Kent still 2 runs in arrears, but the ever-reliable Hardinge steered Kent into a winning lead, batting two hours for his 44 and adding 81 in seventy minutes

'Tich' Freeman's 9 for 11 was his second 9-wicket return against Sussex. He had taken 9 for 87 at Hastings in the previous season.

Sussex won the toss and elected to bat   Umpires: F. Chester and T. Flowers

SUSSEX	1ST INNINGS		2ND INNINGS	
J. Vine	c Collins b Freeman	4	c G.J. Bryan b Freeman	0
E.H. Bowley	c G.J. Bryan b Freeman	24	b Freeman	31
R.A. Young	st Hubble b Freeman	0	c J.L. Bryan b Freeman	8
V.W.C. Jupp	c J.L. Bryan b Freeman	2	c Ashdown b Woolley	0
T.E.R. Cook	c Troughton b Freeman	0	c Seymour b Freeman	4
H.E. Roberts	c Hedges b Freeman	9	c G.J. Bryan b Freeman	31
G.R. Cox	c Ashdown b Freeman	4	c Troughton b Hardinge	4
M.W. Tate	b Freeman	0	b Freeman	0
*A.E.R. Gilligan	c Hedges b Freeman	3	b Freeman	10
†G.B. Street	c Ashdown b Woolley	0	c Ashdown b Freeman	21
A.H.H. Gilligan	not out	0	not out	12
Extras	(NB 1)	1	(B 1, LB 4)	5
TOTAL	(all out)	47	(all out)	126

FOW: 1-25, 2-25, 3-30, 4-30, 5-31, 6-44, 7-44, 8-47, 9-47   1-7, 2-40, 3-42, 4-44, 5-51, 6-82, 7-82, 8-83, 9-103

Bowling

	O	M	R	W
Collins	1	0	6	0
Woolley	10.1	3	29	1
Freeman	10	4	11	9

	O	M	R	W
Woolley	20	5	61	1
Freeman	23.5	6	56	8
Hardinge	4	3	4	1

KENT	1ST INNINGS	
J.L. Bryan	c Street b Bowley	0
H.T.W. Hardinge	c Young b Cox	44
J. Seymour	b Cox	23
F.E. Woolley	b Jupp	14
L.P. Hedges	b Cox	20
G.J. Bryan	c Roberts b Cox	64
W.H. Ashdown	st Street b Cox	0
G.C. Collins	run out	5
†J.C. Hubble	not out	6
*L.H.W. Troughton	b Jupp	11
A.P. Freeman		
Extras	(B 5, LB 3, W 1)	9
TOTAL	(for 9 wickets declared)	196

FOW: 1-0, 2-26, 3-45, 4-69, 5-150, 6-154, 7-175, 8-175, 9-196

Bowling

	O	M	R	W
Bowley	19	3	46	1
Tate	8	2	26	0
Cox	19	2	43	5
Jupp	11.1	0	58	2
A.H.H. Gilligan	4	1	14	0

Kent won by an innings and 23 runs

with Geoffrey Bryan. Nineteen-year-old Geoffrey, a left-hander like elder brother Jack, batted ninety minutes for his 64, which included 7 fours. At the close of play Kent were 196 for 9.

With the pitch still wet but with no sun to turn it vicious, Troughton declared at the overnight total. This time Freeman opened the bowling and Sussex were soon in trouble, losing the veteran Joe Vine to a slip catch in his first over. Sadly he failed to score in the last of his 506 appearances for the county. Ted Bowley, one of the best in the country against spin bowling, had been top scorer in the first innings and once again he was playing Freeman with relative ease. Like many wrist spinners, Freeman was sparing with his googly except against left-handers. Now, with the total at 40, he bowled one. The ball pitched outside off stump, Bowley read it as a leg-break and played no stroke, it broke in and bowled him. The only other serious resistance came from Harry Roberts, who managed to hit Woolley out of the attack, a few blows from Street and some stubborn resistance from Cox who stayed while 31 runs were added. At lunch Sussex had subsided to 97 for 8 and the last wicket fell fifteen minutes after the restart.

Freeman's 17 for 67 remains the second-best bowling analysis in a match for Kent and his first innings 9 for 11 is numerically the best 9 wickets in an innings return in the club's history, as well as being the best match and innings returns for Kent v. Sussex. He did not concede a boundary until his thirty-second over and his total of 194 wickets for the season was the highest until his *annus mirabilis* of 1928 when he achieved his incredible 304.

KENT v. LANCASHIRE

Date: 30 June, 1-2 July 1926   **Location:** Dover

In 1926 Lancashire were generally rated as the strongest side in the country; in the eyes of many, Kent were their closest rivals. Both teams were strong in batting but where the Northerners had a reputation for dourness and solidity, the more adventurous Kent batting was subject to occasional unexpected collapses. Kent relied heavily on Freeman as their main wicket-taker while Lancashire included not only the rotund Dick Tyldesley, who bowled mainly variations of top-spin, but also Australian Test cricketer Ted McDonald. Coming to Lancashire via a stint with Nelson in the Lancashire League, McDonald, even at the age of thirty-five, was still on his day the best fast bowler in the world.

In bright sunshine the Crabble was looking its best for the second match of the week. Lancashire batted all day for 307 for 8 on a fast, true wicket, the liveliest batting coming from Harry Makepeace and Ernest Tyldesley, who added 109 in 105 minutes. Frank Watson took 105 minutes over his first fifty before uncharacteristically getting himself out. Kent's ground fielding was much admired by the experts but, according to *The Times'* correspondent they missed two slip catches and two behind the wicket. Charlie Wright, the pick of the bowlers, was the chief sufferer. Immediately after bowling Halliday, Cornwallis suffered a groin strain that prevented him from bowling again in the match.

Kent were batting by noon on the second day. 'Wally' Hardinge and Bill Ashdown began with a flurry of strokes, 39 coming in the first thirty minutes. McDonald's first 41 balls had cost 29 but from his 42nd Ashdown attempted to hook a bouncer and skied a catch off the back of the bat. Always a bowler of moods, McDonald now gained an extra yard of pace, getting the ball to lift and inducing uncertainty on and outside off stump. Three wickets fell for 13 runs, Hardinge and Chapman edging to Duckworth, Seymour held low down at slip. Woolley, second to none against fast bowling, off-drove the fast bowler for four and square cut him for another before unexpectedly losing his leg stump to Watson's medium pace and, although Hubble resisted for a while, both he and Collins fell to the Duckworth/McDonald combination. Wright contributed a few lusty blows but made a hash of a short ball from Dick Tyldesley to become Duckworth's sixth victim.

Leonard Green did not enforce the follow-on and, although Hallows again went early and Watson succumbed to Freeman's googly, the usually cautious Makepeace hit 37 in fifty minutes, adding 50 in half an hour with Ernest Tyldesley and at tea Lancashire were 79 for 3. After the interval Tyldesley gave

a superb display, scoring 122 with Jack Iddon and reaching his century in 170 minutes. Enjoying a run of form that would propel him back into the England team, Tyldesley's two innings were the second and third in a sequence of ten successive scores of fifty or more, his century the second in a run of seven consecutive matches in which he passed three figures. At the close of play Lancashire were 243 for 5.

Lancashire declared at their overnight total, 425 ahead with play due to finish at 5.30 p.m. Attacking from the first ball, Kent soon lost Ashdown, bowled by a ball swinging in from outside leg stump, and Seymour, caught by Halliday running from deep mid-on to short leg to hold a towering mishit. Woolley joined Hardinge and, gradually accelerating, they scored 140 in ninety-five minutes, lunch being taken at 181 for 2. After lunch they continued in the same vein, reducing the previously dominant Lancashire bowlers to, in the words of Neville Cardus in the *Manchester Guardian* 'merely so much fuel for the bonfire of batsmanship which was burning for the glory of Kent cricket'. When Woolley was lbw the pair had scored 253 in 170 minutes and put Kent

Ernest Tyldesley and Ted McDonald (*top left and right*) and Frank Woolley and 'Wally' Hardinge (*bottom left and right*), key players in a game of fluctuating fortunes.

Lancashire won the toss and elected to bat   Umpires: H.R. Butt and F. Chester

LANCASHIRE	1ST INNINGS		2ND INNINGS	
J.W.H. Makepeace	b Collins	71	c Hubble b Ashdown	37
C. Hallows	c Freeman b Ashdown	12	lbw b Wright	2
G.E. Tyldesley	c Ashdown b Freeman	69	not out	144
F.B. Watson	st Hubble b Freeman	78	b Freeman	3
J. Iddon	lbw b Wright	18	b Chapman	39
T.M. Halliday	b Cornwallis	13	(7) not out	1
*L. Green	c Hubble b Collins	18		
F.M. Sibbles	c Hubble b Wright	17		
E.A. McDonald	c Chapman b Freeman	0	(6) c Woolley b Chapman	13
†G. Duckworth	b Wright	10		
R.K. Tyldesley	not out	15		
Extras	(B 1, LB 12, NB 1, W 1)	15	(B 1, LB 3)	4
TOTAL	(all out)	336	(for 5 wickets declared)	243

FOW: 1-24, 2-133, 3-174, 4-217, 5-255, 6-281, 7-291, 8-292, 9-313   1-11, 2-72, 3-77, 4-199, 5-221

Bowling

	O	M	R	W
Wright	38.2	9	81	3
Cornwallis	7	0	26	1
Ashdown	24	4	69	1
Freeman	50	14	96	3
Woolley	8	2	23	0
Collins	14	3	25	2
Hardinge	2	1	1	0

	O	M	R	W
Wright	16	2	51	1
Ashdown	16	2	46	1
Freeman	12	4	34	1
Collins	5	0	24	0
Woolley	11	1	42	0
Hardinge	7	0	18	0
Chapman	4	0	24	2

KENT	1ST INNINGS		2ND INNINGS	
H.T.W. Hardinge	c Duckworth b McDonald	27	run out	132
W.H. Ashdown	c Duckworth b McDonald	19	b Sibbles	6
J. Seymour	c R.K. Tyldesley b McDonald	1	c Halliday b McDonald	24
F.E. Woolley	b Watson	24	lbw b Watson	137
A.P.F. Chapman	c Duckworth b McDonald	3	c Makepeace b McDonald	49
J.A. Deed	b Watson	8	(8) b McDonald	0
G.C. Collins	c Duckworth b McDonald	17	(6) b R.K. Tyldesley	0
†J.C. Hubble	c Duckworth b McDonald	20	(7) st Duckworth b R.K. Tyldesley	17
A.C. Wright	st Duckworth b R.K.Tyldesley	19	b McDonald	0
A.P. Freeman	b McDonald	14	b McDonald	13
*W.S. Cornwallis	not out	1	not out	1
Extras	(NB 1)	1	(B 8, LB 1, NB 4)	13
TOTAL	(all out)	154	(all out)	392

FOW: 1-39, 2-47, 3-48, 4-52, 5-79, 6-86, 7-104, 8-135, 9-153   1-12, 2-41, 3-294, 4-327, 5-331, 6-361, 7-361, 8-361, 9-390

Bowling

	O	M	R	W
McDonald	17.3	0	81	7
Sibbles	9	3	27	0
R.K. Tyldesley	10	3	35	1
Watson	2	1	10	2

	O	M	R	W
McDonald	30	2	106	5
Sibbles	16	1	75	1
R.K. Tyldesley	22.4	1	93	2
Watson	16	2	58	1
Iddon	9	0	47	0

Lancashire won by 33 runs

in sight of victory. Missed at 82, Woolley hit 15 fours. Belying his supposed weakness against fast bowling, Hardinge was equally in command until, attempting a second run, he was run out by a direct hit from the Lancashire captain. He had batted for 230 minutes and hit 13 fours. Collins was bowled first ball but Chapman continued to blaze away and at tea (4 p.m.) Kent were 331 for 5, needing another 95.

McDonald had been bowling off-cutters from round the wicket. At tea his captain plied him with a large whisky and asked for one more burst of speed. Suitably stimulated, he obliged. Chapman and Hubble added another 30 but the former was caught at cover from a slash at a fast rising ball and the next two deliveries shattered the stumps of Deed and Wright to give McDonald the timeliest of hat-tricks. Hubble and Freeman kept Kent hopes alive, taking the score to 390, but the leg spinner became McDonald's twelfth victim and Hubble was stumped almost on the stroke of 5 p.m. to end an epic run chase.

Lancashire finished champions, 10 points ahead of Kent who were third.

KENT v. LANCASHIRE

Date: 18, 20-21 June 1927   **Location:** Maidstone

For a few years Percy Chapman was the golden boy of English cricket. As a left-handed batsman he was the most exciting in the country, relying less on technique than on a good eye, fast reactions and sheer physical strength. Whatever the situation, he kept playing shots and the crowds loved him for it. Although never approaching Woolley's elegance, timing and ability to defend when necessary, he could, like Woolley, drive from a good length or from just short of a good length, in the air or along the ground. When he flashed outside off stump – which he did frequently – the likely outcome was a six over point or third man. Square on the leg side he revelled in the pull and a devastating short-arm hook. While no tactical genius, he regained the Ashes as captain at The Oval in 1926 and retained them by a 4-1 margin in 1928/29. He was past his best by the time the Kent captaincy came his way but, although his record was hardly outstanding, his youthful, joyous approach to the game was infectious and people enjoyed playing under him. In the field he was outstanding at slip, gully or cover with a penchant for holding the most unlikely catches. Chapman's time at the top was tragically short and, examined dispassionately, his figures for Kent are relatively modest. Nevertheless, nothing he achieved for England, the Gentlemen or Cambridge exceeded his performance in the second half of Maidstone Week 1927 against Lancashire, the reigning champions.

Kent batted first on a pitch damp from overnight rain but after ten minutes a further shower caused a fifty-minute stoppage. With his smooth, balanced, almost silent approach to the wicket – similar to Michael Holding's, according to some of those lucky enough to have seen both – McDonald had less trouble with wet run-ups than most of his contemporaries. With a strong wind behind him Kent lost Ashdown, caught at slip, and captain Evans in the gully with only 3 runs on the board, both to very fast balls. Shortly afterwards Hardinge was run out following a misunderstanding and Kent lunched uneasily at 18 for 3.

After lunch, an unusually circumspect Frank Woolley and Leslie Ames, the latter playing his first full season, took the score to 64 when the left-hander tried and failed to hit the accurate fast-medium Frank Sibbles over mid-off. With the sun out and the wicket beginning to dry, McDonald had switched to bowling off-cutters from round the wicket and 6 runs later he had Ames lbw, which brought in Geoffrey Legge to join Chapman. There followed one of the most memorable periods in the entire history of Kent county cricket. Despite McDonald, who went back to bowling fast off his long run, in 150 minutes Chapman and Legge added 284 in what was described as 'the most remarkable display of sustained attack on fast bowling that has ever been witnessed'.

Told he was wanted on the phone as he was going out to bat at 70 for 5, Chapman had replied 'Tell him to hang on. I'll be back in a minute.' In fact he batted for three hours and was last out, caught at deep mid-on, having hit 5 sixes and 32 fours. His first hundred came in even time, his second in seventy minutes,

his last fifty in under fifteen minutes. He scored 184 between 4.35 p.m. and 6.20 p.m. In hitting his first century for the county, Geoffrey Legge was inevitably overshadowed by the pyrotechnics going on at the other end but nevertheless he played a vital supporting role. All the remaining batsmen struggled against Dick Tyldesley and the 87 added for the last 4 wickets came almost entirely from Chapman. Lancashire sent in Duckworth and Sibbles as dual nightwatchmen and closed at 13 for 0.

As sometimes happens in cricket, the rest of the match was anti-climax. Lancashire batted for almost the whole of the second day and, although at 184 for 6 the follow-on seemed a possibility, Peter Eckersley and Jack Iddon saw them to safety with an eighth-wicket

Percy Chapman's 260 in three hours, 'the most remarkable display of sustained attack on fast bowling that has ever been witnessed.'

Kent won the toss and elected to bat Umpires: J. Hardstaff and J. Stone

KENT	1ST INNINGS		2ND INNINGS	
H.T.W. Hardinge	run out	12	lbw b Sibbles	0
W.H. Ashdown	c Sibbles b McDonald	1	not out	86
*A.J. Evans	c R.K. Tyldesley b McDonald	0	st Duckworth b R.K. Tyldesley	143
F.E. Woolley	c McDonald b Sibbles	9		
L.E.G. Ames	lbw b McDonald	36		
A.P.F. Chapman	c McDonald b R.K. Tyldesley	260	(4) c Taylor b McDonald	4
G.B. Legge	c Duckworth b R.K. Tyldesley	101		
†J.C. Hubble	b R.K. Tyldesley	1		
C.J. Capes	lbw b R.K. Tyldesley	8		
A.C. Wright	b R.K. Tyldesley	6		
A.P. Freeman	not out	0		
Extras	(B 5, LB 2)	7	(B 3, LB 2, W 1)	6
TOTAL	(all out)	441	(for 3 wickets declared)	239

FOW: 1-3, 2-3, 3-18, 4-64, 5-70, 6-354, 7-358, 8-370, 9-394   1-3, 2-227, 3-239

Bowling

	O	M	R	W
McDonald	25	3	118	3
Sibbles	28	6	108	1
R.K. Tyldesley	18.3	3	94	5
Watson	11	0	72	0
Iddon	6	0	42	0

	O	M	R	W
McDonald	11.2	3	39	1
Sibbles	20	2	59	1
R.K. Tyldesley	16	2	64	1
Watson	11	0	56	0
Iddon	4	0	15	0

LANCASHIRE	1ST INNINGS		2ND INNINGS	
†G. Duckworth	b Capes	18		
F.M. Sibbles	lbw b Freeman	28		
C. Hallows	c Wright b Hardinge	82	(1) not out	57
G.E. Tyldesley	lbw b Freeman	8	(3) c & b Ames	40
F.B. Watson	c Woolley b Evans	7	(2) lbw b Capes	10
*L. Green	b Wright	32		
M.L. Taylor	b Freeman	0		
P.T. Eckersley	not out	73		
J. Iddon	c Hardinge b Ashdown	42		
R.K. Tyldesley	b Woolley	13		
E.A. McDonald	c Freeman b Woolley	2		
Extras	(B 12, LB 8, NB 3, W 1)	24	(B 6, LB 1, NB 1)	8
TOTAL	(all out)	329	(for 2 wickets)	115

FOW: 1-46, 2-54, 3-77, 4-92, 5-184, 6-184, 7-207, 8-303, 9-321   1-39, 2-115

Bowling

	O	M	R	W
Wright	19	3	44	1
Evans	20	4	33	1
Capes	23	7	61	1
Freeman	42	14	71	3
Woolley	9.5	3	23	2
Ames	1	0	3	0
Ashdown	18	2	43	1
Hardinge	11	5	27	1

	O	M	R	W
Wright	7	0	23	0
Ashdown	5	0	8	0
Capes	10	3	14	1
Freeman	6	3	13	0
Hardinge	6	2	4	0
Woolley	3	0	15	0
Legge	4	0	17	0
Chapman	4	0	13	0
Ames	0.1	0	0	1

Match Drawn

partnership of 96. For Kent, Evans used eight bowlers (including Les Ames) but only Freeman looked more than steady on the slow wicket. Kent lost Hardinge before close of play.

On the final morning Kent attempted quick runs but although Evans played brilliantly for his 143, Ashdown was tied down and the declaration was delayed until half an hour after lunch. Lancashire made no serious effort to score 351 in a little over three hours but there was time for Les Ames to pick up the first wicket of his career. Kent used nine bowlers, ten in the match.

Chapman ended his season for Kent with 985 runs at 70.35 including three hundreds. While his triumphs on the 1928/29 tour still lay ahead of him, for the rest of his career with Kent – he retired in 1938 – he only twice averaged over 30 and hit only three more centuries.

KENT v. WARWICKSHIRE

Date: 29-30 June 1932   **Location:** Folkestone

The first game of the 1932 Folkestone Festival had provided 'Tich' Freeman with a match return of 13 for 144 and Kent with a two-day victory over Lancashire. In the previous year, both matches had similarly ended in two days and doubts about the Folkestone wicket were expressed in the press. On the other hand, in 1931 Herbert Sutcliffe had hit a double century there and shared a second-wicket partnership of 258 with Edgar Oldroyd. Frank Woolley too had hit a second-innings hundred against Warwickshire and, while Freeman had done the damage for the home side, most of Kent's wickets had fallen to pace so possibly it was not as simple as that.

Kent won the toss and batted against the two quick bowlers largely responsible for Warwickshire's victory on the same ground in 1931, 'Danny' Mayer and Derek Foster. After the latter bowled Aidan Crawley with only 5 on the board, Ashdown and Woolley added 83 in an hour but both were dismissed before lunch, taken at 150 for 4. Woolley scored his 92 out of 139 with 1 six and 13 fours. Kent were prone to sudden collapses and they suffered one after lunch, losing their remaining 6 wickets in forty minutes for just 24 runs, all to Mayer and Foster, Mayer claiming 3 for 5 in 5 overs, Foster 3 for 19 in 4 overs and 3 balls.

Warwickshire started well but after Kemp-Welch ran himself out, Freeman began to make life difficult. Bates hit 14 in one over from Ashdown but fell to the predatory Ames/Freeman partnership. Bob Wyatt was not among the most quick-footed of batsman and seldom flourished against the Australian leg-spinners, but he rarely seems to have been troubled by Freeman. Now he quickly settled in, presenting resolute defence to Freeman but taking 12 from Hardinge's first over and hitting him into a marquee in the next, injuring one of the Brotherhood of Cheerful Sparrows in doing so. At tea Warwickshire were 114 for 4 and, with Wyatt still there, looking likely to take the lead. Once again tea and Freeman changed the situation. Five of the remaining 6 wickets fell to him in half an hour in 4 overs at the cost of 4 runs, leaving Wyatt without a partner. Always at his best in a crisis, he batted faultlessly for eighty-five minutes and hit 9 fours as well as his Cheerful Sparrow-endangering six. Freeman had bowled unchanged. Kent had to bat for an hour and lost Crawley, Ashdown and Ames cheaply, all to Mayer and Foster. Close: Kent 47 for 3 (Woolley 21*).

The second day began badly for Kent with the loss of 3 wickets for 17 but Hardinge led a rally, adding 44 with Leslie Todd and 46 with Ian Akers-Douglas. Undefeated when the last wicket fell, he had batted for 130 minutes and guided Kent to a lead of 214. All Kent's wickets fell to the two Warwickshire pace bowlers, Mayer (9-73) and Foster (11-163).

Once again Freeman opened the bowling and at 22 Kemp-Welch gave him his first wicket and Ames his fourth stumping of the match. Bates and Croom took the total to 49 when, at the same score, Croom

was lbw to Freeman's googly and Bates was caught off Alan Watt. As in the first innings, Wyatt played all the bowling without obvious difficulty and, after losing Parsons and Kilner cheaply, he shared a partnership

A Kent team in 1932. From left to right: 'Wally' Hardinge, Alec Pearce, 'Tich' Freeman, Alan Watt, 'Father' Marriott, Bryan Valentine, Percy Chapman, Bill Ashdown, Les Ames, Aidan Crawley and Frank Woolley.

Kent won the toss and elected to bat   Umpires: F. Chester and T.W. Oates

KENT	1ST INNINGS		2ND INNINGS	
A.M. Crawley	b Foster	5	lbw b Mayer	2
W.H. Ashdown	c Santall b Foster	30	b Foster	5
F.E. Woolley	c Wyatt b Mayer	92	c Foster b Mayer	25
†L.E.G. Ames	c Croom b Mayer	12	lbw b Foster	16
H.T.W. Hardinge	c Kilner b Mayer	18	not out	66
*A.P.F. Chapman	c Kilner b Mayer	3	c Smart b Mayer	1
I.S. Akers-Douglas	b Mayer	1	(9) c Smart b Foster	20
B.H. Valentine	c Wyatt b Foster	3	(7) c Wyatt b Foster	3
L.J. Todd	b Foster	2	(8) c Roberts b Foster	13
A.E. Watt	not out	1	b Foster	4
A.P. Freeman	b Foster	4	b Mayer	4
Extras	(NB 2, W 1)	3	(B 2, LB 8)	10
TOTAL	(all out)	174	(all out)	169

FOW: 1-5, 2-88, 3-133, 4-144, 5-150, 6-164, 7-167, 8-169, 9-169   1-7, 2-15, 3-47, 4-53, 5-55, 6-64, 7-108, 8-154, 9-162

Bowling

	O	M	R	W
Mayer	13	2	25	5
Foster	18.3	1	81	5
Wyatt	5	1	23	0
Roberts	3	0	28	0
Santall	3	0	14	0

	O	M	R	W
Mayer	21.2	4	48	4
Foster	24	5	82	6
Santall	5	2	5	0
Wyatt	5	0	15	0
Croom	3	0	9	0

WARWICKSHIRE	1ST INNINGS		2ND INNINGS	
G.D. Kemp-Welch	run out	9	st Ames b Freeman	3
A.J.W. Croom	lbw b Freeman	12	lbw b Freeman	28
L.T.A. Bates	st Ames b Freeman	18	c Valentine b Watt	14
*R.E.S. Wyatt	not out	59	not out	49
J.H. Parsons	c Ashdown b Freeman	11	c Hardinge b Freeman	1
N. Kilner	lbw b Freeman	13	lbw b Freeman	1
F.R. Santall	st Ames b Freeman	1	b Freeman	21
H.J. Roberts	st Ames b Freeman	0	c Ashdown b Freeman	0
†J.A. Smart	lbw b Freeman	1	b Freeman	6
D.G. Foster	b Freeman	0	b Freeman	6
J.H. Mayer	c Ames b Watt	0	lbw b Freeman	3
Extras	(B 4, LB 1)	5	(B 3, LB 3, NB 2)	8
TOTAL	(all out)	129	(all out)	140

FOW: 1-22, 2-28, 3-48, 4-86, 5-116, 6-118, 7-118, 8-124, 9-124   1-22, 2-49, 3-49, 4-55, 5-58, 6-104, 7-108, 8-114, 9-126

Bowling

	O	M	R	W
Ashdown	14	3	63	0
Freeman	19	7	31	8
Hardinge	2	0	19	0
Watt	3.3	1	11	1

	O	M	R	W
Watt	23	3	71	1
Freeman	22.4	5	61	9

Kent won by 74 runs

of 46 in twenty-five minutes with Croom until the latter was lbw trying to sweep a ball pitching a yard outside leg stump. The remaining 4 wickets fell to Freeman at the cost of 13 runs, giving him a match return of 17 for 92, 30 for 236 for the week and Kent a 74-run victory. Freeman bowled unchanged throughout the match for the second 17-wicket return of his career. Once again undefeated, Wyatt, who had seldom played better, hit 1 six (off Freeman) and 6 fours.

According to *The Daily Telegraph*, by the second day the pitch was little more than 'powdered chalk', 'characterised by players and other principals as absurd', which, if true, would detract somewhat from Freeman's performance. Wyatt too, in his autobiography *Three Straight Sticks*, described the pitch as 'badly crumbled' but, curiously, no other spinner managed to take a wicket and neither *The Times* nor *Wisden* commented on the state of the pitch. Freeman picked up another 20 wickets in the two matches of the 1933 Folkestone Festival but, despite the presence among the opposition of spinners such as Charlie Parker, Tom Goddard and Reg Sinfield (Gloucestershire) and Peter Smith (Essex), Les Ames achieved the highest score of his career, 295, Bryan Valentine hit two centuries and Les Todd one. Nevertheless, after the Second World War, the wicket was dug up and relayed with more durable blue clay.

KENT v. YORKSHIRE

Date: 19, 21-22 August 1933   **Location:** Dover

Few stronger teams have competed in the County Championship than those fielded by Yorkshire in the 1930s. In the last decade before the Second World War they won the title seven times and only once finished lower than third. Of the players taking the field against Kent at Dover in 1933, six had been capped for England; three more would be capped within the next five years. The team had already won the championship.

When Kent opened on a good wicket, Todd was soon caught fencing at a rising ball on leg stump and Woolley afforded the bowling due respect, taking half an hour over his first 2 runs. Meanwhile, Bill Ashdown had been indulging in his favourite square cut until, once again, his main strength proved his chief weakness when, attempting to cut Verity, he was caught at the wicket. His 59 had been scored out of 75. At lunch Kent were 112 for 2.

Bodyline was very much in the news and Bowes was one of its chief exponents. Shortly after lunch Ames was bowled leg stump backing away trying to hit a shortish ball through the covers. With Bryan Valentine's arrival Yorkshire lost their customary control. Woolley hit Bowes for six between point and cover and drove Verity a vast distance over long-on for another. Valentine hooked Rhodes for a third. Once the great left-hander went down the wicket to Bowes and edged him over the slips for four. Thanks to an error in transmission this was reported in one Yorkshire paper as 'Woolley advanced on Bowes and hit him over the cliffs into the sea' – if true the longest hit of all time. When Bowes took the new ball, Woolley hit him for 3 fours, a two and a single in one over. An hour's batting had produced 99 runs when Woolley skied a ball from Macaulay to mid-on.

Valentine and Gerry Chalk added a further 50 when Brian Sellers turned to the left-arm wrist spin of Morris Leyland. Almost immediately Valentine was lbw after hitting 1 six and 13 fours and the remaining 5 wickets fell for 57, 3 of them to Leyland. Yorkshire scored 36 for the loss of Percy Holmes.

Next day Sutcliffe ran himself out, Verity edged a leg-break and Mitchell fell to Freeman's top-spinner, but Leyland dominated the Kent bowlers from his first ball. With Marriott and Freeman bowling in tandem the Kent attack was theoretically at its strongest but few Englishmen have played wrist spin better than the Yorkshire left-hander and at lunch the score was 145 for 3, Leyland 75*, Wilf Barber 14*. After the break Leyland reached his hundred with a six over long-on, having batted for 110 minutes and scored his runs out of 136. Barber was caught at square leg when the partnership was worth 147 but Leyland carried on scoring all round the wicket without a hint of risk, reaching his 200 and Yorkshire's 300 with an off-driven four off Marriott shortly before tea. Shortly after tea a rainstorm of monsoon proportions ended play. Yorkshire were 330 for 6 (Leyland 207*, Sellers 2*).

Next day Yorkshire batted only long enough to secure a first-innings lead (worth 5 points in a drawn game). Leyland's 210* was the highest at the Crabble, scored in 220 minutes with 1 six and 28 fours. With the wicket now receptive to spin, Sellers opened with Hedley Verity bowling to a close field and

Morris Leyland and Hedley Verity (*top left and right*) and Bryan Valentine and Bill Ashdown (*bottom left and right*). An unexpected victory for Kent over the champions.

Kent won the toss and elected to bat   Umpires: L.C. Braund and D. Hendren

KENT	1ST INNINGS		2ND INNINGS	
W.H. Ashdown	c Wood b Verity	59	c Sellers b Verity	0
L.J. Todd	c Verity b Bowes	11	lbw b Verity	10
F.E. Woolley	c Bowes b Macaulay	86	c Mitchell b Verity	8
†L.E.G. Ames	b Bowes	12	c & b Verity	15
*B.H. Valentine	lbw b Leyland	90	c Rhodes b Verity	8
F.G.H. Chalk	c Wood b Verity	20	c Sutcliffe b Verity	39
C.H. Knott	b Leyland	19	c & b Verity	4
H.T.W. Hardinge	c & b Leyland	0	hit wicket b Leyland	19
A.E. Watt	c Sellers b Verity	23	c Macaulay b Verity	4
A.P. Freeman	not out	0	not out	7
C.S. Marriott	b Leyland	0	st Wood b Verity	9
Extras	(B 6, LB 4, NB 2)	12	(B 5, LB 5)	10
TOTAL	(all out)	332	(all out)	133

FOW: 1-28, 2-103, 3-124, 4-223, 5-273, 6-305, 7-305, 8-315, 9-332   1-1, 2-21, 3-41, 4-42, 5-51, 6-58, 7-101, 8-106, 9-123

Bowling

	O	M	R	W
Bowes	19	3	70	2
Macaulay	17	3	39	1
Rhodes	13	0	57	0
Verity	29	8	78	3
Sellers	4	0	20	0
Leyland	12.1	3	56	4

	O	M	R	W
Verity	30	10	59	9
Macaulay	14	5	26	0
Rhodes	3	1	10	0
Leyland	12	1	28	1

YORKSHIRE	1ST INNINGS		2ND INNINGS	
P. Holmes	c Valentine b Freeman	19	c Ashdown b Marriott	10
H. Sutcliffe	run out	17	b Freeman	12
H. Verity	c Ames b Freeman	2	(8) c Chalk b Freeman	0
A. Mitchell	lbw b Freeman	13	(3) lbw b Freeman	0
M. Leyland	not out	210	(4) c Woolley b Freeman	10
W. Barber	c Freeman b Ashdown	40	(5) c Ashdown b Marriott	25
†A. Wood	lbw b Marriott	15	(6) c Knott b Freeman	19
*A.B. Sellers	not out	2	(7) b Freeman	4
G.G. Macaulay			c Watt b Marriott	4
A.C. Rhodes			not out	3
W.E. Bowes			absent hurt	
Extras	(B 7, LB 8)	15	(LB 1)	1
TOTAL	(for 6 wickets declared)	333	(all out)	88

FOW: 1-32, 2-36, 3-44, 4-106, 5-253, 6-320   1-19, 2-19, 3-27, 4-33, 5-65, 6-70, 7-70, 8-80, 9-88

Bowling

	O	M	R	W
Watt	23	3	71	0
Freeman	46.4	16	100	3
Marriott	43	10	113	1
Ashdown	9	1	34	1

	O	M	R	W
Freeman	23	8	51	6
Marriott	22.4	8	36	3

Kent won by 44 runs

Kent were soon 58 for 6. Ashdown and Woolley fell to close catches in front of the wicket, victims of the unexpected bounce characteristic of Verity's bowling. Ames was caught and bowled, Todd lbw, Valentine and Knott caught from attempts to drive. With the wicket easing, Chalk and Hardinge added a further 19 before lunch. Post lunch, by sensible aggressive batting they took the score to 101 when Hardinge trod on his stumps trying to hook a long hop. Chalk was ninth out, top scorer with 39 and, although there was an unexpected, not to say improbable, bonus when Marriott – reputedly the worst batsman in the country – hit 2 fours, Kent were all out by 3.15 p.m., leaving Verity with 9 for 59 and 133 as Yorkshire's target.

Valentine opened with his two leg-spinners and by the time the score had reached 19 Sutcliffe, arguably the best in the world on a turning wicket, and Mitchell had both fallen to Freeman. At tea, Holmes and Leyland had also gone, the latter superbly caught by Woolley at forward short leg, and the total was 41 for 4 with any of three results possible. Not out at tea, Barber, who batted for an hour, and Wood took the score to 65 but once they were out the end came swiftly. Bowes was injured and unable to bat but, as a born number eleven, he was hardly likely to have affected the result – an unexpected victory for Kent over the reigning champions, thanks largely to their two leg-spinners who bowled unchanged.

KENT v. ESSEX

Date: 30-31 May, 1 June 1934   **Location:** Brentwood

Essex were in their first season since forsaking their headquarters among the bricks and mortar of Leyton in favour of a policy of playing around the county. Brentwood, a picturesque ground in semi-rural surroundings, had not seen first-class cricket since 1922. Over the next three days it would gain immortality of a sort.

The ground is small, some thought too small. Essex captain Tom Pearce said that at one end it was only possible to score one, four or six unless somebody fumbled. A young E.W. Swanton had played there in a club match and declared it unfit for county cricket but if he was referring to the wicket, things had changed. *The Times'* correspondent thought the pitch 'superlatively good' and the outfield 'as fast as glass'. The wicket had been liberally treated with liquid manure and the man from *The Daily Telegraph* considered the smell a bigger threat to the batsmen than the bowling.

Kent won the toss and batted against an Essex attack lacking two of its fast bowlers, Kenneth Farnes and 'Hopper' Read, and with all-rounder Laurie Eastman unable to bowl due to a shoulder strain. After Ashdown and Fagg had batted relatively sedately for 70, the pattern for the innings was set with the appearance of Frank Woolley at the crease. At lunch the total was 153 for 1 (Ashdown 81*, Woolley 40*). The first forty-five minutes after lunch produced 100 runs and for the rest of the day the average

Bill Ashdown, Frank Woolley and Leslie Ames in front of scoreboard when Kent declared before lunch on the second day.

KENT v. ESSEX

Kent won the toss and elected to bat   Umpires: J.W. Hitch and A.E. Street

KENT	1ST INNINGS	
W.H. Ashdown	c Ashton b Nichols	332
A.E. Fagg	lbw b R. Smith	31
F.E. Woolley	b Ashton	172
†L.E.G. Ames	not out	202
A.E. Watt	c R. Smith b Ashton	11
I.D.K. Fleming	not out	42
L.J. Todd		
B.H. Valentine		
*A.P.F. Chapman		
D.V.P. Wright		
A.P. Freeman		
Extras	(B 8, NB 1, W 4)	13
TOTAL	(for 4 wickets declared)	803

FOW: 1-70, 2-422, 3-667, 4-707

Bowling

	O	M	R	W
Nichols	20	1	93	1
R. Smith	22	1	115	1
Ashton	31	2	185	2
T.P.B. Smith	36	2	208	0
O'Connor	16.2	0	83	0
Cutmore	12	0	63	0
Taylor	7	0	36	0
Pope	2	0	7	0

ESSEX	1ST INNINGS		2ND INNINGS	
L.C. Eastman	c Chapman b Wright	52	(8) c Woolley b Freeman	4
D.F. Pope	c Woolley b Valentine	100	(1) c Ames b Wright	11
*T.N. Pearce	c Ames b Valentine	79	(4) c Woolley b Freeman	17
J. O'Connor	not out	105	(2) lbw b Freeman	25
M.S. Nichols	c Valentine b Wright	3	lbw b Wright	20
J.A. Cutmore	c Ames b Watt	30	(3) c Fleming b Wright	0
C.T. Ashton	st Ames b Freeman	11	(6) not out	71
R.M. Taylor	st Ames b Freeman	1	(7) st Ames b Freeman	1
T.P.B. Smith	c Woolley b Freeman	11	c Ashdown b Freeman	0
†J.R. Sheffield	c Woolley b Freeman	0	c Watt b Ashdown	31
R. Smith	b Freeman	0	st Ames b Freeman	1
Extras	(B 7, LB 8, NB 1)	16	(B 14, LB 8)	22
TOTAL	(all out)	408	(all out)	203

FOW: 1-75, 2-231, 3-242, 4-259, 5-333, 6-358, 7-360, 8-394, 9-408   1-35, 2-36, 3-42, 4-86, 5-92, 6-97, 7-105, 8-115, 9-201

Bowling

	O	M	R	W
Watt	23	4	85	1
Ashdown	6	2	22	0
Freeman	50.5	15	116	5
Wright	38	9	117	2
Todd	6	0	11	0
Woolley	7	2	10	0
Valentine	9	2	31	2

	O	M	R	W
Watt	9	0	20	0
Valentine	5	2	16	0
Freeman	34.2	13	60	6
Wright	27	12	59	3
Woolley	5	0	26	0
Ashdown	1	1	0	1

Kent won by an innings and 192 runs

rate never fell below 100 an hour. The outfield was so fast that, to quote *The Times*' correspondent again, 'unless the ball went straight to an outfielder – he had little chance of saving it', the ball travelling 'like an electric hare pursued by a particularly ferocious pair of greyhounds'. Ashdown reached his hundred in 140 minutes and doubled it in another ninety. Woolley's hundred arrived in even time. At tea the pair were still together with the score 400 for 1 (Ashdown 205*, Woolley 161*).

When another 22 had been added after tea, Woolley played back to Claude Ashton and was bowled. His 172 contained 1 six and 21 fours. The partnership, worth 352, was at the time the highest for any Kent wicket and was to remain so until 1990. Jimmy Cutmore, handicapped by stitches over one eye, had missed Woolley at square leg when he had scored 2 and shortly after reaching his hundred there were chances to Stan Nichols at long-off and Dudley Pope at long-on in successive overs from Peter Smith. The wicket brought no let-up. Although the only six maiden overs bowled in the innings were in this session after tea, with two right-handers together and less time lost to field changes, the pace

KENT v. ESSEX

The Brentwood ground, small but picturesque.

if anything increased. By the close Kent were 623 for 2, Ashdown 307*, the highest in Kent's history, Ames – missed at 30 – 106*.

With short boundaries and a fast outfield, Chapman decided to bat on. Ashdown added another 25 before giving a low catch in the gully. *Wisden* testifies that his 332 contained 'nothing resembling a chance' in a stay of six-and-a-quarter hours. He hit 1 six (overthrows) and 45 fours, a high proportion in his favoured hunting ground between cover-point's left hand and third man's right. The Ashdown/Ames partnership had yielded 245 in a fraction over two hours. When Chapman's attempt to raise the tempo still further by sending in Alan Watt did not quite come off, he allowed Ian Fleming to make his first-class debut with the total 707 for 4. With orders to give the strike to Ames ringing in his ears and understandably afraid of making a fool of himself, he helped add 96 in twenty-three minutes, enabling Chapman to declare and give Essex seventy minutes' batting before lunch. Kent's total, scored at 5.5 runs an over, was the highest by a county since 1899.

Essex scored 77 in the remainder of the morning session for the loss of Eastman. With an attack based primarily on leg-spin, Kent were not ideally suited to containment and, without taking risks, Pope and Pearce took the score to 201 for 1 at tea (Pope 88*, Pearce 54*). When Pope was caught at slip from Valentine's outswinger immediately after reaching his hundred, 156 had been added for the second wicket in 160 minutes. He batted a little over 200 minutes and hit 1 five (overthrows) and 9 fours. Pearce gave Valentine his second wicket 11 runs later, followed shortly by Nichols, who had the doubtful distinction of being the first batsman in the match to fail to reach double figures. Jack O'Connor and Cutmore attacked the bowling but when 74 had been scored in half an hour, the latter was caught behind off Watts, followed shortly by Ashton and Taylor, both Ames/Freeman stumping victims. At the close of play Essex were 365 for 7 (O'Connor 80*, Peter Smith 1*).

On the final morning O'Connor carried on as before but Freeman was too much for the tail, leaving Essex 395 in arrears. O'Connor, frequently at his best against Freeman, batted a little over two hours for his unbeaten century. Opening the second innings with Pope, he hit 25 of the first 35 before falling to Freeman's top-spinner. Two more wickets fell for 7 runs, Cutmore hitting a long hop to mid-wicket and Pope caught behind from a vicious leg-break. Nichols was missed at slip by Woolley off Doug Wright when he had scored 6 but, with his captain, he played through to lunch, taken at 78 for 3. After lunch, with the total 86 and the pitch at last showing signs of wear, Pearce edged a leg-break to slip and with 6 runs added Nichols was deceived by Wright's googly. Although normally only playing when Marriott was unavailable, Wright was beginning to be noticed with his leg-breaks and googlies bowled at near medium pace.

Taylor, Eastman and Peter Smith all fell to Freeman but Claude Ashton, out of county cricket for five years, played superbly. With wicketkeeper Roy Sheffield standing firm at the other end, he hit sixes off Freeman and Woolley and 86 had been added when Sheffield succumbed to the new ball via a catch at short leg. The end came through yet another 'st Ames b Freeman'. In the most hopeless of rearguard actions, Ashton had batted eighty minutes for his 71*.

Pearce's strictures on the size of the ground may have been an exaggeration but throughout Kent's innings there were only 14 threes and 55 twos, which, with due allowance for misfields, is not many. There was an interesting postscript to the match. Surrey's next fixture was at Brentwood. On the second evening of the Kent game Jack Hobbs phoned Bill Ashdown to enquire about the wicket. Bill, no doubt euphoric after his triple century, gave the only reply possible: 'I suggest you look at the score Jack.' Three days later Essex too were celebrating victory. Surrey were dismissed for 115 and 263. O'Connor hit 248, Ashton 118, 'Hopper' Read had match figures of 10 for 103 and Essex triumphed by the same margin as Kent, an innings and 192 runs. Cricket is, as somebody somewhere once observed, a funny game.

On a sadder note, at the end of the season the stalwart Dudley Pope was killed in a car crash.

KENT v. SURREY

Date: 14, 16-17 July 1934   **Location:** Blackheath

In the 1920s and 1930s there was a large following for Kent cricket in south-east London – now hardly catered for – and the traditional rivalry with Surrey was at its liveliest in the annual meeting between the two at Rectory Field. The ground was not the most attractive in Kent but the fact that it was usually the only first-class fixture played there brought a sense of occasion often absent at The Oval.

Heavy rain on Friday night had ruined the pitch originally chosen but, on winning the toss, Errol Holmes chose to bat on a hastily prepared substitute. It began to look the wrong decision with Bob Gregory out to the third ball of the day and Andy Sandham following shortly afterwards. For a while the Kent opening bowlers looked lethal. Winlaw was caught at forward short leg and Tom Barling, twice missed at slip before he had scored, edged a ball into his face without the ball going to hand but while Stan Squires defended, Barling began to display an array of strokes, reaching his 50 in forty-five minutes. Together they had added 108 when Barling was stumped in the last over before lunch. With the pitch easing, Squires, who survived an easy stumping chance immediately after the interval, played steadily while first Errol Holmes and then Monty Garland-Wells – known to the Surrey pros as the 'Biff Bang Boys' – went through their repertoire, including a towering six to square leg by Garland-Wells off Bill Ashdown. Neither stayed long, however, and Kent were batting by 4 p.m.

Ashdown opened with three boundaries in Eddie Watts' first over, two hooks and a deliberate upper cut over the slips, but was out in his next. Frank Woolley began with a superb on-drive but lifted another into mid-on's hands and it was not until the arrival of Bryan Valentine at 68 for 4 that any Kent batsman looked likely to play an innings. His strokes included a hooked six onto the roof of the pavilion. At stumps Kent were 141 for 6 (Valentine 45*, Fagg 11*).

On the second morning the remaining Kent wickets fell for 41 runs in forty-five minutes, giving the visitors a lead of 58. Alan Watt was absent through injury and runs came quickly until Valentine turned to his spinners, when Sandham was bowled off his boot. At lunch Surrey were 75 for 1. Afterwards, despite frequent bowling changes, Bob Gregory and Squires scored runs 'when and where they chose', 60 coming in the first half-hour. The partnership was worth 167 when Freeman made a dramatic intervention. First he ran out Gregory with a direct hit and in his next over claimed 2 wickets in 2 balls, Squires lbw and Barling bowled. Holmes stopped the hat-trick but in his following over Freeman did it again, bowling Winlaw and Garland-Wells with successive deliveries. His sixth scalp came just before tea, Fender caught by Arthur Fagg, who had taken over behind the stumps to give Les Ames a run around the field.

After tea the game swung back in Surrey's favour, via a vigorous partnership of 94 between Holmes and Watts, but again Freeman intervened. First he had Watts out to a superbly judged catch on the long-on boundary in front of the 'ginger beer tent'. The batsmen had crossed and from the next ball Holmes was caught at slip. The next ball trapped Brooks lbw, giving Freeman his hat-trick after twice taking 2 in 2 – the thirty-seventh time he had taken eight or more wickets in an innings. Faced

Bob Gregory. His second-innings century looked to be taking Surrey to victory until Freeman's direct hit from cover.

Surrey won the toss and elected to bat   Umpires: W.A. Buswell and J. Stone

SURREY	1ST INNINGS		2ND INNINGS	
A. Sandham	c Ames b Ashdown	12	b Lewis	24
R.J. Gregory	c & b Watt	0	run out	104
H.S. Squires	b Ashdown	76	lbw b Freeman	73
R. de W. K. Winlaw	c Lewis b Ashdown	1	b Freeman	1
H.T. Barling	st Ames b Freeman	71	b Freeman	0
*E.R.T. Holmes	b Todd	27	c Woolley b Freeman	89
H.M. Garland-Wells	c Woolley b Freeman	31	b Freeman	0
P.G.H. Fender	c Ames b Watt	2	c Fagg b Freeman	18
E.A. Watts	c sub b Ashdown	1	c Todd b Freeman	34
A.R. Gover	not out	8	not out	0
†E.W.J. Brooks	b Freeman	3	lbw b Freeman	0
Extras	(B 6, LB 2)	8	(B 9, LB 3)	12
TOTAL	(all out)	240	(all out)	355

FOW: 1-1, 2-13, 3-15, 4-123, 5-174, 6-221, 7-228, 8-228, 9-231

1-37, 2-204, 3-206, 4-206, 5-207, 6-207, 7-261, 8-355, 9-355

Bowling

	O	M	R	W
Watt	21	3	66	2
Ashdown	20	9	41	4
Lewis	6	1	21	0
Freeman	21.4	3	85	3
Todd	6	1	19	1

	O	M	R	W
Ashdown	20	2	83	0
Valentine	4	0	14	0
Lewis	27	4	106	1
Freeman	41.3	5	136	8
Todd	3	0	4	0

KENT	1ST INNINGS		2ND INNINGS	
W.H. Ashdown	b Watts	19	c Brooks b Gover	12
A.M. Crawley	c Brooks b Gover	11	(8) not out	9
F.E. Woolley	c sub b Watts	8	(2) lbw b Watts	132
†L.E.G. Ames	c Brooks b Gover	30	b Watts	0
L.J. Todd	b Fender	5	not out	83
*B.H. Valentine	c Gregory b Holmes	52	c Brooks b Gover	15
F.G.H. Chalk	c & b Fender	1	c Winlaw b Gover	62
A.E. Fagg	c Brooks b Holmes	21	(3) b Gover	80
A.P. Freeman	c Squires b Gover	3		
C. Lewis	not out	9		
A.E. Watt	b Gover	8		
Extras	(B 9, LB 4, NB 2)	15	(B 12, LB 3, NB 7, W 1)	23
TOTAL	(all out)	182	(for 6 wickets)	416

FOW: 1-19, 2-31, 3-63, 4-68, 5-74, 6-84, 7-152, 8-155, 9-169

1-17, 2-236, 3-236, 4-242, 5-261, 6-380

Bowling

	O	M	R	W
Gover	20.4	5	39	4
Watts	13	2	62	2
Fender	9	0	38	2
Holmes	7	1	28	2

	O	M	R	W
Gover	32.1	4	119	4
Watts	19	2	75	2
Holmes	15	1	76	0
Fender	21	0	93	0
Gregory	15	4	30	0

Kent won by 4 wickets

with scoring 414, Kent had fifty minutes' batting. Ashdown ventured fatally outside off stump but Woolley survived despite one or two narrow escapes. Kent were 50 for 1 at the close (Woolley 19*, Fagg 17*).

On the final morning Woolley commenced with 14 runs from the first over and the 100 came up in eighty-four minutes, mostly through hooks and pulls by the left-hander when the pace bowlers dropped short. Having survived a difficult chance to slip off Alf Gover and another when Watts was unable to hold on to a drive that struck his left hand, Woolley's 100 took only 130 minutes. At lunch Kent were 184 for 1 and looking set for victory. Lunch changed the picture. When the partnership had added 219, Woolley was lbw trying to turn a full toss to leg and without addition Fagg was bowled after an invaluable supporting innings. Six runs later Ames departed before he had scored. When Valentine followed caught at the wicket (261 for 5), the odds were back in Surrey's favour, only for Les Todd and Gerry Chalk to turn the game back again. Without attempting to score at Woolley's pace, defending when necessary but punishing anything loose, they had added 119 when Chalk was caught in the gully. Both had given chances against the spinners but Kent were almost home. Todd and Crawley did the rest.

KENT v. SURREY

Date: 27, 29-30 July 1935   **Location:** The Oval

More than 15,000 turned up to see Surrey play Kent on the first day of Andrew Sandham's second benefit match. His first in 1927 had been ruined by rain. The two sides were well matched. Kent started the season by winning 7 of their first 10 matches. Then, during July, they lost 6, 5 in succession, and won only 1. Surrey too lacked consistency. In the words of their captain Errol Holmes, they were 'like the New York Stock Exchange, first up to great heights and then down to the depths'.

Percy Chapman won the toss and, with the weather set fair, chose to bat on a typical Oval wicket of the period. Alf Gover, the cutting edge of Surrey's attack, had strained a muscle in his side in one of the early matches and for the rest of the season bowled strapped up and at little above medium pace. The rest of the bowling was not much more than steady and the Kent openers were untroubled until shortly before lunch, when Ashdown gave a catch to cover with the score 136.

After lunch Woolley began an assault on the bowling exceptional even by his standards. His second scoring stroke was a straight six into the pavilion off Bob Gregory and in half an hour he had scored 52 out of 74. His hundred came in eighty minutes, 150 in 125 minutes, 200 in 160 minutes. One ball from the unfortunate Gregory, pitching outside off stump, was hit out of the ground into Harleyford Road, where it bounced on the tramlines and into a garden on the opposite side. Towards the end Woolley, who was now forty-eight, began to tire and when Freddie Brown landed one in the rough outside off stump he offered no stroke and was bowled. He had batted for 185 minutes, hitting 4 sixes and 30 fours.

Woolley hit 87 out of 133 in seventy minutes with Arthur Fagg and 68 out of 106 in an hour with Leslie Todd. Fagg's hundred took 190 minutes with 16 fours. When Woolley was out at 480 for 5, Valentine carried on the mayhem, hitting 71 out of 91 in thirty-five minutes with 3 sixes and 6 fours. There was time before the close for Chapman to provide the beneficiary with a rare wicket. At stumps Kent were 579 for 8 (Sunnucks 33*).

On Monday morning Surrey began quietly against the new ball but accelerated with the introduction of the spinners until, with the total 81, Freeman's top-spinner accounted for Sandham and Squires in the same over. At lunch Surrey were 123 for 2 (Gregory 46*, Barling 23*).

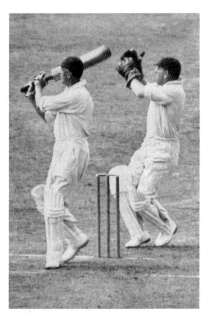

Gregory reached his fifty soon after lunch but, after adding 71 with Tom Barling, he too was lbw, triggering a mini-collapse. Fishlock fell to a typical Chapman spectacular at mid-off, Holmes went down the wicket to Freeman with fatal results and Monty Garland-Wells was caught on the boundary attempting a lofted straight drive. Barling continued to play the spinners with comfort if not dominance but Brown was caught at mid-on after a few powerful blows. At tea Surrey were 233 for 7.

Shortly after the interval Barling's invaluable innings was ended by a superb leg-side stumping in Alan Watt's first over with the new ball and by 5.30 p.m. Surrey were following on. At close of play they were 73 for the loss of Gregory, Sandham 59*.

Despite the loss of Squires, runs came quickly on the final morning until Sandham, who had looked set for a thoroughly deserved century, tried to drive Todd and was caught in the gully. Fishlock began to score freely, hitting 35 out of 51 but,

Frank Woolley's immortal hit out of The Oval off Bob Gregory. It bounced on the tramlines and into a garden on the far side of Harleyford Road.

Kent won the toss and elected to bat   Umpires: W.A. Buswell and D. Hendren

KENT	1ST INNINGS		2ND INNINGS	
W.H. Ashdown	c Gregory b Gover	61	not out	50
A.E. Fagg	c Fishlock b Watts	111	not out	28
F.E. Woolley	b Brown	229		
†L.E.G. Ames	b Gover	12		
L.J. Todd	lbw b Holmes	38		
P.R. Sunnucks	not out	33		
B.H. Valentine	c Barling b Gover	71		
*A.P.F. Chapman	c Watts b Sandham	2		
A.E. Watt	b Gover	2		
A.P. Freeman				
C.S. Marriott				
Extras	(B 7, LB 6, NB 3, W 4)	20	(NB 2)	2
TOTAL	(for 8 wickets declared)	579	(for no wicket)	80

FOW: 1-136, 2-269, 3-297, 4-403, 5-480, 6-571, 7-574, 8-579

Bowling

	O	M	R	W
Gover	29.4	4	144	4
Watts	18	1	97	1
Brown	25	4	135	1
Holmes	17	2	86	1
Gregory	14	4	65	0
Garland-Wells	3	0	11	0
Squires	2	0	13	0
Sandham	2	0	8	1

	O	M	R	W
Gover	8.1	1	33	0
Watts	2	0	18	0
Brown	6	0	27	0

SURREY	1ST INNINGS		2ND INNINGS	
A. Sandham	lbw b Freeman	47	c Chapman b Todd	93
R.J. Gregory	lbw b Freeman	62	c Ames b Marriott	8
H.S. Squires	lbw b Freeman	1	c Woolley b Freeman	16
H.T. Barling	st Ames b Watt	87	c Watt b Marriott	113
L.B. Fishlock	c Chapman b Marriott	1	c Ashdown b Freeman	35
*E.R.T. Holmes	st Ames b Freeman	6	c Ames b Freeman	28
H.M. Garland-Wells	c Fagg b Freeman	0	c Valentine b Watt	40
F.R. Brown	c Ashdown b Marriott	16	run out	2
E.A. Watts	not out	24	lbw b Marriott	6
†E.W.J. Brooks	st Ames b Marriott	30	not out	4
A.R. Gover	lbw b Marriott	0	st Ames b Freeman	4
Extras	(B 11, LB 5)	16	(B 11, LB 8)	19
TOTAL	(all out)	290	(all out)	368

FOW: 1-81, 2-83, 3-154, 4-155, 5-172, 6-182, 7-205, 8-238, 9-290   1-43, 2-102, 3-145, 4-196, 5-266, 6-332, 7-343, 8-355, 9-364

Bowling

	O	M	R	W
Watt	17	4	37	1
Todd	23	3	57	0
Freeman	30	5	99	5
Marriott	37	8	81	4

	O	M	R	W
Watt	12	1	38	1
Todd	12	1	39	1
Freeman	46	8	137	4
Marriott	41	7	135	3

Kent won by 10 wickets

deceived by Freeman's flight, he was caught at mid-off. At lunch Surrey were 222 for 4 with Barling looking even safer than in the first innings.

After lunch the bulk of the runs came from Barling. The normally fast-scoring Holmes was oddly subdued and when he was caught at the wicket Surrey were still only 79 ahead with 5 wickets in hand. Garland-Wells, never one to hang around, launched an immediate assault, hitting Freeman for two sixes, but he failed to survive the new ball and when Brown was the victim of a misunderstanding and Watts was lbw, Kent looked likely winners. At 364 for 8, faced with the prospect of running out of partners, Barling tried to force the pace and sent a towering hit to square leg. His 113, scored out of 262, included 12 fours. Gover, an archetypal tailender, pulled Freeman for four before providing Ames with his fourth stumping and the game was over by 5.15 p.m. Kent scored the runs in forty-two minutes, time enough for Ashdown to register his second fifty of the match.

Woolley's double hundred, his last, had been the key to victory. *Wisden* rated it 'one of the finest displays of his long career.' To *The Times* it was 'one of those innings which defy analysis and criticism'.

KENT v. GLOUCESTERSHIRE

Date: 18-20 August 1937   **Location:** Dover

When county matches lasted three days, final-day run chases were not uncommon but nothing before or since can match the events at the Crabble in August 1937, a game all the more remarkable in that there was no contrivance or 'joke' bowling. Of the Gloucestershire bowlers, Tom Goddard was the country's leading off-spinner with 3 Test caps and more to come; Reg Sinfield would be capped in the following season.

Gloucestershire won the toss and batted. Contrary to the impression given by most current commentators, opening batsmen who attack from the first ball are no new phenomenon. In the first thirty-five minutes Charles Barnett hit 70 out of 90 including 9 fours and 1 six. His opening partner, the Cambridge Double Blue and rugby international Grahame Parker, batted steadily through the morning session but wickets fell at the other end and at lunch Gloucestershire were 175 for 4. All but the most fanatical Kent supporters will have felt a twinge of disappointment at the departure of Wally Hammond, caught at slip before he had settled. After the interval Parker opened out, reaching his second successive century, going on to the highest score of his career and adding 214 with Sinfield. Missed three times in the slips and once at cover, Parker's 210 came in a little over four hours with 3 sixes and 20 fours. Nobody else was able to stay with Sinfield, the remaining 5 wickets falling for 45. Watt (6 for 129) was the pick of the Kent bowlers. The fastest, Norman Harding, making his county debut, had slip catches missed off three successive balls with only number eleven's wicket at a cost of 108 runs as consolation. In the absence of Fagg (missing the season with rheumatic fever), Woolley was now opening with Ashdown and when bad light brought an early close the scoreboard showed 38 for 0.

On the second morning runs came quickly until, with the total on 90, Parker had Ashdown caught at slip in his second over. When Woolley and Gerry Chalk had taken the score to 183, 3 wickets fell for the addition of 6 runs, Woolley's to a simple return catch immediately after reaching his second hundred of the week, scored in two hours. After lunch, a stand of 100 in sixty-five minutes between Alec Pearce and Tom Spencer averted a possible collapse and Kent finished only 35 short of the Gloucestershire total. When bad light again intervened, Gloucestershire were 47 for 3 (Hammond 17*, Crapp 0*).

On the final morning, with the exception of former captain Beverley Lyon, none of the Gloucestershire batsmen made any obvious attempt to force the pace. Even Hammond took seventy-five minutes to add 35 to his overnight score, in the process reaching 3,000 runs for the season. When the last wicket fell half an hour after lunch a draw seemed inevitable, with Kent needing 218 in a maximum of 110 minutes.

According to Les Ames, when asked by his captain 'Can we win?' he replied 'I doubt it but it all depends if Frank can give us a start.' Frank did just that. Gloucestershire had no bowler above medium pace but from Barnett's first over, accurate, just short of a length with a hint of in-swing, he hit 9 runs and after eighteen minutes Kent were 51 for 0. The advent of the spinners did nothing to check the scoring until, after 68 had come in twenty-five minutes, Sinfield had Woolley superbly caught by Barnett in front of the sightscreen. With the arrival of Ames, runs came even faster. Despite five men on the boundary, he hit Goddard for 2 sixes and 5 fours

To end an epic run chase, Alan Watt hit 39 out of 51 in ten minutes with 3 sixes and 3 fours.

Gloucestershire won the toss and elected to bat Umpires: F. Chester and W. Reeves

GLOUCESTERSHIRE

1ST INNINGS			2ND INNINGS	
C.J. Barnett	b Watt	70	c Valentine b Harding	0
G.W. Parker	b Watt	210	b Watt	20
*B.O. Allen	c Spencer b Watt	21	c Woolley b Todd	9
W.R. Hammond	c Ashdown b Woolley	3	c Woolley b Wright	52
J.F. Crapp	c Ashdown b Watt	2	b Watt	1
R.A. Sinfield	not out	74	b Watt	26
B.H. Lyon	c Pearce b Watt	0	b Watt	21
W.L. Neale	lbw b Watt	0	c Chalk b Todd	3
E.J. Stephens	c Ashdown b Woolley	4	run out	15
T.W.J. Goddard	c Ames b Woolley	6	c & b Harding	9
†B.T.L. Watkins	b Harding	25	not out	11
Extras	(B 9, LB 9, W 1)	19	(B 7, LB 4, NB 4)	15
TOTAL	(all out)	434	(all out)	182

FOW: 1-90, 2-157, 3-164, 4-175, 5-389, 6-389, 7-391, 8-397, 9-409   1-0, 2-27, 3-43, 4-56, 5-104, 6-134, 7-137, 8-155, 9-160

Bowling

	O	M	R	W
Harding	24.1	2	104	1
Watt	29	2	129	6
Todd	8	0	22	0
Wright	25	7	78	0
Woolley	24	6	82	3

	O	M	R	W
Harding	14.1	2	43	2
Watt	26	7	69	4
Todd	18	8	26	2
Wright	12	4	29	1

KENT

1ST INNINGS			2ND INNINGS	
W.H. Ashdown	c Hammond b Parker	45	not out	62
F.E. Woolley	c & b Sinfield	100	c Barnett b Sinfield	44
F.G.H. Chalk	b Neale	34		
†L.E.G. Ames	b Neale	1	(3) c Barnett b Sinfield	70
L.J. Todd	b Parker	12		
*B.H. Valentine	c Hammond b Parker	30		
T.A. Pearce	b Sinfield	59		
T.W. Spencer	b Sinfield	53		
D.V.P. Wright	c Watkins b Goddard	29		
A.E. Watt	c Barnett b Sinfield	0	(4) not out	39
N.W. Harding	not out	14		
Extras	(B 22)	22	(B2, LB 2)	4
TOTAL	(all out)	399	(for 2 wickets)	219

FOW: 1-94, 2-183, 3-189, 4-189, 5-219, 6-240, 7-340, 8-367, 9-367   1-68, 2-168

Bowling

	O	M	R	W
Barnett	16	2	45	0
Lyon	8	0	39	0
Sinfield	31	5	83	4
Goddard	23.1	2	77	1
Parker	24	5	78	3
Neale	11	0	55	2

	O	M	R	W
Barnett	3	0	23	0
Parker	3	0	25	0
Sinfield	9	0	69	2
Goddard	8.2	0	98	0

Kent won by 8 wickets

including 17 in one over. By now the scorers were struggling to keep up and the scoreboard – a young Godfrey Evans was one of the operators – was in a state of total confusion.

After fifty-five minutes the total had reached 150 and a Kent victory was looking a possibility. The biggest obstacle appeared to be the time taken in retrieving the ball from the pine trees at the Crabble Avenue end of the ground and a party of members volunteered or were press-ganged into patrolling the vulnerable area to see the ball returned promptly. When Ames gave Barnett his second boundary catch he had contributed 70 out of 100 in thirty-six minutes and the score was 168 for 2. At this point, with 50 needed, Valentine sent in Alan Watt, who seldom played a long innings but was a mighty smiter of sixes. In the next ten minutes Watt hit 39 out of 51 including 3 sixes and 3 fours and Kent were home with more than half an hour to spare. With Ashdown keeping one end secure and feeding the strike to his partners, Kent had scored 218 in seventy-one minutes. In that time Gloucestershire, to their lasting credit, bowled 23.2 overs or 140 balls. The ball from Alan Watt's final blow was lost and not recovered until after the Second World War.

KENT v. ESSEX

Date: 13-15 July 1938   **Location:** Castle Park, Colchester

Remarkable events often occur when Kent play Essex; Brentwood in 1934 for example. In the opening match of the 1938 season, when Kent won by 6 wickets at Gravesend, 1,422 runs were scored with centuries from Ames, Valentine, Nichols, Peter Smith and O'Connor. There were more runs to come.

It is largely forgotten that when Arthur Fagg first appeared he was widely considered (outside Yorkshire of course) as a better prospect than Len Hutton. Picked for the MCC tour of Australia in 1936/37, he had not found form when rheumatic fever caused an early return. He missed the whole of the 1937 season but was back in 1938 and by the beginning of the Colchester Festival was averaging 40, with 1,000 runs and 4 centuries to his credit. Sections of the Southern press were agitating for his return to the England side.

Kent were without Frank Woolley, who was captaining the Players at Lord's. The same traditional fixture had deprived Essex of more than half their attack – pace bowlers Kenneth Farnes, currently the best fast bowler in England and probably the world, Stan Nichols and John Stephenson, together with leg-spinner Peter Smith. When Kent won the toss, the spectre of Brentwood 1934 cannot have been far from the thoughts of the Essex faithful.

The pitch was soft and early movement accounted for Peter Sunnucks and 'Hopper' Levett, but Fagg, totally unruffled, monopolised the scoring to reach his first 50 out of 55 in forty minutes and his hundred before lunch out of 125 in ninety-four minutes. After lunch he slowed down but continued to dominate, reaching his double hundred out of 305. With Les Todd he added 133 for the third wicket and with his captain Gerry Chalk 137 for the fifth in eighty-five minutes. When he was eventually out lbw he had batted a little under five hours without giving a chance and hit 31 fours, most of them in his favoured area, the arc from fine leg to mid-on. The closing stages of the Kent innings were enlivened by some lusty hitting by Alan Watt and there was time for Essex to knock 12 off the arrears (Eastman 11*, Wilcox 1*).

Todd's late in-swing triggered an early breakthrough on the second morning and, despite a lively contribution from Jack O'Connor, who hit 9 fours, Essex were in dire trouble at 207 for 8. Wright, by now an England cricketer, was getting his leg-breaks and googlies to turn and lift and in one devastating four-over spell claimed 4 wickets for 6 runs, including Tom Wade bowled and Frank Vigar lbw from successive deliveries. In contrast with the clatter of wickets at the other end, the Essex captain Tom Pearce had been in no difficulty and when joined by Ray Smith 131 runs came in 110 minutes. By the time he ran out of partners, Pearce had batted for just over three hours and hit 16 fours. When Kent batted again with a lead of 79, Fagg forced the pace from the first over, outpacing Sunnucks and reaching his second hundred of the match out of 134 in sixty-nine minutes. At close of play Kent were 142 for 0 (Fagg 104*, Sunnucks 35*).

Next day the Kent openers resumed their assault and when Sunnucks was run out 283 runs had come in 155 minutes. This stood as a Kent first-wicket record until 1991. Scoring at almost twice the pace of the first

innings, Fagg reached his second double hundred of the match, an unprecedented feat, in 170 minutes. Scoring a higher-than-usual proportion of his runs on the off side, he hit 27 fours, once again without giving a discernible chance. Once the 200 was reached Chalk declared, leaving Essex needing 393. Both Essex openers were out before lunch, but a heavy downpour during the interval and another around 3 p.m. ruined any further chance of play, a sad anticlimax to what, for Fagg if not for the Essex bowlers, had been a memorable three days.

Arthur Fagg. His two double hundreds in a match is still unequalled.

Kent won the toss and elected to bat — Umpires: J.A. Newman and C.W.L. Parker

KENT	1ST INNINGS		2ND INNINGS	
A.E. Fagg	lbw b Taylor	244	not out	202
P.R. Sunnucks	c Wade b Smith	3	run out	82
†W.H.V. Levett	c Wilcox b Daer	0		
L.J. Todd	b Smith	39		
T.W. Spencer	c Taylor b Vigar	14		
*F.G.H. Chalk	c Lavers b Eastman	61		
F.G. Foy	c & b Taylor	25		
N.W. Harding	st Wade b Vigar	9		
D.V.P. Wright	c Wade b Taylor	2		
A.E. Watt	not out	24	(3) not out	24
C. Lewis	c Vigar b Taylor	5		
Extras	(LB 3)	3	(B 2, LB 2, NB 1)	5
TOTAL	(all out)	429	(for 1 wicket declared)	313

FOW: 1-15, 2-28, 3-161, 4-195, 5-332, 6-386, 7-397, 8-399, 9-401   1-283

Bowling

	O	M	R	W
Smith	22	4	96	2
Daer	10	3	51	1
Eastman	40	15	68	1
Lavers	9	1	30	0
Vigar	19	3	91	2
O'Connor	2	0	6	0
Pearce	10	0	43	0
Taylor	10.1	1	41	4

	O	M	R	W
Smith	10	3	46	0
Daer	9	0	46	0
Eastman	17	2	52	0
Taylor	10	0	46	0
O'Connor	5	0	23	0
Vigar	13	0	75	0
Wilcox	4	0	20	0

ESSEX	1ST INNINGS		2ND INNINGS	
D.R. Wilcox	c Harding b Todd	5	b Watt	1
L.C. Eastman	lbw b Todd	44	c Wright b Todd	0
R.M. Taylor	b Lewis	37	not out	7
J. O'Connor	c Lewis b Wright	63	not out	0
A.V. Avery	b Wright	1		
*T.N. Pearce	not out	137		
A.B. Lavers	lbw b Wright	1		
†T.H. Wade	b Wright	4		
F.H. Vigar	lbw b Wright	0		
R. Smith	c Fagg b Wright	37		
H.B. Daer	lbw b Wright	4		
Extras	(B 5, LB 6, NB 6)	17		0
TOTAL	(all out)	350	(for 2 wickets)	8

FOW: 1-44, 2-57, 3-127, 4-128, 5-194, 6-198, 7-207, 8-207, 9-338   1-0, 2-8

Bowling

	O	M	R	W
Todd	19	6	46	2
Watt	22	3	63	0
Harding	5	1	34	0
Wright	31.3	7	107	7
Lewis	26	7	83	1

	O	M	R	W
Todd	2	0	6	1
Watt	1.3	0	2	1

Match Drawn

Fagg's achievement attracted a lot of notice and he was among eight batsmen in the party chosen for the final Test match at The Oval, 'Hutton's match'. Although he had a better record at that stage of the season than Joe Hardstaff or Bill Edrich, he was left out of the final XI and did not get a chance to bat on a wicket on which even the great Bill O'Reilly could not get a ball to deviate. Invited to tour South Africa that winter, he declined on health grounds and, although he played once against the West Indies in 1939, that ended his Test career.

Unfit for military service, he spent the Second World War coaching at Cheltenham College and by the time he returned to full-time cricket in 1947, increasing weight and lack of mobility in the field, combined with the success of Cyril Washbrook and the likes of Robertson, Simpson, Brookes, Gimblett, Place etc. waiting in the wings, meant he was never again in serious contention for an England place.

Remarkably, after sixty-seven years Arthur Fagg's performance remains unique although among others Maurice Hallam (twice), Herschelle Gibbs, Derek Randall and Zaheer Abbas (four times) have all come close.

KENT v. HAMPSHIRE

Date: 3, 5-6 August 1946   **Location:** Canterbury

The traditional festival of Canterbury Cricket Week returned for the ninety-fifth time after a break of six years during the Second World War. For the nineteenth time since 1908 Kent played hosts to near neighbours Hampshire, a fixture that was to become recognised almost as a permanent part of the week in the years prior to and following the Second World War.

There was an impatience to get back to something close to normality and on this Bank Holiday weekend Men of Kent and Kentish men and women flocked in their thousands to the St Lawrence ground. The match was designated as a benefit for Joe Murrin, who had been groundsman for forty-one years.

Only four of the Kent side from the corresponding match in 1939 were present on this occasion with Gerry Chalk, who captained the pre-war side, having been killed in action. The same fate had befallen J.P. Blake and D.F. Walker of the Hampshire side, although five of their XI had appeared in the last pre-war fixture.

Hampshire dominated the early proceedings with an opening partnership of 156 between the attractive right-hand batsman John Arnold, who had played just a single Test match for England in 1931, and Arthur Holt. Arnold's share in that partnership was 83 while Holt reached 90 before being bowled by right-arm off-break and seam-up bowler Ray Dovey. But from then on it was downhill all the way with only extras reaching double figures. All 10 wickets fell for just 73 runs with four of Kent's bowlers sharing them.

Conditions were certainly not to blame. Kent's reply was led by experienced left-hand opener Leslie Todd who anchored the innings. In four hours he scored 122 while skipper Bryan Valentine's 110 was scored in half that time. Valentine's innings included a six and 14 fours. Todd was well supported by the up-and-coming wicketkeeper Godfrey Evans, who was batting at number three in the order due to an injury to Leslie Ames. He gave the large crowd an early indication of what they could look forward to in the future with a typically fast-scoring 72 out of a partnership of 110. Half his runs came in boundaries. Kent's lower order was well marshalled by amateur debutant Tony Pawson, the Winchester captain of 1939-40, who scored a typical quick-fire 90 that included 12 fours. His was the final wicket to fall, run out in his first innings for the county, a mode of dismissal that he was to experience on an above-average number of occasions throughout his career. Kent's total of 477

Leslie Todd got the highest score in the first post-war Canterbury Week

Hampshire won the toss and elected to bat   Umpires: H.W. Lee and J.A. Smart

HAMPSHIRE	1ST INNINGS		2ND INNINGS	
J. Arnold	c Evans b Davies	83	lbw b Ridgway	19
A.G. Holt	b Dovey	90	c Evans b Harding	20
G. Hill	b Harding	8	(6) c Evans b Harding	24
J. Bailey	c Ames b Todd	3	(5) c Valentine b Ridgway	27
*E.D.R. Eagar	b Dovey	6	(7) b Ridgway	20
N.H. Rogers	b Dovey	7	(3) lbw b Ridgway	0
F.A.V. Parker	c Dovey b Harding	5	(4) c Davies b Harding	4
†N.T. McCorkell	lbw b Dovey	1	c Davies b Ridgway	28
O.W. Herman	c Ames b Harding	0	c & b Ridgway	19
C.J. Knott	not out	9	b Harding	2
G.E.M. Heath	run out	5	not out	0
Extras	(B 1, LB 7, NB 4)	12	(B 6, LB 3, NB 1)	10
TOTAL	(all out)	229	(all out)	173

FOW: 1-156, 2-168, 3-179, 4-201, 5-206, 6-213, 7-215, 8-215, 9-215   1-35, 2-35, 3-41, 4-45, 5-97, 6-99, 7-134, 8-170, 9-173

Bowling

	O	M	R	W
Harding	22	4	52	3
Ridgway	10	2	30	0
Todd	13	3	22	1
Dovey	20.3	5	55	4
Davies	17	2	45	1
Ames	3	1	13	0

	O	M	R	W
Harding	21.1	2	78	4
Ridgway	26	8	59	6
Todd	10	6	9	0
Davies	11	4	11	0
Dovey	8	5	6	0

KENT	1ST INNINGS	
L.J. Todd	b Eagar	122
J.G.W. Davies	b Knott	29
†T.G. Evans	c Holt b Knott	72
L.E.G. Ames	b Heath	1
*B.H. Valentine	c Eagar b Hill	110
A.H. Phebey	b Knott	16
H.A. Pawson	run out	90
T.W. Spencer	c Hill b Knott	0
N.W. Harding	b Hill	3
R.R. Dovey	b Knott	19
F. Ridgway	not out	5
Extras	(B 3, LB 7)	10
TOTAL	(all out)	477

FOW: 1-85, 2-195, 3-200, 4-257, 5-322, 6-364, 7-389, 8-394, 9-461

Bowling

	O	M	R	W
Herman	23	3	78	0
Heath	35	5	153	1
Hill	21	5	49	2
Knott	38.5	3	159	5
Eagar	5	0	28	1

Kent won by an innings and 75 runs

was reached off 1 ball short of 123 overs. It was the county's second-highest innings score of the season. On only two other occasions did the side exceed 400. Two Hampshire bowlers conceded between them more than 300 of Kent's total runs. The pick of them was Charlie Knott who, with a mixture of right-arm medium pace and off-breaks, took 5 wickets but at a cost of 159 runs off 38.5 overs. George Heath's fast-medium bowling cost him 153 runs for the sole wicket of Leslie Ames.

Collectively, Hampshire's batsmen fared even worse in their second innings although individually they all contrived to get in and then get out when set. By the end of the second day Hampshire were well into their second innings and had it not been for the careful batting of Hill and Bailey the match may well have been concluded in two days. However, a hostile spell of bowling by right-arm fast bowler Fred Ridgway, in his first season for the county, paved the way for Kent's decisive victory early on the third day. His 6 for 59 was his best performance to date. Norman Harding, a right-arm fast-medium bowler with a near-perfect sideways action, was to die tragically young from infantile paralysis at the end of the following season. He took 7 wickets in the match and shared with Ridgway all 10 second-innings dismissals.

This was Kent's sixth victory of that first post-war season and the third by an innings.

KENT V. MIDDLESEX

Date: 13-15 August 1947   **Location:** Lord's

Kent arrived at Lord's to face a rampant Middlesex who, after an early defeat at the hands of Somerset, had won 12 of their next 14 championship matches. That Kent triumphed after one of the most exciting matches of the season just five minutes from the end of extra time on the final day owed much to the bowling of Doug Wright. His 11 wickets in the match came from bowling medium-pace leg-breaks and googlies to an accurate length, employing the top-spinner and getting lift as well as turn. It was the main bowling contribution in what was Wright's best season, during which he took 177 wickets at 21 apiece.

At the end of play on the first day, honours were close to even with Kent, having scored 301, possibly holding a slight advantage in that the 3 Middlesex wickets to fall in their overnight score of 133 included Edrich and Compton, who between them managed fewer than 50 runs. But Middlesex would have been well satisfied to have dismissed Kent for a modest score on a wicket that, while taking some spin, provided pretty good conditions for the batsmen.

In the pre-lunch period Kent's experienced opening pair, Fagg and Todd, scored at more than a run a minute but almost immediately after the interval Todd, who had been the quicker of the two, played on. When Ames, who had been in great form and finished the season with more than 2,000 runs, was out cheaply, hopes of a large score were dimmed. But an aggressive innings by the captain Bryan Valentine and cameos by Old Harrovian Geoffrey Anson and Doug Wright took Kent up to 300. The Middlesex reply began disastrously with Brown steering a catch to Valentine in the gully off Harding in the first over. Edrich and Robertson steadied things with a stand of 77 but an attempted yahoo by Edrich had him clean bowled by Ray Dovey. Worse was to follow before play ended for the day when Denis Compton, after a perfect beginning, was bowled round his legs by a huge Wright leg-break.

On the second day there was a sense among the supporters of both counties that this could be where the championship might be won or lost, although at this point in the season Kent were third in the table trailing leaders Gloucestershire by 48 points. With Middlesex lying second there was an air of tension and anticipation. At the start of play much depended on the partnership between the overnight batsmen, Robertson, undefeated on 73, and Robins. Both had played Wright with great skill and for the best part of an hour all went well. Robertson completed his twelfth century of the season and his fifth in successive matches, immediately after which Robins got a top edge off Wright and was well caught by Harding at long leg. George Mann quickly followed, well caught by Fagg at slip at which point Robertson decided that there would be little further support and after one or two desperate blows departed. Despite late resistance from Young, the Middlesex total left Kent with an advantage of 72.

Middlesex hopes were raised with the cheap dismissal of Kent's opening pair, but there then followed two-and-a-half hours of high-quality batting from Ames and Valentine. While Ames batted well within himself, his captain treated the large crowd – there were an estimated 35,000 on the first two days – to some brilliant stroke play. The score had reached 170 when Ames played a ball from Young straight into the hands of Denis Compton at silly point. Soon after, Valentine drove Compton just inches above the ground only to see Laurie Gray take a brilliant catch. Davies again went cheaply but Anson, after his modest but valuable first innings, was 33* at the close, leaving supporters of both counties eagerly anticipating the final day's proceedings.

These were the days when cricket was governed by time rather than overs bowled and on day three Kent continued their second innings for just short of two hours before the declaration came. When play began their lead was 298 with 5 wickets still in hand. They added 98 runs in double-quick time with Anson and Evans both batting adventurously and enjoying some luck. The declaration challenged Middlesex to score 397 runs at a rate of 100 an hour and left them half an hour of pre-lunch batting, during which Brown was bowled off his pads. Then, the first ball after the interval saw Robertson dismissed lbw. Two wickets had fallen for 28 runs and with Wright bowling accurately the task facing Edrich and Compton was immense. Could they first get on top of the bowling, then score at sufficient a rate to bring off a

Kent won the toss and elected to bat   Umpires: H.G. Baldwin and C.A.R. Coleman

KENT	1ST INNINGS		2ND INNINGS	
L.J. Todd	b Sims	62	b Hever	7
A.E. Fagg	b Young	66	c L.H. Compton b Gray	6
L.E.G. Ames	c L.H. Compton b Sims	8	c D.C.S. Compton b Young	69
*B.H. Valentine	b Gray	61	c Gray b D.C.S. Compton	92
J.G.W. Davies	c L.H. Compton b Sims	4	lbw b Young	11
G.F. Anson	lbw b Sims	25	c Mann b Young	51
†T.G. Evans	lbw b D.C.S. Compton	18	c Robertson b D.C.S. Compton	56
R.R. Dovey	run out	7	not out	10
D.V.P. Wright	b Hever	36	c Edrich b Young	11
F. Ridgway	b D.C.S. Compton	0		
N.W. Harding	not out	5		
Extras	(B 5, LB 4)	9	(B 5, LB 6)	11
TOTAL	(all out)	301	(for 8 wickets declared)	324

FOW: 1-97, 2-113, 3-179, 4-196, 5-221, 6-246, 7-254, 8-263, 9-275   1-9, 2-13, 3-170, 4-181, 5-199, 6-298, 7-298, 8-324

Bowling

	O	M	R	W
Gray	17	3	44	1
Hever	10.1	2	32	1
Robertson	3	1	12	0
Young	16	8	24	1
D.C.S. Compton	24	2	87	2
Robins	2	0	6	0
Sims	19	0	87	4

	O	M	R	W
Gray	19	3	70	1
Hever	15	3	37	1
Young	38.2	12	65	4
D.C.S. Compton	31	10	86	2
Sims	12	1	37	0
Robins	3	0	18	0

MIDDLESEX	1ST INNINGS		2ND INNINGS	
S.M. Brown	c Valentine b Harding	0	b Harding	5
J.D.B. Robertson	c Evans b Wright	110	lbw b Harding	12
W.J. Edrich	b Dovey	28	c & b Wright	31
D.C.S. Compton	b Wright	16	c Davies b Wright	168
*R.W.V. Robins	c Harding b Wright	24	b Davies	21
F.G. Mann	c Fagg b Wright	1	b Wright	57
†L.H. Compton	c Harding b Wright	6	st Evans b Wright	7
J.M. Sims	b Dovey	7	b Davies	7
L.H. Gray	c Todd b Wright	7	not out	4
J.A. Young	c Fagg b Wright	17	c Evans b Davies	0
N.G. Hever	not out	8	b Davies	2
Extras	(LB 2, W 2, NB 1)	5	(LB 4, NB 3)	7
TOTAL	(all out)	229	(all out)	321

FOW: 1-0, 2-77, 3-104, 4-172, 5-173, 6-189, 7-192, 8-202, 9-218   1-12, 2-28, 3-88, 4-135, 5-296, 6-305, 7-312, 8-317, 9-317

Bowling

	O	M	R	W
Harding	5	1	22	1
Wright	33.2	5	92	7
Dovey	28	5	59	2
Ridgway	13	1	46	0
Davies	2	0	5	0

	O	M	R	W
Harding	13	0	56	2
Ridgway	5	0	29	0
Wright	24	3	102	4
Dovey	20	2	69	0
Davies	19	3	58	4

Kent won by 75 runs

spectacular but certainly not impossible victory? When, with the score on 88, Edrich, who had added a quick 60 with Compton, was brilliantly caught and bowled, defeat looked inevitable. With Robins bowled by Jack Davies and a long tail, play in the hour before tea suggested that Middlesex had decided to settle for a draw.

At the interval, which lasted just five minutes and with the players not leaving the field, Compton was given orders to go for the runs and for the next forty minutes the crowd witnessed batting that they were unlikely to ever forget. He had played strokes outside the imagination of any but a Trumper or a Macartney. Mann had supported him bravely and with skill. In that short period 102 runs were scored with Compton's contribution being 71. That left three-quarters of an hour to score a further 101 runs for

victory. At that point, in attempting to force a ball wide of the leg stump over cover-point he failed to clear the fielder. When Mann quickly followed, Middlesex did not have quite the batting skill to withstand the final overs of Kent's spinners.

This was one of the outstanding matches of a summer in which Middlesex secured the County Championship. Kent finished in fourth position, which was to prove their best for the next twenty years.

Opposite:
Doug Wright took 11 wickets in the match, and was instrumental in Kent's win.

Above:
Denis Compton in 1947. This was his year, but his 168 was not enough to give the eventual champions victory.

KENT v. MIDDLESEX

Date: 9-11 August 1950   **Location:** Canterbury

What better occasion can there have been for a Kent batsman to become the twelfth player to record 100 centuries in first-class cricket than the most famous of all cricket festivals?

On 11 August 1950, in a chase that required Kent to score 237 runs in two-and-a-half hours to beat Middlesex, Leslie Ames, outstanding wicketkeeper-batsman for his county and country, followed Frank Woolley as the second Kent player to reach this milestone. He is the only wicketkeeper to have done so. In an innings that lasted exactly two hours he hit 2 sixes and 17 fours. His 131 runs were scored out of 211, while his partnership with Tony Pawson added 85 runs in only thirty-five minutes. With little time remaining it guaranteed an unexpected Kent victory. And for good measure it was his final appearance keeping wicket for Kent, being called on to do so following an injury to Godfrey Evans' hand.

Middlesex began the match in lively fashion, scoring 101 for 1 in the pre-lunch session but from then until the close of play batting was desperately slow against a fine bowling performance by all the Kent bowlers, especially Doug Wright, who bowled for hour after hour with hardly a loose ball. It was 6.30 p.m. when the Middlesex innings was brought to a close and with a 7 p.m. finish Kent were left on 18 for 1 at the close.

At the end of day two the match was very much in the balance. There were fine batting performances by Arthur Fagg, whose innings included 13 fours, while Tony Pawson's 103 came in under two hours and was his second century of the summer. Fagg particularly batted well first thing, countering the movement that J.J. Warr and the nineteen-year-old Alan Moss were able to get before a heavy dew had dried from the wicket. The thousands of spectators who had come on the traditional Ladies' Day in the hope of seeing Leslie Ames record his hundredth hundred were to be disappointed. He was an early victim of the conditions, touching one from Warr that moved away. Fagg's dismissal, just twelve short of a century, came about through the sort of misunderstanding comic and embarrassing in equal measure when both he and Pawson found themselves at the same end. Pawson's keenness for the short single was a key element in his scoring technique but went down not too well with Fagg who, coming to the end of his career, was

not an enthusiastic runner. On this occasion both batsmen were in their 80s when Pawson had a cut brilliantly stopped in the covers. According to his account it was four or nothing but Fagg quite uncharacteristically had charged down the pitch. Pawson was aware of an expletive in his ear and, after what seemed like a full minute glaring at each other, decided as the amateur that he should do the honourable thing by giving himself out. He was halfway to the pavilion when called back by the umpire who declared Fagg out as Pawson had not left his crease!

Once Kent had passed the Middlesex total the declaration came, but the challenge to make a game of it was not taken up in the final session of day two. While Robertson and Dewes batted well, the latter pushed about for almost two hours before being dismissed. Edrich also batted slowly but Sharp showed much greater confidence than

Leslie Ames, with Peter Hearn, going out to bat after lunch on the third day prior to completing his hundredth hundred.

Middlesex won the toss and elected to bat   Umpires: J.T. Bell and H. Elliott

MIDDLESEX	1ST INNINGS		2ND INNINGS	
J.D.B. Robertson	st Evans b Wright	40	b Dovey	54
J.G. Dewes	c Evans b Wright	60	c Pawson b Dovey	32
*W.J. Edrich	b Ridgway	6	not out	77
H.P.H. Sharp	b Dovey	62	c Clark b Wright	21
S.M. Brown	b Wright	19	not out	51
†L.H. Compton	b Wright	7		
F.J. Titmus	c Evans b Ridgway	9		
J.M. Sims	c Fagg b Ridgway	13		
J.J. Warr	b Wright	4		
J.A. Young	b Dovey	14		
A.E. Moss	not out	7		
Extras	(B 4, LB 4)	8	(B 6)	6
TOTAL	(all out)	249	(for 3 wickets declared)	241

FOW: 1-99, 2-106, 3-114, 4-142, 5-156, 6-179, 7-207, 8-212, 9-242   1-80, 2-89, 3-125

Bowling

	O	M	R	W
Ridgway	31	9	86	3
Mallett	20	5	58	0
Dovey	19.5	4	36	2
Wright	30	8	61	5

	O	M	R	W
Ridgway	22	8	59	0
Mallett	27	8	65	0
Wright	11	2	47	1
Dovey	20	4	64	2

KENT	1ST INNINGS		2ND INNINGS	
A.E. Fagg	run out	88	c Compton b Warr	0
*D.G. Clark	c Compton b Warr	6	run out	3
L.E.G. Ames	c Compton b Warr	4	c Moss b Young	131
P. Hearn	st Compton b Sims	17	b Young	30
H.A. Pawson	not out	103	b Warr	57
†T.G. Evans	c Sims b Warr	6		
A.F. Woollett	c Young b Warr	10	(8) not out	0
A.W.H. Mallett	not out	15	(6) b Warr	9
R.R. Dovey			(7) not out	5
D.V.P. Wright				
F. Ridgway				
Extras	(LB 4, W 1)	5	(B 4)	4
TOTAL	(for 6 wickets declared)	254	(for 6 wickets)	239

FOW: 1-18, 2-34, 3-77, 4-183, 5-197, 6-232   1-0, 2-16, 3-126, 4-211, 5-234, 6-235

Bowling

	O	M	R	W
Warr	26	8	67	4
Moss	21	4	76	0
Sims	16	2	53	1
Young	14	8	15	0
Titmus	11	2	38	0

	O	M	R	W
Warr	11	1	57	3
Moss	5	2	18	0
Sims	14	1	53	0
Young	19	3	90	2
Edrich	1	0	13	0
Titmus	0.5	0	4	0

Kent won by 4 wickets

in the first innings. Nevertheless, in close on three hours Middlesex had scored just 140 runs. The game was heading for a draw.

There must have been an overnight change of heart in the Middlesex camp for, in the first hour of the final day, Edrich and Brown added 101 runs before declaring. Edrich, who led the side with a sure and easy touch, batted in his best vein. With Brown also scoring at a fast rate the declaration came just after noon. It set the stage for Ames. Before lunch he found it slow going, with Fagg and Clark having gone cheaply. But he found a solid partner in Peter Hearn. Both were tempted by Edrich, who bowled an over of donkey-drops to encourage them in the chase. The arrival of Pawson coincided with a spate of fours from Ames's bat and his hundred was greeted with great excitement. He celebrated by bombarding the tents of the president and the Band of Brothers, scoring 22 of his final 31 runs in boundaries. Following Ames's dismissal Pawson continued with the onslaught, Kent reaching their target with seven minutes to spare.

This was the last of Ames's 78 hundreds for Kent. His career ended with the first match of the following season when, on a chill day at Gillingham, his suspect back let him down for a final time.

KENT v. SURREY

Date: 9, 11-12 July 1955   **Location:** The Oval

The fortunes of Kent and Surrey could barely have been more different in the mid-1950s. Surrey were in the midst of their famous run that saw them champions in seven successive seasons. Kent had not finished in the top half of the table for eight years. The lack of a settled side, and of any consistency in the batting, a limited opening attack and often poor out-cricket condemned the side to also rans. 1955 was typical. Their potential star batsman Colin Cowdrey, fresh from success in Australia, missed much of the season through injury, as did their main strike bowler Fred Ridgway through illness. Thus the side that appeared against the might of Surrey had very much a makeshift look about it. The opening attack in particular looked almost non-existent, with only the extremely inexperienced Oxford Blue John Phillips, playing in the first of only four games for Kent, providing any real pace. Godfrey Evans was also missing on Test duty, but it is arguable that his loyal substitute Derek Ufton was, on day-to-day form, a more competent and reliable wicketkeeper than Evans, who did not always rise to the grind of county cricket.

The gulf between the two sides had been all too apparent only the week before at Blackheath when Surrey were triumphant by an innings in two days. Thus, when Kent were dismissed in ideal conditions on the first day for 181, with only the Australian all-rounder Jack Pettiford reaching 50, the outcome seemed inevitable.

Yet on the second day, completely unexpectedly, Kent secured a first-innings lead. On a pitch inclined to be dusty, the two Kent spinners in this match, Doug Wright and Jimmy Allan, secured a 35-run advantage. Wright was nearing the end of his career, but he was still Kent's principal wicket-taker and, as an indication of Kent's weakness, often carried the attack. Indeed, in 1955 he took nearly half all the wickets taken.

Jimmy Allan was an Oxford Blue whose golden summer this was. In all matches for the university and Kent, he was just 5 wickets short of completing the season 'double'. A Scotsman, he was a slow left-hander who gave the ball plenty of air. He was also a useful batsman who had progressed from a number eleven to open for Oxford, and for Kent scored two centuries in a match. Surrey collapsed remarkably just before lunch on the second day, losing 6 wickets for just 9 runs, Allan's nagging length bowling worrying batsmen into indiscretions.

By the time rain enforced the close of day two, thanks to 49 by the veteran Arthur Fagg, the lead had been increased to 126, but with 5 wickets down. On a damp pitch, drying under a hot sun, the remaining 5 soon fell mainly to the spin of Laker and Eric Bedser for the addition of just 25, leaving Surrey 152 to win. They were proceeding on their untroubled way at 123 for 4 with Ken Barrington and Ron Pratt in control, adding 50 in forty minutes.

Jimmy Allan, Kent's underrated Scottish all-rounder, whose 9 wickets in the match were critical.

Kent won the toss and elected to bat   Umpires: H. Elliott and K. McCanlis

KENT	1ST INNINGS		2ND INNINGS	
A.E. Fagg	b Cox	28	lbw b Laker	49
A.H. Phebey	c Pratt b Loader	5	lbw b Loader	5
J.M. Allan	c Stewart b Surridge	0	(7) lbw b Laker	10
R.C. Wilson	b Cox	24	(3) c Surridge b Laker	13
J. Pettiford	lbw b Cox	50	c Pratt b Bedser	12
J.F. Pretlove	c Laker b Loader	5	c Surridge b Laker	8
P. Hearn	c McIntyre b Surridge	14	(4) c Stewart b Cox	0
†D.G. Ufton	b Laker	14	c Surridge b Bedser	0
*D.V.P. Wright	not out	17	c Clark b Bedser	3
J.C.T. Page	c Constable b Laker	3	not out	3
J.B. Phillips	c Stewart b Laker	0	lbw b Laker	4
Extras	(B14, LB 4, NB 2, W 1)	21	(B 4, LB 5)	9
TOTAL	(all out)	181	(all out)	116

FOW: 1-14, 2-15, 3-43, 4-74, 5-92, 6-119, 7-148, 8-178, 9-181   1-19, 2-52, 3-65, 4-71, 5-91, 6-95, 7-96, 8-104, 9-108

Bowling

	O	M	R	W
Loader	17	4	35	2
Surridge	19	1	45	2
Laker	20.5	8	34	3
Cox	14	5	23	3
Bedser	10	2	23	0

	O	M	R	W
Loader	9	3	25	1
Surridge	4	1	7	0
Laker	23.5	9	48	5
Cox	6	3	10	1
Bedser	13	6	17	3

SURREY	1ST INNINGS		2ND INNINGS	
T.H. Clark	c Wilson b Wright	32	c Ufton b Phillips	0
M.J. Stewart	c Allan b Wright	20	c & b Allan	11
B. Constable	run out	30	c Phebey b Wright	14
K.F. Barrington	c Wilson b Allan	27	lbw b Allan	72
E.A. Bedser	lbw b Wright	12	lbw b Wright	6
R.E.C. Pratt	st Ufton b Allan	1	c Fagg b Allan	23
†A.J.W. McIntyre	b Allan	2	c & b Allan	4
J.C. Laker	c Phillips b Wright	1	c Wilson b Allan	1
*W.S. Surridge	b Allan	15	b Wright	0
D.F. Cox	b Wright	0	c Phebey b Wright	0
P.J. Loader	not out	2	not out	0
Extras	(LB 3, NB 1)	4	(LB 4, NB 3)	7
TOTAL	(all out)	146	(all out)	138

FOW: 1-49, 2-56, 3-108, 4-123, 5-126, 6-126, 7-129, 8-129, 9-132   1-0, 2-15, 3-30, 4-46, 5-123, 6-127, 7-133, 8-134, 9-134

Bowling

	O	M	R	W
Phillips	19	2	39	0
Allan	31.3	12	49	4
Wright	17	3	45	5
Page	4	1	9	0

	O	M	R	W
Phillips	3	1	3	1
Allan	22.4	4	60	5
Wright	14	1	45	4
Page	6	1	23	0

Kent won by 13 runs

But with Pratt's dismissal to a slip catch by Fagg off Allan, the County Champions collapsed alarmingly, generally through reckless strokes. The last 6 wickets fell for just 15 runs in 20 deliveries, with Barrington last out trying to sweep Allan to leg to farm the bowling. He scored 72 – an innings not without luck, but it should have won the match. Four of the last 6 wickets fell to Allan in 15 deliveries. In all Wright had match figures of 9 for 90, and Allan 9 for 109.

Surrey won the championship and Kent finished an indifferent thirteenth in the table. It was the only match at The Oval that year they did not win. Jimmy Allan never reached the heights of 1955 again. His batting fell away, although he still topped the Kent bowling averages in a limited number of matches in 1956. He played 7 matches in 1957 with no success and did not reappear for Kent again. A falling out with Les Ames was hinted at. Allan continued to play for Scotland and reappeared for Warwickshire with some success for three seasons in the mid-1960s.

KENT v. WORCESTERSHIRE

Date: 15 June 1960   **Location:** Tunbridge Wells

The events at Tunbridge Wells on a mid-June day in 1960 would have sent today's pitch inspectors running around like headless chickens. Had the present-day requirements on pitch preparation been applied the penalty imposed on Kent does not bear thinking about. A period of unsettled weather and heavy thunderstorms had not been helpful to a groundsman who had been appointed only earlier in the year and who was immediately required to commence preparation of the wickets for the traditional Tunbridge Wells Week.

There had been heavy overnight rain to add to his concerns but the morning of 15 June dawned warm and sunny. Worcestershire's previous match had been against Lancashire at Old Trafford. It had gone to its full extent with the visitors holding out for a draw. They were then faced with the long journey from Manchester to Tunbridge Wells, arriving at their hotel at 4 a.m. Kent faced no such problems in getting to the venue, having just completed a match at The Oval. Of more serious concern was their recent form, having drawn 2 and lost 4 of their last 6 matches, including an innings defeat by Surrey the previous day.

On a wicket that was described as grassless, damp and with a marl-covered surface, there was a feeling that it would break up as it dried out. That proved to be the case, for thirty batsmen were dismissed in the day and, despite being all out for 187, Kent won by an innings and 101 runs.

After winning the toss, Colin Cowdrey spent some time before deciding that Kent would bat first. Early exchanges gave no indication of what was to follow. Arthur Phebey and Peter Richardson batted freely against the new-ball attack of Jack Flavell and Derek Pearson. But, after just 8 overs slow left-arm bowler Doug Slade was brought into the attack. Having conceded 16 runs in 4 overs he was replaced by Norman Gifford, making his first-class debut. His slow left-arm bowling brought immediate success for, with only his third ball, he bowled Phebey for 16. Two further wickets fell with only 3 runs added, Kent slipping from 40 without loss to 43 for 3. The surface was already beginning to break up but with slow progress Stuart Leary and Colin Cowdrey took the score on to 68. However, Cowdrey, after hitting a six and a four in his 17, was caught close in attempting to drive.

This brought to the wicket, just fifteen minutes before lunch, the first of Kent's heroes of the day, the all-rounder Peter Jones who, after five seasons on the staff, had finally won a regular first-team spot. He and Leary added 36 valuable runs before Leary was dismissed. Alan Dixon joined Jones and with both batting positively they were able to take the score on to 151, recording the highest stand of a remarkable day. Three wickets fell for the addition of just 10 runs and when Jones was ninth out with the score at 179 he had hit 73 out of 111, including 9 fours and 2 sixes. Kent's innings had lasted just three-and-a-half hours, closing at 3.40 p.m.

What followed was nothing short of sensational. Dave Halfyard, whose leg-cutter was to prove lethal on that wicket, opened from the Pavilion End. His first ball to West Indian Ron Headley, son of George Headley (the 'Black Bradman') and father of Dean (Middlesex, Kent and England), exploded as it hit the pitch, leaving what was described as a crater where it had landed. Alan Brown, opening from the Railway End, proved equally hostile. However, it was not until the final ball of the third over that the first wicket fell, Headley being dismissed by what was described as a 'fast leg-spinner' that broke back fiercely and hit his leg stump. Six runs were on the board and only 3 more were added while a further 5 wickets fell. At that stage five of the Worcestershire batsmen had been dismissed without scoring. Each of Kent's opening bowlers had bowled 4 overs, Halfyard conceding 3 runs for his 2 wickets and Brown 4 runs for 4 wickets. Doug Slade and Roy Booth added 15 for the seventh wicket, which included two successive fours by Slade off Brown. But with the score on 24 came the second and final collapse, the last 4 wickets falling for the addition of 1 run. The innings had lasted seventy-five minutes with Brown and Halfyard bowling unchanged throughout. Worcestershire's score was the second lowest in the club's history, exceeding by just one their 24 against Yorkshire in 1903.

Kent won the toss and elected to bat   Umpires: T.J. Bartley and J.S. Buller

KENT — 1ST INNINGS

A.H. Phebey	b Gifford	16
P.E. Richardson	b Flavell	23
*M.C. Cowdrey	c Broadbent b Pearson	17
R.C. Wilson	c Headley b Flavell	0
S.E. Leary	st Booth b Slade	23
P.H. Jones	c Broadbent b Slade	73
A.L. Dixon	c Dews b Pearson	17
†A.W. Catt	st Booth b Gifford	0
D.J. Halfyard	st Booth b Gifford	0
A. Brown	b Gifford	1
P.A. Shenton	not out	7
Extras	(B 7, LB 2, NB 1)	10
TOTAL	(all out)	187

FOW: 1-41, 2-43, 3-43, 4-68, 5-104, 6-151, 7-154, 8-161, 9-179

Bowling

	O	M	R	W
Flavell	18	8	25	2
Pearson	16	7	35	2
Slade	18	5	54	2
Gifford	17	5	63	4

WORCESTERSHIRE — 1ST INNINGS / 2ND INNINGS

	1st innings		2nd innings	
J.B. Sedgley	c Leary b Brown	7	(2) c Richardson b Brown	2
R.G.A. Headley	b Halfyard	0	(1) c Wilson b Halfyard	0
A.H. Spencer	b Brown	0	c Leary b Brown	4
D.W. Richardson	b Brown	0	b Halfyard	2
R.G. Broadbent	b Halfyard	0	c Catt b Halfyard	22
*G. Dews	lbw b Brown	0	b Brown	0
†R. Booth	b Brown	2	c Wilson b Halfyard	7
D.N.F. Slade	b Halfyard	9	c Leary b Shenton	11
N. Gifford	not out	0	c Brown b Shenton	4
D.B. Pearson	b Halfyard	0	c Cowdrey b Halfyard	2
J.B. Flavell	b Brown	1	not out	0
Extras	(B 1, LB 5)	6	(B 5, LB 1, W 1)	7
TOTAL	(all out)	25	(all out)	61

FOW: 1-6, 2-7, 3-8, 4-9, 5-9, 6-9, 7-24, 8-24, 9-24

1-0, 2-6, 3-7, 4-17, 5-18, 6-40, 7-51, 8-51, 9-61

Bowling

	O	M	R	W
Halfyard	9	4	7	4
Brown	8.1	5	12	6

	O	M	R	W
Halfyard	13	2	20	5
Brown	8	2	22	3
Shenton	4.5	0	12	2

Kent won by an innings and 101 runs

Inevitably, with a lead of 162 runs – an enormous one in the circumstances – Cowdrey invited them to follow on. So, less than ninety minutes after the start of the first innings, Sedgley and Headley, doubtless full of foreboding, once more made their way to the wicket. Little was to change, although at least all but three batsmen recorded a score, whereas in the first innings there were seven ducks. For a time it looked like a repeat performance. The first 5 wickets fell with only 18 scored. A recovery of sorts saw a sixth-wicket partnership of 22, with the last 4 wickets going down for an additional 21 runs. In the first Worcestershire innings eight batsmen were bowled, but only two suffered that fate second time around.

A truly remarkable match ended at 7.15 p.m. after Cowdrey had claimed the extra half-hour. In under three hours Worcestershire had lost 20 wickets. That the wicket was sub-standard there is little doubt. Colin Cowdrey described it as a 'travesty' and felt it necessary to apologise to the Worcestershire team. It remains the last first-class match to be completed in one day.

Fears expressed about the state of the wicket for the traditional fixture against Sussex, scheduled as the second match of the week, seemed confirmed when the visitors were dismissed for 69 on the first day. But proceedings got back to something like normality when Kent replied with a score of almost 400.

Alan Brown (*opposite*) and David Halfyard (*above*) dismissed Worcestershire twice in a single day.

KENT v. YORKSHIRE

Date: 9, 11-12 May 1964   **Location:** Bradford

Yorkshire had been County Champions in the two previous seasons, and indeed had not been out of the top two since 1958. Kent were in a period of slow progression up the championship table under the leadership of Colin Cowdrey as captain and Les Ames as manager. They had not won in Yorkshire since 1930, and even in Kent could only boast three wins over these opponents in that time.

It was Kent's first game of the season, so it was mainly their first-choice team that appeared. The match saw the reappearance of David Halfyard, who had missed all of 1963 because of serious injuries sustained in a motor accident near the end of the previous season. The Kent side also included the phenomenon of 1963, Derek Underwood, the eighteen-year-old left-arm slow/medium-pace bowler who had grabbed the bowling berth vacated by Halfyard and had become the youngest player ever to take 100 wickets in his debut season.

On the first day, thanks to a delightful innings by Cowdrey, 85 including 1 six and 13 fours, Kent made a reasonable 249, Brian Close taking six wickets for just 29. With no play on the second day, the initial intention by Close, the Yorkshire captain, was to go for first-innings points, but his plans were thwarted by the introduction of Underwood, who took 2 quick wickets in a spell of 9 overs, 8 of which were maidens. In the hope of a successful run chase, Close declared 147 behind as soon as Boycott reached his fifty. To this Kent advantage, 67 runs were added in seventy minutes before lunch, whereupon Cowdrey declared. This decision was probably aided by a misfortune to Jackie Hampshire, who suffered a serious blow when Richardson hit the ball straight to his head, an injury that resulted in five stitches over his eye, and the warning to bat only if necessary.

A target of 215 to win at 76 an hour was on first

Derek Underwood took 7 wickets in an innings for the first time in his career.

Kent won the toss and elected to bat   Umpires: W.H. Copson and R.S. Lay

KENT	1ST INNINGS		2ND INNINGS	
P.E. Richardson	c Binks b Ryan	13	c Boycott b Ryan	21
M.H. Denness	c Boycott b Trueman	14	c Close b Trueman	0
R.C. Wilson	c & b Trueman	20	not out	33
*M.C. Cowdrey	st Binks b Close	85		
S.E. Leary	c Binks b Close	32	not out	3
B.W. Luckhurst	not out	31		
†A.W. Catt	c Sharpe b Close	6	(4) b Ryan	6
A.L. Dixon	c Binks b Close	29		
D.L. Underwood	b Close	0		
D.J. Halfyard	c Hampshire b Close	4		
J.C.J. Dye	b Trueman	2		
Extras	(B 7, LB 4, NB 2)	13	(LB 4)	4
TOTAL	(all out)	249	(for 3 wickets declared)	67

FOW: 1-20, 2-38, 3-61, 4-165, 5-176, 6-186, 7-225, 8-229, 9-235   1-1, 2-35, 3-61

Bowling

	O	M	R	W
Trueman	26.5	6	61	3
Ryan	10	0	25	1
Wilson	28	9	65	0
Illingworth	10	1	38	0
Taylor	8	1	18	0
Close	24	13	29	6

	O	M	R	W
Trueman	9	2	20	1
Ryan	8	0	43	2

YORKSHIRE	1ST INNINGS		2ND INNINGS	
G. Boycott	not out	53	c Cowdrey b Underwood	30
J.H. Hampshire	lbw b Dixon	1	(11) not out	7
D.E.V. Padgett	b Underwood	34	c Catt b Halfyard	16
*D.B. Close	b Underwood	0	run out	67
P.J. Sharpe	not out	10	c Leary b Underwood	18
K. Taylor			(2) c Halfyard b Dixon	7
R. Illingworth			(6) b Underwood	17
D. Wilson			(7) b Underwood	8
F.S. Trueman			(8) c Leary b Underwood	14
†J.G. Binks			(9) c Leary b Underwood	9
M. Ryan			(10) b Underwood	3
Extras	(NB 3, W 1)	4	(B 1, LB 2, NB 1)	4
TOTAL	(for 3 wickets declared)	102	(all out)	200

FOW: 1-7, 2-77, 3-81   1-32, 2-52, 3-68, 4-105, 5-131, 6-143, 7-173, 8-189, 9-189

Bowling

	O	M	R	W
Dye	8	0	49	0
Dixon	8	1	19	1
Halfyard	11	6	17	0
Underwood	9	8	3	2
Leary	4.2	2	10	0

	O	M	R	W
Halfyard	20	3	79	1
Dixon	8	4	20	1
Underwood	24.1	4	97	7

Kent won by 14 runs

sight generous. The carrot was accepted and a period of absorbing cricket with runs and wickets falling regularly ensued. With an hour to play, Yorkshire needed 85 with 5 wickets to fall, thirty minutes later it was 42 but with 3 wickets left. Brian Close was playing a captain's innings until Underwood swung the match as a fieldsman, running out the Yorkshire captain as he went for second run. He followed this by getting Jimmy Binks caught in the covers and finishing the game by bowling Mel Ryan. Hampshire, appearing in that emergency at number eleven, was left not out. Kent had won the match with just three minutes to spare by 14 runs, Underwood taking 7 for 97, at that point his career-best figures.

Halfyard played only one further game for Kent. He had helped put the brake on the Yorkshire scoring in the first innings, but was less successful in the second. Thus ended a Kent career that had carried much of the county's opening attack for seven or eight years. He did return to county cricket, after a few years as an umpire, to play for Nottinghamshire and afterwards for various minor counties, putting in some remarkable performances. For his successor as Kent's main wicket taker, Derek Underwood, the rest, as they say, is history.

KENT v. YORKSHIRE

Date: 9-11 August 1967   **Location:** Canterbury

This second match of Canterbury Week brought together the two counties vying for the championship. It produced one of the most exciting games of the season. Played in front of large crowds, it saw the reappearance for Kent of the ever-popular Godfrey Evans, eight years after his retirement.

Both sides were weakened by Test calls; Kent's Derek Underwood, Colin Cowdrey and Alan Knott – playing in his first Test – and for Yorkshire Geoffrey Boycott and Brian Close. Knott's absence was the reason for the reappearance of Godfrey Evans.

It was tough, tense cricket with drama from the outset when Kent's ever-reliable opener Brian Luckhurst fell victim to an early hostile ball from Trueman. With only 2 runs on the board he was struck on the hand, breaking a bone. As was inevitable he took no effective further part in the match. Trueman's hostility earned him an official warning from the umpire after he had bowled three successive short balls.

Mike Denness and David Nicholls, whose maiden century in 1963, when just nineteen, had been a double, set about recovering from the loss of Luckhurst. With only 31 scored and with Richard Hutton replacing Trueman after only 5 overs, Nicholls tried to hook and was caught at backward square leg. Worse followed when, with just 10 added to the score, West Indian all-rounder John Shepherd attempted to pull a similar short ball and was caught at deep fine leg. Denness became the third victim in quick succession, caught and bowled by Don Wilson. Three wickets then fell quickly, all to Ray Illingworth, the third being Evans, but not before a note of humour entered the proceedings. A great ovation greeted Evans' appearance in which the Yorkshire players joined. His progress to the wicket was accompanied by Trueman humorously sweeping a path for him with his cap. Back with the serious business, while those 3 wickets were falling, Stuart Leary had held one end for three-and-a-half hours. But he was eventually bowled off his left foot. His was a valuable innings. But there was still fun for the crowd in a swashbuckling knock of 33 from bowler Alan Brown, who hit Trueman for 4, 6, 4, 4 off successive balls.

Yorkshire were left with just over an hour to bat out the first day, which they did without any mishap. By day two the pitch was starting to take spin and with the score at 90 for 1, Alan Dixon changed the picture. Bowling his right-arm medium-pace off-spin he accounted for the five middle-order batsmen, reducing Yorkshire to a precarious 157 for 8. Yorkshire's hopes of a first-innings lead and an invaluable 4 points seemed a long

way off. But that was to forget the reputations of Trueman and Don Wilson as attacking tail-end batsmen. In a stand of 62 for the ninth wicket, during which Wilson survived an easy chance, they got within 6 runs of Kent's total. Then yet another sensational twist: Trueman produced a mighty pulled drive but

Stuart Leary hooks a short ball from Fred Trueman to the long leg boundary during the Kent first innings.

Kent won the toss and elected to bat   Umpires: A.E. Alderman and R. Aspinall

KENT	1ST INNINGS		2ND INNINGS	
M.H. Denness	c & b Wilson	42	c Binks b Trueman	2
B.W. Luckhurst	not out	1	(11) c Illingworth b Nicholson	0
D. Nicholls	c Hampshire b Hutton	12	(2) b Nicholson	0
J.N. Shepherd	c Nicholson b Hutton	5	(3) b Nicholson	13
S.E. Leary	b Hutton	66	(4) c Trueman b Nicholson	0
R.C. Wilson	c Sharpe b Illingworth	19	(5) c & b Hutton	50
*A.L. Dixon	c Hutton b Illingworth	18	(6) lbw b Illingworth	18
†T.G. Evans	b Illingworth	10	(7) c Padgett b Hutton	6
G.W. Johnson	b Trueman	8	(8) b Illingworth	2
A. Brown	b Trueman	33	(9) not out	0
J.N. Graham	b Nicholson	3	(10) b Nicholson	1
Extras	(LB 2, NB 4)	6	(LB 3, NB 5)	8
TOTAL	(all out)	223	(all out)	100

FOW: 1-31, 2-41, 3-69, 4-128, 5-156, 6-170, 7-184, 8-201, 9-219   1-2, 2-2, 3-5, 4-37, 5-77, 6-88, 7-95, 8-99.9-100

Bowling

	O	M	R	W
Trueman	10.1	2	39	2
Nicholson	12	2	29	1
Hutton	17	2	65	3
Wilson	23	15	26	1
Illingworth	26	7	58	3

	O	M	R	W
Trueman	4	2	3	1
Nicholson	11.3	3	37	5
Hutton	10	4	15	2
Illingworth	14	5	25	2
Wilson	10	4	12	0

YORKSHIRE	1ST INNINGS		2ND INNINGS	
P.J. Sharpe	c Johnson b Brown	56	c Shepherd b Dixon	37
K. Taylor	c Evans b Brown	20	c Denness b Graham	9
D.E.V. Padgett	c Leary b Dixon	18	not out	30
J.H. Hampshire	c Johnson b Dixon	26	c Brown b Johnson	21
J.C. Balderstone	lbw b Dixon	1	not out	1
R. Illingworth	c Evans b Dixon	0		
R.A. Hutton	b Dixon	8		
†J.G. Binks	c Shepherd b Graham	14		
D. Wilson	b Dixon	37		
*F.S. Trueman	c sub b Dixon	33		
A.G. Nicholson	not out	1		
Extras	(B 8, LB 2, NB 1)	11	(LB 1)	1
TOTAL	(all out)	225	(for 3 wickets)	100

FOW: 1-48, 2-92, 3-98, 4-100, 5-102, 6-116, 7-141, 8-157, 9-217   1-19, 2-65, 3-97

Bowling

	O	M	R	W
Graham	37	13	60	1
Brown	18	3	61	2
Dixon	29.2	7	93	7

	O	M	R	W
Graham	5	1	20	1
Brown	7	1	12	0
Shepherd	12	4	28	0
Dixon	4	1	31	1
Johnson	5	2	7	1

Yorkshire won by 7 wickets

this time Alan Ealham, fielding as substitute for the injured Luckhurst, pulled off what was described as the catch of the season. He raced round the boundary edge and took the ball one-handed while running at full speed. With the last two batsmen at the wicket and courtesy of another dropped catch, Yorkshire gained a first innings lead, and those 4 points, by just 2 runs.

With parity after two completed innings the enthralled crowd looked forward to their favourites building a lead that would have Yorkshire facing a large total on a wearing pitch. It was not to be! By close on the second day Kent had struggled to 99 for 8 off little more than 40 overs. Had it not been for a gritty half century by Bob Wilson, who was batting with a dislocated finger, the match would have been all over in two days. As it was, Kent's innings just went into the final day, with the injured Luckhurst batting at eleven. Their opponents had little difficulty in scoring the 99 runs needed for victory.

It had been a tense, exciting and riveting contest with plenty of incident and memorable moments for the large crowd. It was also the match that decided that the County Championship would return to Yorkshire for the sixth time in nine years.

KENT v. NOTTINGHAMSHIRE

Date: 29, 31 August, 1 September 1970   **Location:** Folkestone

Kent arrived for the first game of the Folkestone Festival on the back of 10 matches undefeated, which included 5 wins. They had been bottom of the County Championship table at the beginning of July with only 1 win in their first 7 matches. However, hopes were beginning to rise that in the club's centenary year the county might gain its first championship success in fifty-seven years.

Kent included in their side two recently capped players, Graham Johnson and Bob Woolmer, while Nottinghamshire had David Halfyard, who had played 185 matches for Kent between 1956 and 1964 before joining Notts in 1968 after recovering from a serious road accident and serving a period as a first-class umpire.

On a perfect wicket, Nottinghamshire, who scored more runs in the championship than any other county in the season, set about the task of making a big score with Mike Harris and Brian Bolus leading the way. Both had been prolific run scorers throughout the season. The Cornishman Harris, a forcing right-handed batsman, was not far short of 2,000 for the season, while Bolus was to reach that magic figure during the second innings of this match. It was a solid first innings by the Robin Hood county, the highlight being a brilliant hundred by captain Garry Sobers, whose 123 came in a partnership of 203 with Mike Smedley. His century was reached in two-and-three-quarter hours. It included 17 fours and 1 six. On the dismissal of Smedley, Sobers declared, leaving Kent an awkward twenty minutes before the close during which time they lost Denness.

Disaster struck early on the second day and it was the ex-Kent fast-medium bowler Halfyard who inflicted it. Within forty-five minutes the hosts were reduced to 27 for 5. Nightwatchman Derek Underwood, together with Graham Johnson, Colin Cowdrey and Asif Iqbal, were all back in the pavilion. At that stage Halfyard had taken 3 for 8 in 9 overs. Brian Luckhurst, supported firstly by Alan Ealham and then John Shepherd, set about building a recovery. Ealham's 57 came in a stand of 113. That performance earned him his county cap, which was presented to him on his return to the pavilion. The seventh-wicket stand of 105 with Shepherd came in seventy-two minutes. Following their dismissals Bob Woolmer helped to extend the score to 310, at which point Colin Cowdrey declared. Luckhurst was the backbone of what from unpromising beginnings had become a very respectable total. He finished with 156*, including 22 fours, and he had batted for five-and-a-quarter hours.

Nottinghamshire were left with just under an hour to bat on this second day, during which they lost Harris. After surviving twenty minutes before the close without scoring, Kenyan-born Basharat Hassan was dismissed in the second over of the morning. Despite that early setback, they went about their task with an urgency, seeking a declaration to give themselves sufficient time to dismiss Kent. Sobers scored 44 out of 53, including eight boundaries in thirty-five minutes. He was well supported by Bolus, Smedley and Graham Frost. Ten minutes after lunch came the declaration, Kent being required to score 282 to win in two hours plus the statutory last-hour 20 overs.

It was a confident start by Denness and Luckhurst, their partnership of 103 coming in just eighty minutes. When

Colin Cowdrey, John Shepherd, Garry Sobers, Graham Frost and Brian Luckhurst leave the field at Folkestone.

KENT v. NOTTINGHAMSHIRE

Nottinghamshire won the toss and elected to bat Umpires: H.D. Bird and A.E. Fagg

NOTTINGHAMSHIRE 1ST INNINGS

				2ND INNINGS	
M.J. Harris	run out		53	b Shepherd	11
J.B. Bolus	c Denness b Dye		43	c Denness b Underwood	73
S.B. Hassan	c Knott b Woolmer		55	c Shepherd b Dye	0
M.J. Smedley	b Shepherd		92	c Knott b Underwood	23
*G.S. Sobers	not out		123	b Johnson	44
G. Frost				not out	49
R.A. White				b Johnson	3
M.N.S. Taylor					
D.J. Halfyard					
P.J. Plummer					
†D.A. Pullan					
Extras	(LB 6, NB 3, W 1)		10	(B 6, LB 5, NB 1)	12
TOTAL	(for 4 wickets declared)		376	(for 6 wickets declared)	215

FOW: 1-80, 2-110, 3-173, 4-376

1-16, 2-21, 3-71, 4-124, 5-206, 6-215

Bowling

	O	M	R	W
Dye	22	2	88	1
Shepherd	27	6	91	1
Woolmer	20	3	67	1
Underwood	22	7	64	0
Johnson	17	2	56	0

	O	M	R	W
Dye	11	3	29	1
Shepherd	15	8	29	1
Underwood	28	10	63	2
Woolmer	6	1	23	0
Johnson	14.1	2	48	2
Asif	3	0	11	0

KENT 1ST INNINGS

				2ND INNINGS	
M.H. Denness	c Pullan b Taylor		2	b Taylor	90
B.W. Luckhurst	not out		156	c Plummer b White	58
D.L. Underwood	c Pullan b Taylor		1		
G.W. Johnson	c Smedley b Halfyard		0	(7) c Hassan b Sobers	0
*M.C. Cowdrey	c Sobers b Halfyard		4	(4) c Hassan b Sobers	18
Asif Iqbal	c Plummer b Halfyard		10	(3) b Sobers	56
A.G.E. Ealham	b Harris		57	(6) c White b Taylor	11
J.N. Shepherd	lbw b Sobers		47	(5) lbw b Taylor	22
R.A. Woolmer	not out		26	(8) not out	2
†A.P.E. Knott				(9) not out	12
J.C.J. Dye					
Extras	(B 1, LB 2, NB 3, W 1)		7	(LB 8, NB 6)	14
TOTAL	(for 7 wickets declared)		310	(for 7 wickets)	283

FOW: 1-2, 2-6, 3-7, 4-13, 5-27, 6-140, 7-245

1-103, 2-197, 3-221, 4-253, 5-262, 6-268, 7-269

Bowling

	O	M	R	W
Taylor	25	7	62	2
Halfyard	30.2	9	85	3
White	3	2	8	0
Plummer	13	1	46	0
Sobers	15	2	49	1
Harris	9	1	53	1

	O	M	R	W
Sobers	19.4	2	103	3
Taylor	23	2	107	3
Halfyard	5	0	31	0
White	5	0	28	1

Kent won by 3 wickets

Luckhurst was dismissed Asif took over. There could be no better batsman to come to the crease at such a time than the dashing Pakistani. He hit 50 out of 86 in forty-seven minutes. Needing only 112 from the final 20 overs Kent were in a strong position. But Cowdrey became Sobers' second victim, then just 9 runs later Denness departed, having batted just under three hours for his 90, during which he hit eleven boundaries. Shepherd and Ealham departed after brief but useful knocks. At that point Mike Taylor had taken 3 wickets in 8 balls without conceding a run. Sobers then removed Johnson, which left Knott and Woolmer to score 13 off the last 3 overs. With Knott hitting three successive fours the target was achieved with 8 balls remaining. Given the way Halfyard had sliced through Kent's middle order in the first innings it was something of a mystery that he was given only 5 overs during Kent's run chase.

This sensational win stamped Kent with the hallmark of champions, an achievement that was confirmed just ten days later when the title returned to the Hop County after their long wait.

KENT v. SURREY

Date: 4-6 July 1973   **Location:** Maidstone

Colin Cowdrey relinquished the Kent captaincy after the 1971 season. He had held the reins for fifteen years; a period only equalled by the founding father of Kent cricket himself, Lord Harris. In that time he had taken the county from the nether regions of the County Championship to the title and had confirmed himself as one of the great cricketers in Kent history.

After 1971, however, Cowdrey's career was in a state of limbo. The Kent selection committee was often in some doubt what to do with him. He slipped down the batting order and sometimes was dropped altogether, the argument being to make way for younger players. The needs of a middle order to chase bonus points or late runs in limited-overs games did not help his cause. Nevertheless, he still put together 1,000 runs in 1972 and in 1973 was scoring consistently. Most significantly, Cowdrey was approaching a notable milestone in his career, 100 hundreds. He had ended 1972 on ninety-eight, a figure he had not added to by the time he came to Maidstone Week at the end of June. The auspices that the feat would be achieved on the picturesque Mote were not good. Strangely, in 35 innings on the ground, Cowdrey had never made a hundred and averaged less than 30. It was easily his least successful ground in Kent. It was also a ground with the bad memory of his dreadful Achilles injury that ended his final reign as England captain during a Sunday match in 1969.

Yet in the first match of the week, against Somerset, Cowdrey scored century number ninety-nine, 123* in four-and-three-quarter hours, adding 241 with Mike Denness. Batsmen remained in control when it came to the second match against Surrey. The visitors dominated the first day, with New Zealander Geoff Howarth making his highest first-class score to date – it was, to quote *The Times*, 'a batsman's dreamland set in an outfield of grass'.

However, Kent faltered on day two due to poor batting and Intikhab Alam's spin, and were 124 for

5 when Cowdrey, remarkably batting at number seven, joined the Pakistani star Asif Iqbal. Five runs were added before lunch. By tea the score was 310 for 5 (Asif 114*, Cowdrey 89*). It was Cowdrey at his best, all scientific placing, even the odd hook. In the over he reached 50, he stroked Intikhab effortlessly past cover and then lapped a leg-side ball almost straight behind the wicketkeeper. Shortly after tea, with the 138th ball he faced, he reached his milestone. Denness promptly declared and Cowdrey was enthusiastically cheered off the field by invading Kent supporters. Cowdrey thus became the sixteenth player to reach 100 hundreds and the

Colin Cowdrey. The hundredth run of his hundredth hundred.

Surrey won the toss and elected to bat   Umpires: J.F. Crapp and C.G. Pepper

SURREY	1ST INNINGS				2ND INNINGS		
*J.H. Edrich	c Nicholls b Shepherd			59	c Asif b Topley		40
M.J. Edwards	c Nicholls b Shepherd			6	c Luckhurst b Johnson		15
G.P. Howarth	c Asif b Shepherd			159	not out		42
Younis Ahmed	c Topley b Woolmer			12	st Nicholls b Johnson		0
D.R. Owen-Thomas	not out			89	c Nicholls b Johnson		3
S.J. Storey	c Nicholls b Shepherd			7	c Denness b Johnson		7
Intikhab Alam	c Asif b Woolmer			19	c Asif b Luckhurst		20
†A. Long					c Denness b Luckhurst		0
R.D. Jackman					lbw b Luckhurst		11
D.M. Smith							
P.I. Pocock							
Extras	(B 4, LB 9, NB 1,W 2)			16	(B 3, LB 6)		9
TOTAL	(for 6 wickets declared)			367	(for 8 wickets declared)		147

FOW: 1-9, 2-141, 3-177, 4-305, 5-322, 6-367

1-27, 2-71, 3-72, 4-76, 5-96, 6-121, 7-121, 8-147

Bowling

	O	M	R	W
Elms	21	1	67	0
Shepherd	30	8	85	4
Woolmer	16.2	3	63	2
Johnson	26	1	93	0
Topley	8	2	26	0
Cowdrey	1	0	17	0

	O	M	R	W
Elms	5	1	15	0
Shepherd	8	5	6	0
Woolmer	7	2	13	0
Johnson	31	8	57	4
Topley	15	5	24	1
Luckhurst	12.4	4	23	3

KENT	1ST INNINGS				2ND INNINGS		
B.W. Luckhurst	run out			20	c Long b Jackman		4
G.W. Johnson	b Intikhab			51	c Owen-Thomas b Jackman		16
†D. Nicholls	c Pocock b Intikhab			14	c Smith b Pocock		35
*M.H. Denness	c & b Smith			15	(8) not out		4
Asif Iqbal	not out			119	st Long b Pocock		10
A.G.E. Ealham	c Howarth b Intikhab			4	c Jackman b Intikhab		11
M.C. Cowdrey	not out			100	not out		9
J.N. Shepherd					(4) c Edwards b Smith		10
R.A. Woolmer							
P.A. Topley							
R.B. Elms							
Extras	(LB 2, W 1)			3	(LB 3)		3
TOTAL	(for 5 wickets declared)			326	(for 6 wickets)		102

FOW: 1-47, 2-77, 3-94, 4-105, 5-124

1-4, 2-25, 3-35, 4-61, 5-84, 6-94

Bowling

	O	M	R	W
Jackman	24.2	3	81	0
Smith	15	4	37	1
Intikhab	25	4	88	3
Storey	15	1	45	0
Pocock	13	1	72	0

	O	M	R	W
Jackman	6	0	34	2
Smith	4	0	31	1
Pocock	4	1	16	2
Intikhab	3	0	18	1

Match Drawn

third after Kent legends Frank Woolley and Les Ames. With the already declining first-class programme, the potential for too many others in the years to come joining this distinguished company was becoming less likely.

However, even Cowdrey admitted that Asif had played the greater innings in their unbeaten partnership of 202. Driving, pulling and cutting, Surrey found it impossible to bowl a length at him – 'a fabulous innings', Cowdrey is quoted as saying afterwards.

Rain ended play soon after Surrey started their second innings and continued to have the decisive say in the rest of match. Again, Howarth stood in Kent's way as Surrey, helped by at least four fairly easy dropped catches, progressed to give a Kent a target of 189 off what was to be 32 overs. They slipped to 94 for 6, but with two unlikely numbers seven and eight, Cowdrey and Denness, there was still hope when, 87 runs short of victory and with 15 overs left, the weather intervened.

It was, for Cowdrey on the day, 'the last milestone of his career'. But one remarkable innings remained.

KENT v. AUSTRALIANS

Date: 25-27 June 1975   **Location:** Canterbury

Kent had not beaten the Australians since 1899. The Australian side that played in this opening first-class match of a shortened tour that followed the inaugural World Cup competition was hardly a full-strength XI. A number of individuals who had had a part in crucifying the England side during the previous winter were rested, including Greg Chappell, Max Walker and Jeff Thomson. But Ian Chappell, Ashley Mallett and, notably, Dennis Lillee did play.

The Kent side was also not at full strength. Mike Denness, the captain, was missing because of a knee injury and David Nicholls was keeping wicket in place of Alan Knott. Included was Colin Cowdrey, fresh from his unexpected summons back into Test cricket the previous winter against these very same visitors. Cowdrey had continued to play an uncertain role in the Kent side. He did top the Kent averages in 1974. However, he had to all intents announced his retirement, stating that, not wanting to stand in the way of the county's developing younger players, he would not play regularly. Others thought there was more life in the Cowdrey career. Rumours linking him to a future career with Sussex were prevalent during the match. On the other hand, the MCC clearly thought the end was nigh by appointing him captain for their upcoming traditional Lord's match against the tourists.

The Australians won the toss on an excellent wicket and in front of a near-capacity crowd. Almost inevitably they piled up a large total, 415 off 120 overs with Alan Turner, thought to have been fortunate to be chosen for the tour, scoring 156. Just about everybody else who batted got a reasonable score at least. Kent's innings on the second day was soon in trouble and they only struggled up to 202 thanks to Alan Ealham, John Shepherd and Bernard Julien down the order. However, the follow-on was not enforced. Ian Chappell chose batting practice after a mass of limited-over games, feeling play in the longer game may have been a bit rusty.

When Chappell declared on the third day, Kent had the hopeless task of 354 to win or five-and-a-quarter hours to survive; a situation not helped with Julien injured and unlikely to bat and Richard Elms only able to do so with a runner. Luckhurst and Johnson made a patient start, but both were out before lunch and soon afterwards Woolmer, going well, was hit a painful blow on the arm by Lillee bowling a multitude of styles including fearsome bouncers and leg-spinners. Ealham followed first ball, leaving Kent

at 116 for 3, possibly 5, even 6. Not surprisingly the tourists thought the match was over and the tour bus was manoeuvred into position behind the pavilion for a swift getaway.

Enter Colin Cowdrey. Perhaps characteristically he was a little shaky at the start, particularly against the spinners, but imperceptibly the scoreboard was ticking along. Cowdrey passed 50 and found in Nicholls a courageous and skilful partner. No further wickets were lost, so that at tea the scoreboard registered 226 for 3. There were at least hopes the game would be saved, perhaps amazingly won.

Lillee had clearly come to that conclusion and in a fearsome spell immediately after tea disposed of Nicholls and Shepherd in short time. An unexpected bonus of 30 runs came from Rowe and 300 was nigh when Woolmer returned. Together with Cowdrey the runs flowed and indeed the final 79 runs came off 10 overs; only 28 were needed off the last 10. The game was up.

Colin Cowdrey. The highest score by a Kent player in a Kent match against the Australians.

Australians won the toss and elected to bat   Umpires: D.J. Constant and B.J. Meyer

AUSTRALIANS	1ST INNINGS		2ND INNINGS	
R.B. McCosker	c Nicholls b Shepherd	58	c Ealham b Shepherd	26
A. Turner	c Luckhurst b Shepherd	156	(5) not out	25
B.M. Laird	st Nicholls b Underwood	27	(2) not out	63
*I.M. Chappell	c Rowe b Woolmer	27	(3) b Johnson	0
K.D. Walters	lbw b Underwood	50	(4) lbw b Underwood	21
G.J. Gilmour	c Woolmer b Julien	30		
†R.D. Robinson	b Johnson	36		
D.K. Lillee	b Underwood	0		
A.A. Mallett	not out	8		
A.G. Hurst				
J.D. Higgs				
Extras	(B 2, LB 16, NB 4, W 1)	23	(B 3, LB 2)	5
TOTAL	(for 8 wickets declared)	415	(for 3 wickets declared)	140

FOW: 1-121, 2-230, 3-273, 4-300, 5-367, 6-377, 7-377, 8-415   1-55, 2-55, 3-88

Bowling

	O	M	R	W
Julien	18	3	80	1
Elms	8	0	42	0
Shepherd	18	4	70	2
Woolmer	22	5	85	1
Johnson	15.3	2	48	1
Underwood	24	3	67	3

	O	M	R	W
Shepherd	7	0	18	0
Woolmer	4	1	10	0
Johnson	24	4	65	2
Underwood	21	9	38	1
Rowe	2	0	4	0

KENT	1ST INNINGS		2ND INNINGS	
*B.W. Luckhurst	c Robinson b Gilmour	2	lbw b Hurst	40
G.W. Johnson	c Mallett b Gilmour	19	b Gilmour	11
M.C. Cowdrey	c Robinson b Gilmour	22	(4) not out	151
R.A. Woolmer	c Robinson b Hurst	4	(3) not out	71
A.G.E. Ealham	lbw b Hurst	41	c McCosker b Lillee	0
†D. Nicholls	b Higgs	16	c Robinson b Lillee	39
J.N. Shepherd	c Walters b Higgs	38	lbw b Lillee	2
B.D. Julien	st Robinson b Mallett	41		
C.J.C. Rowe	st Robinson b Higgs	3	(8) c Robinson b Gilmour	30
R.B. Elms	st Robinson b Higgs	0		
D.L. Underwood	not out	0		
Extras	(B 4, LB 6, NB 6)	16	(LB 7, NB 3)	10
TOTAL	(all out)	202	(for 6 wickets)	354

FOW: 1-3, 2-39, 3-44, 4-58, 5-96, 6-137, 7-164, 8-186, 9-202   1-39, 2-77, 3-116, 4-242, 5-246, 6-295

Bowling

	O	M	R	W
Lillee	8	1	28	0
Gilmour	13	5	40	3
Hurst	15	4	44	2
Higgs	15	6	49	4
Mallett	5.1	1	25	1

	O	M	R	W
Lillee	22	3	95	3
Gilmour	21.5	2	92	2
Hurst	13	0	48	1
Higgs	12	2	67	0
Mallett	13	3	42	0

Kent won by 4 wickets

Cowdrey's massive contribution was 151*, including 25 glorious fours. When set, the runs flowed over a fast outfield from a pitch that offered a little spin but no spite. Lillee's bouncers were hooked, balls outside the off stump were impudently cut fine or square and spinners pulled to all corners on the leg-side field. 'Cowdrey,' wrote John Arlott in *The Guardian*, 'batted with the calm authority and complete accomplishment of his finest days.' Alan Gibson in *The Times* added, 'As he [Cowdrey] came running triumphantly in after what must have been one of the most satisfying innings of his life, he looked less like the familiar archdeaconal personage than a skipping lamb finding another spring.'

Inevitably the call for another return to the colours came from the media. But the postscript was a severe anti-climax. In the MCC match Lillee had the last laugh, dismissing the great man for a sad pair. He made one further century (his 107th) before the end of 1975 and, although still offering his services, he played just one match in 1976 during Canterbury Week before, as a player, passing into history.

KENT v. WARWICKSHIRE

Date: 7-9 September 1977   **Location:** Edgbaston, Birmingham

It is rarely the case that the destination of the County Championship is decided on the final afternoon of the season but that was how the situation developed during this game.

When the last round of matches commenced any one of three sides, Gloucestershire, who headed the table by 5 points, Kent or Middlesex could have been crowned champions. A further piece of spice in the mix was that, rather controversially, Middlesex would have not been in contention at all had they not been able to rearrange a fixture to accommodate a Gillette Cup semi-final delayed by bad weather. If the fixture had been kept as planned it would almost certainly, like Kent's at the same time, have been abandoned because of rain. As it was Middlesex won the rearranged game (at Chelmsford).

By mid afternoon on 9 September Gloucestershire had been unexpectedly but soundly beaten by Hampshire in front of what was described as the biggest last-day crowd at Bristol that anyone could remember, while Middlesex had won a comfortable victory over Lancashire, putting them at least for an hour or two at the top of the table.

So Kent knew that only a victory would give them a chance of the title. Their quest could not have started more disastrously. In conditions ideal for seam bowling they struggled to their lowest first innings score of the season. Consequently, they won not a single batting point. However, with John Shepherd taking advantage of the conditions, Warwickshire fared little better and half the side was out for just 81. But a brave innings by Alvin Kallicharran secured at the close of play a small but significant lead of 23 with 4 wickets still in hand, a potentially important advantage. Early on the second day John Shepherd quickly disposed of the remaining resistance, leaving Warwickshire with a first-innings lead of 60. The popular all-rounder's return of 5 for 63, together with his single wicket in the second innings, gave him a total of 87 for the season – the third highest in the country.

Conditions had improved by the time Kent started their second innings. Nevertheless, before the deficit had been wiped off, Graham Clinton and Chris Tavaré had both been dismissed cheaply. Faultless batting by Bob Woolmer began to repair the situation and in partnership with Asif the scoring rate started to accelerate. But when they, followed by Alan Knott and Charles Rowe, were dismissed, Kent were still a long way short of a total that would bring them the required victory. However, Alan Ealham and Shepherd responded magnificently. Both went for their shots and progressed the score to 285 for 6 by close of the day's play, a lead of 222. Their final 4 wickets, however, added only 31 runs on the final morning, leaving Warwickshire the far-from-insurmountable task of scoring 254 for victory in exactly five hours.

The tensions of the occasion certainly did not get to the Kent bowlers. In a short space of time Kevin Jarvis, wicketless in the first innings, accounted for England star Dennis Amiss, John Whitehouse and David Smith, while John Shepherd had opener Neil Abberley lbw. All were dismissed for single figures. But the prize wicket was that of Kallicharran, brilliantly caught by Ealham off the bowling of all-rounder Richard Hills who, along with Jarvis and Rowe, had been capped earlier in the season. At that stage the hosts' early batting was in disarray.

John Shepherd hits the ball past a diving John Whitehouse. He managed 106 runs and 6 wickets in a decisive match.

Kent won the toss and elected to bat Umpires: W.L. Budd and P.B. Wight

KENT	1ST INNINGS		2ND INNINGS	
R.A. Woolmer	c Humpage b Willis	2	lbw b Willis	59
G.S. Clinton	c Whitehouse b Perryman	22	lbw b Brown	8
C.J. Tavaré	lbw b Rouse	3	c Humpage b Perryman	5
*Asif Iqbal	b Perryman	19	c sub b Willis	38
A.G.E. Ealham	b Brown	15	c Whitehouse b Willis	62
†A.P.E. Knott	lbw b Brown	2	(8) lbw b Hemmings	28
C.J.C. Rowe	c Humpage b Brown	2	(6) lbw b Hemmings	13
J.N. Shepherd	b Willis	29	(7) c Whitehouse b Perryman	77
R.W. Hills	retired hurt	19	c sub b Perryman	6
D.L. Underwood	c Smith b Perryman	2	lbw b Willis	1
K.B.S. Jarvis	not out	0	not out	2
Extras	(NB 3)	3	(B 1, LB 9, NB 7)	17
TOTAL	(all out)	118	(all out)	316

FOW: 1-8, 2-11, 3-38, 4-61, 5-65, 6-65, 7-79, 8-105, 9-118

1-51, 2-56, 3-108, 4-117, 5-148, 6-222, 7-289, 8-311, 9-314

Bowling

	O	M	R	W
Willis	14	2	34	2
Brown	19	2	27	3
Rouse	8	2	21	1
Perryman	14.1	3	33	3

	O	M	R	W
Willis	28	6	91	4
Brown	19	8	47	1
Perryman	40.3	13	96	3
Hemmings	20	5	65	2

WARWICKSHIRE	1ST INNINGS		2ND INNINGS	
D.L. Amiss	c Knott b Shepherd	4	c Tavaré b Jarvis	7
R.N. Abberley	c Asif b Woolmer	22	lbw b Shepherd	1
J. Whitehouse	lbw b Shepherd	0	b Jarvis	2
K.D. Smith	b Woolmer	15	b Jarvis	4
A.I. Kallicharran	b Hills	79	c Ealham b Hills	3
†G.W. Humpage	c Knott b Woolmer	4	c Asif b Underwood	104
S.J. Rouse	not out	21	(8) lbw b Woolmer	25
E.E. Hemmings	c Woolmer b Underwood	0	(7) c Tavaré b Jarvis	25
R.G.D. Willis	c Ealham b Shepherd	10	b Woolmer	8
S.P. Perryman	c Asif b Shepherd	1	(11) c Woolmer b Jarvis	25
*D.J. Brown	b Shepherd	6	(10) not out	19
Extras	(B 1, LB 8, NB 7, W 3)	19	(LB 2, W 1)	3
TOTAL	(all out)	181	(all out)	226

FOW: 1-18, 2-23, 3-32, 4-77, 5-81, 6-119, 7-150, 8-150, 9-173

1-6, 2-9, 3-15, 4-16, 5-29, 6-121, 7-173, 8-173, 9-181

Bowling

	O	M	R	W
Jarvis	16	7	27	0
Shepherd	20.1	6	63	5
Woolmer	17	8	32	3
Asif	2	0	10	0
Underwood	6	2	15	1
Hills	8	3	15	1

	O	M	R	W
Jarvis	20.1	3	83	5
Shepherd	19	6	42	1
Hills	7	0	34	1
Underwood	11	4	22	1
Woolmer	15	4	42	2

Kent won by 27 runs

With Warwickshire reduced to 29 for 5, Kent looked well on their way to at least a share of the title.

But an outstanding hundred by wicketkeeper-batsman Geoff Humpage almost turned the tide. He scored his runs in little over even time and had good support from Steve Rouse, Eddie Hemmings and Steve Perryman. His was the ninth wicket to go down and at that point the tension in the Kent camp became almost unbearable, for news had got through of the Middlesex victory at Blackpool. Kent needed a win to guarantee a share of the title.

The last-wicket pair resisted with apparent ease and Asif's bowling changes made little difference. Perryman and Brown inched nearer to the required target of 254. Shepherd, Underwood and Woolmer all tried to break the partnership but to no avail. Jarvis, the hero of the early-order collapse, was recalled and with his first ball after tea he forced Perryman to edge the ball to Woolmer at first slip.

So Kent were home by just 27 runs and celebrated a half share in the championship, the first time since 1950 that it had ended in a tie. But, given the circumstances of Middlesex's rearranged match, for Kent at least it was not entirely a satisfactory outcome.

KENT v. MIDDLESEX

Date: 17, 19-20 June 1978   **Location:** Canterbury

On a cold and windy day Kent began their eighth championship match of 1978 against the reigning joint-champions. The controversy surrounding the shared championship of the previous season was certainly in the minds of Kent supporters, who were still feeling aggrieved at being deprived of an outright title win. Nevertheless, the season so far had promised much, 5 of their matches having been won against 1 defeat.

It had been a troublesome period with disruption threatening as a result of the Packer Affair. Asif was relieved of the captaincy in favour of Alan Ealham and Alan Knott decided to take a season off. But there were advantages. With their Packer players having been banned from international cricket it meant that the county could be at full strength for the whole season. However, the situation caused quite a bit of ill feeling, both among sections of the paying public (mainly outside Kent) and in dressing rooms.

Bob Woolmer and Charles Rowe produced Kent's highest opening stand in five years. Their 187-run partnership was scored off 67 overs but once they had been dismissed, only Chris Tavaré and Asif Iqbal briefly built on the fine start. After their dismissal no one was able to maintain the early advantage, with 4 wickets falling for only 8 runs and the last 3 going down in 4 balls. Eight wickets had fallen for just 50 runs. Allan Arthur Jones, who throughout his first-class career appeared for four counties, produced his best figures for Middlesex up to that point.

Before play ended on the first day Kevin Jarvis dismissed Wilf Slack with a brutal lifter. John Emburey, in the unfamiliar position of opening batsman, struggled to come to terms with the bowler-friendly conditions on the Monday morning and became Jarvis's second victim. Meanwhile, Folkestone-born Graham Barlow was seeking to build a partnership but no one was able to stay with him. When he was sixth out, bowled by Underwood, Middlesex were still 154 behind. The inexperienced Keith Tomlins and wicketkeeper Ian Gould retrieved the situation with a stand of 113 in good time. But when Derek Underwood dismissed Tomlins the way was open for a speedy end to the innings. Selvey was well caught by Paul Downton without scoring and with the score on 278 the last 3 wickets went down. Kent's lead of just 19 was far short of what had been hoped for earlier in the day.

Kent commenced their second innings in the late afternoon, needing to build on their slight first innings advantage. However, there was to be no repeat of the strong first-innings early showing. They started disastrously, losing both Rowe and Tavaré to the big Barbadian fast bowler Wayne Daniel in his first 3 overs. A partnership of 61 ended when Mike Gatting

Bob Woolmer. His 92 and 52 were the mainstay of the Kent batting.

Kent won the toss and elected to bat   Umpires: J.G Langridge and P.B. Wight

KENT	1ST INNINGS		2ND INNINGS	
R.A. Woolmer	lbw b Selvey	92	c & b Emburey	50
C.J.C. Rowe	b Selvey	84	c Gould b Daniel	4
C.J. Tavaré	c Gould b Jones	18	lbw b Daniel	0
Asif Iqbal	c Gould b Selvey	38	c Gatting b Selvey	29
*A.G.E. Ealham	c Gould b Jones	23	c Slack b Emburey	7
C.S. Cowdrey	run out	0	(7) c Barlow b Daniel	10
G.W. Johnson	c Gould b Jones	0	(8) c sub b Jones	35
†P.R. Downton	not out	13	(6) b Daniel	6
G.R. Dilley	lbw b Jones	0	b Emburey	8
D.L. Underwood	b Jones	0	not out	20
K.B.S. Jarvis	b Jones	0	b Daniel	0
Extras	(B 2, LB 10, NB 14, W 3)	29	(B 4, LB 6, NB 4)	14
TOTAL	(all out)	297	(all out)	183

FOW: 1-187, 2-190, 3-247, 4-255, 5-255, 6-255, 7-289, 8-297, 9-297   1-10, 2-14, 3-75, 4-90, 5-103, 6-113, 7-113, 8-135, 9-173

Bowling

	O	M	R	W
Daniel	8	3	7	0
Selvey	27	5	81	3
Jones	29.5	8	89	6
Emburey	27	6	64	0
Featherstone	6	0	27	0

	O	M	R	W
Daniel	18.1	5	49	5
Selvey	15	2	51	1
Jones	7	0	30	1
Emburey	19	8	31	3
Featherstone	1	0	8	0

MIDDLESEX	1ST INNINGS		2ND INNINGS	
W.N. Slack	c Downton b Jarvis	0	b Underwood	8
J.E. Emburey	c Tavaré b Jarvis	18	(8) b Johnson	13
G.D. Barlow	b Underwood	72	c Cowdrey b Jarvis	10
M.W. Gatting	c Downton b Jarvis	14	c Woolmer b Jarvis	0
N.G. Featherstone	run out	16	b Underwood	10
*M.J. Smith	c Downton b Underwood	0	(2) b Jarvis	0
K.P. Tomlins	c Downton b Underwood	42	(6) lbw b Underwood	6
†I.J. Gould	c Ealham b Underwood	83	(7) c Tavaré b Johnson	42
M.W.W. Selvey	c Downton b Jarvis	0	not out	19
W.W. Daniel	not out	0	b Underwood	3
A.A. Jones	b Jarvis	0	b Dilley	33
Extras	(B 19, LB 5, NB 8, W 1)	33	(B 4, LB 13, NB 2)	19
TOTAL	(all out)	278	(all out)	163

FOW: 1-0, 2-38, 3-68, 4-124, 5-125, 6-143, 7-256, 8-278, 9-278   1-0, 2-18, 3-18, 4-18, 5-37, 6-50, 7-77, 8-108, 9-113

Bowling

	O	M	R	W
Jarvis	15.5	3	56	5
Dilley	15	2	43	0
Underwood	28	8	72	4
Johnson	23	9	54	0
Rowe	5	0	20	0

	O	M	R	W
Jarvis	6	1	17	3
Dilley	6.1	0	14	1
Underwood	22	6	55	4
Johnson	18	4	54	2
Rowe	1	0	4	0

Kent won by 39 runs

caught Asif. Then, right on the close of play, Ealham departed, caught by Slack off Emburey. Kent ended the day on 90 for 4. Some resistance by Graham Johnson and a valuable little knock by Underwood took Kent's lead to 202, the last 3 wickets adding 48.

For their second innings Middlesex dropped Emburey down the order and opened with Slack and their captain Mike Smith, in his twentieth season with the county. But the change of order did little for them. Within a short time they were 18 for 4 and it was Jarvis again who did the early damage, dismissing Smith, Barlow and Gatting in his first 4 overs at a cost of just 15 runs. With Johnson and Underwood replacing Jarvis and Graham Dilley, the ball began to turn prodigiously. Underwood disposed of Slack, Featherstone and Tomlins in quick succession, leaving Middlesex in the precarious position of 77 for 7. But Ian Gould again held up the Kent attack with an innings of 42 and the bowlers were further frustrated by Mike Selvey and Allan Jones with a last-wicket stand of 50 before Jones was finally bowled by Dilley.

Kent were victorious by 39 runs. From that point on they led the championship table almost continuously until the season's end.

KENT v. SUSSEX

Date: 30 June, 2-3 July 1984   **Location:** Hastings

Real classic matches when fortunes continue to waver throughout the game even to the bitter end are very rare. This, however, was one of these and for good measure an outstanding, indeed unusual, personal performance was also thrown in.

Sussex and Kent had a long tradition of meetings at the Hastings Central Ground. This was the forty-eighth since the first back in 1865. Usually these games were in August, high holiday time. Increasingly, the future of the ground was being threatened by the pressures of commercial development on its town centre location.

Derek Underwood's affinity with Hastings was remarkable. The great Kent bowler played just 9 matches here, yet he took 61 wickets in those games, including five times 5 wickets in an innings and three times 10 wickets in a match. It included his career-best bowling of 9 for 28 in 1964 and the formidable figures of 8 for 9 on a rain-affected pitch in 1973. During this weekend, he added two further career bests to that record.

On the first day 21 wickets fell in conditions described as 'encouraging'. Kent batted first and were rapidly dismissed for a paltry 92, a score that would have been infinitely worse but for Neil Taylor who, opening, was last out for 50, a stubborn and brave innings that set the record for the lowest Kent total

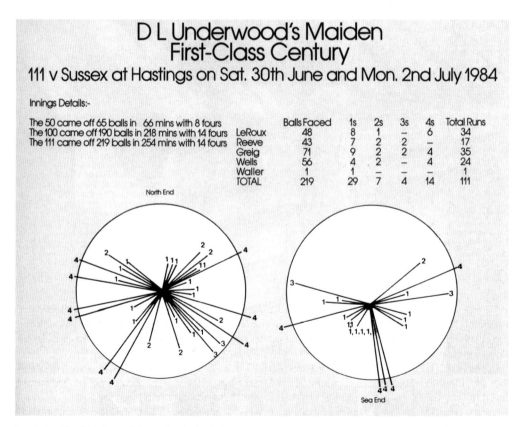

Run charts of Derek Underwood's famous hundred.

Kent won the toss and elected to bat   Umpires: H.D. Bird and A.G.T. Whitehead

KENT	1ST INNINGS				2ND INNINGS		
L. Potter	c Greig b le Roux			2	c Greig b le Roux		14
N.R. Taylor	c Parker b Greig			50	c Smith b le Roux		7
*C.J. Tavaré	c Smith b Greig			2	(4) c Barclay b C.M. Wells		1
D.G. Aslett	run out			12	(5) c Waller b Greig		0
C.S. Cowdrey	b C.M. Wells			8	(6) c Green b C.M. Wells		5
G.W. Johnson	lbw b C.M. Wells			0	(7) c Reeve b C.M. Wells		0
R.M. Ellison	b C.M. Wells			0	(8) c & b le Roux		18
†A.P.E. Knott	b C.M. Wells			0	(9) c A.P. Wells b Greig		21
D.L. Underwood	c Smith b C.M. Wells			6	(3) lbw b Reeve		111
T.M. Alderman	b le Roux			3	not out		52
K.B.S. Jarvis	not out			0	b Reeve		1
Extras	(LB 5, NB 4)			9	(B 1, LB 3, NB 7, W 2)		13
TOTAL	(all out)			92	(all out)		243

FOW: 1-10, 2-18, 3-33, 4-47, 5-52, 6-58, 7-59, 8-77, 9-87   1-22, 2-23, 3-67, 4-68, 5-86, 6-86, 7-110, 8-155, 9-208

Bowling

	O	M	R	W
le Roux	15	5	30	2
Reeve	10	5	13	0
Greig	8.3	1	15	2
C.M. Wells	13	4	25	5

	O	M	R	W
le Roux	27	7	69	3
Reeve	18.5	6	28	2
C.M. Wells	16	4	35	3
Greig	23	4	87	2
Waller	3	0	11	0

SUSSEX	1ST INNINGS				2ND INNINGS		
G.D. Mendis	c Knott b Jarvis			1	lbw b Alderman		16
A.M. Green	c Knott b Alderman			29	c Alderman b Underwood		25
*J.R.T. Barclay	c Alderman b Jarvis			0	(4) c Tavaré b Alderman		10
P.W.G. Parker	c Knott b Alderman			14	(5) c Knott b Jarvis		16
C.M. Wells	c Tavaré b Jarvis			51	(6) c Taylor b Alderman		81
A.P. Wells	c Cowdrey b Alderman			8	(7) c Underwood b Jarvis		6
D.A. Reeve	c Knott b Ellison			0	(3) c Ellison b Alderman		3
I.A. Greig	lbw b Jarvis			15	c Potter b Ellison		27
G.S. le Roux	c Alderman b Ellison			18	c Tavaré b Ellison		0
†D.J. Smith	c Johnson b Alderman			2	c Tavaré b Alderman		1
C.E. Waller	not out			0	not out		1
Extras	(LB 1, NB 4)			5	(LB 1, NB 4, W 1)		6
TOTAL	(all out)			143	(all out)		192

FOW: 1-1, 2-2, 3-40, 4-67, 5-79, 6-84, 7-105, 8-125, 9-143   1-39, 2-45, 3-58, 4-58, 5-89, 6-113, 7-186, 8-190, 9-190

Bowling

	O	M	R	W
Alderman	16	7	46	4
Jarvis	16	7	34	4
Ellison	14.4	4	29	2
Cowdrey	6	1	15	0
Underwood	2	0	14	0

	O	M	R	W
Jarvis	11	2	33	2
Ellison	17	5	29	2
Cowdrey	4	0	21	0
Alderman	23.1	7	60	5
Underwood	13	3	43	1

Match Tied

to include a fifty. Sussex fared little better with Terry Alderman and Kevin Jarvis taking 4 wickets each. The home team too were dismissed in the day with a lead of 51. By close of play, Kent had reduced that to 29, but had lost a wicket. Hence the appearance in his familiar role as nightwatchman of Derek Underwood.

Underwood's uniquely obdurate batting style had made him over the years an obvious choice for this role. His only fifty, 80 against Lancashire at Old Trafford in 1969, was so scored and he had served England well on a number of occasions. His ability just to hang around could prove priceless.

The match was broken by a Sunday League match, where Underwood's love of the Hastings ground was increased by taking 6 for 12, his career-best figures in that competition.

KENT v. SUSSEX

Derek Underwood reaches his maiden (and only) hundred.

Resuming on the Monday at 22 for 1, it was soon 23 for 2 with the loss of Laurie Potter off the South African quick Garth le Roux. Underwood then got his characteristic cross-bat cover drive working to such staggering effect that, in the next partnership, Chris Tavaré contributed but 1 out of 44. Derek Aslett followed soon after but Underwood progressed to the second fifty of his career with a textbook drive through mid-on.

The pitch was still theoretically helping the bowlers. It continued to offer bounce and movement to the seamers, aided further by the cloud cover that persisted for much of the day. So while Underwood continued on his merry way, his technically more correct batting colleagues struggled. At one time Kent were 110 for 7, only 59 ahead. Underwood had one enormous piece of luck, being well on the way to the pavilion before realising he had been caught off a no ball. He was also dropped in the slips in the nineties. Alan Knott added 45 for the eighth wicket before a partnership of 53 with another tail-end 'rabbit' Terry Alderman began to extend the lead into manageable proportions. A hook, his fourteenth four, off Ian Greig brought Underwood his first and only first-class hundred at the 618th attempt. He was finally dismissed for 111. Yet this almost surreal Kent innings continued and, in the same conditions that had defeated their batting betters, Alderman and Jarvis added 35 for the last wicket with the Australian, who had never even approached fifty before, left undefeated on 52. With 193 to win, Sussex had reached 40 for 1 by the close.

On the final morning the game had turned dramatically to Kent as 40 for 1 became 89 for 5, Alderman as a bowler proving decisive. The game, however, turned again when Colin Wells, who had had an outstanding all-round match, added 73 in 14 overs with Ian Greig, taking Sussex from seeming defeat to the edge of victory, just 7 runs short at lunch on 186 for 6. But both were out to injudicious strokes in successive overs, so 186 for 6 become 186 for 7 and then 190 for 8. Off the next ball, le Roux was caught at slip (190 for 9). It was left to David Smith, the reserve wicketkeeper, making one of his very few appearances for the county, and number eleven Chris Waller to see Sussex through. Waller survived the hat-trick ball from Richard Ellison and edged a single to retain the strike. Two to win. After a maiden over from Alderman, Smith levelled the scores with a single off Ellison but off the first ball of the next over Alderman found Smith's outside edge and the match, after all its twists and turns, was tied.

This was the only tied match in Hastings' history and the first in the championship for ten years. Oddly, within a fortnight Kent were involved in another tie when their match at Northampton finished likewise. Apart from Underwood's momentous innings, Alderman had a heroic match with his fifty, 9 wickets and 3 catches. The two seasons he spent with county marked the Australian, with possibly Arthur Fielder apart, as the best seam bowler ever to play for the county.

As for Hastings, sadly within a few years the ground did become history. A shopping centre now stands on the picturesque area that had seen well over a century of cricket. In September 1998 Derek Underwood, along with a number of other distinguished England and Sussex cricketers, appeared in the commemorative last match to be played there and few could have mourned its passing more.

KENT v. MIDDLESEX

Date: 25, 27-28 July 1987   **Location:** Lord's

Kevin Jarvis was a wholehearted right-arm fast-medium bowler who played for Kent over a period of thirteen seasons. At his best he was capable of real pace, particularly when coming down a slope. Indeed he was selected for the England Test team in 1982 but did not make the final XI. However, too often he was afflicted by a succession of niggles and more serious injuries as well as problems with his line and length and his run-up. It was a career that did deliver to some degree – he stands ninth on Kent's list of post-war wicket takers – but frustratingly he should probably have achieved more. Additionally, Jarvis stands as one of the more notable number eleven batsman, one of the select band who have taken more wickets than scored runs. For Kent one exceeded the other by over 300.

By 1987, Jarvis's Kent career was by wide consent drawing to a close. The previous year he had taken only 12 wickets in 7 games and in 1987, his benefit season, injury had meant he had only appeared in 5 games prior to meeting Middlesex at Lord's. But he had one more memorable day's play in his locker.

Middlesex won the toss and batted very consistently down the order, reaching 300 without, strangely, anyone making fifty. Declaring, the home side took the wicket of Neil Taylor before the close. Monday morning was lost through rain but, making up for time, Mark Benson and Simon Hinks added 179 in 40 overs. Hinks was another player who promised much but did not always deliver. An aggressive left-handed batsman who could dominate a bowling attack, he was too often out to an indifferent stroke when going well. 1987 was rather typical; he was not a regular member of the side with only one score over fifty in the championship. This time the gods were with him when what he himself described as 'a horrendous

shot' saw him ready to walk when, on 95, he holed out to Wilf Slack standing on the square leg boundary. But the fielder jumped to take the catch and landed on the wrong side of the rope. Six runs and Hinks's first championship hundred of the season. Earlier Benson had tried the same shot on 97 but was not so lucky.

With time short, Kent declared overnight and Jarvis began his memorable day by bowling Slack for 1. Only John Carr offered any resistance as Middlesex crumbled to 87 for 6. A brief revival took place when Andy Needham joined Carr but, at 125, Jarvis bowled possibly the most memorable over of his career. Carr lost his middle stump to one that moved in, next ball Angus Fraser was trapped leg before and with the next Norman Cowans failed to protect his stumps against a ball that kept straight and true. A hat-trick achieved without the intervention of a fielder and, perhaps unusually given the numerous matches played by Kent at Headquarters, the first instance of a Kent one there. Jarvis then ended the innings somewhat precipitously

Kevin Jarvis took the first hat-trick by a Kent player in a match for the county at Lord's.

KENT v. MIDDLESEX

Middlesex won the toss and elected to bat   Umpires: H.D. Bird and R.A. White

MIDDLESEX	1ST INNINGS		2ND INNINGS	
J.D. Carr	c Cowdrey b Pienaar	41	(2) b Jarvis	77
W.N. Slack	c Marsh b Cowdrey	49	(1) b Jarvis	1
K.R. Brown	c Marsh b Cowdrey	39	c Benson b Igglesden	0
C.T. Radley	c Cowdrey b Igglesden	17	lbw b Jarvis	4
R.O. Butcher	c Benson b Underwood	44	c Marsh b Igglesden	2
*†P.R. Downton	c Tavaré b Pienaar	49	lbw b Pienaar	3
A. Needham	not out	32	c Marsh b Cowdrey	20
N.F. Williams	not out	7	retired hurt	18
A.R.C. Fraser			lbw b Jarvis	0
N.G. Cowans			b Jarvis	0
W.W. Daniel			not out	1
Extras	(B 4, LB 4, NB 10, W 7)	25	(LB 2, NB 3)	5
TOTAL	(for 6 wickets declared)	303	(all out)	131

FOW: 1-86, 2-94, 3-127, 4-182, 5-210, 6-286

1-3, 2-14, 3-33, 4-44, 5-51, 6-87, 7-125, 8-125, 9-125

Bowling

	O	M	R	W
Igglesden	16	4	65	1
Jarvis	21	2	66	0
Cowdrey	30	7	87	2
Pienaar	17.3	6	44	2
Underwood	14	7	33	1

	O	M	R	W
Igglesden	13	1	43	2
Jarvis	10	1	48	5
Pienaar	5	0	25	1
Cowdrey	2	0	13	1

KENT	1ST INNINGS		2ND INNINGS	
M.R. Benson	c Slack b Brown	97	lbw b Cowans	10
N.R. Taylor	c Downton b Cowans	6	b Daniel	42
†S.A. Marsh	b Cowans	12	(8) not out	38
S.G. Hinks	c Fraser b Needham	112	(3) lbw b Fraser	10
C.J. Tavaré	not out	14	(4) c Downton b Fraser	0
D.G. Aslett	not out	3	(5) lbw b Cowans	28
*C.S. Cowdrey			(6) lbw b Cowans	9
R.F. Pienaar			(7) c Downton b Fraser	4
A.P. Igglesden			c Radley b Daniel	2
D.L. Underwood			b Cowans	13
K.B.S. Jarvis			not out	0
Extras	(NB 17, W 1)	18	(LB 8, NB 9)	17
TOTAL	(for 4 wickets declared)	262	(for 9 wickets)	173

FOW: 1-13, 2-35, 3-214, 4-259

1-32, 2-64, 3-67, 4-80, 5-92, 6-101, 7-119, 8-121, 9-159

Bowling

	O	M	R	W
Daniel	12	2	52	0
Cowans	15	5	43	2
Fraser	6	0	26	0
Williams	12	2	56	0
Brown	7	0	33	1
Butcher	1	0	5	0
Needham	16	0	47	1

	O	M	R	W
Daniel	17	0	74	2
Cowans	17	4	47	4
Fraser	21	6	44	3

Kent won by 1 wicket

and unfortunately when he bowled Neil Williams a bouncer that the batsman misjudged and was forced to retire with severe facial swelling. Kent were left at least 66 overs to score 173.

Kent started steadily with 42 from Neil Taylor, but stuttered very badly in mid-innings against the pace attack of Angus Fraser, Wayne Daniel and Cowans (Williams could not take the field). At 121 for 8, the odds favoured Middlesex. But skilful farming of the bowling by Steve Marsh, and Underwood at his obdurate best saw a valuable 38 added for the ninth wicket. When Underwood was bowled by Cowans, 14 was still needed. Enter Jarvis, who superbly survived the might of the Middlesex attack for 10 balls without troubling the scorers, while Marsh scored the required runs to give Kent a memorable win amid great tension.

Jarvis played 5 more first-class games for Kent after Lord's without any great success, indeed on a couple of occasions proving somewhat expensive. He was not retained by Kent at the end of the season and subsequently played 18 matches for Gloucestershire over three seasons.

KENT v. MIDDLESEX

Date: 28-31 August 1991

Location: Canterbury

This was one of the six four-day matches that formed a part of the County Championship programme in the late 1980s and early 1990s. Three were played in the early part of the season with the remaining three at the end.

Kent v. Middlesex has always been a fixture for supporters of both counties to savour, be the fixture at Lord's or, as is so often the case, at the St Lawrence Ground. Indeed, it was in the earlier match between the two sides at Lord's in late May/early June that Kent's wicketkeeper Steve Marsh equalled the world record for the number of dismissals in an innings and then went on to score an undefeated hundred in Kent's second innings.

Kent entered this return match with a chance of being in the championship prize money should they finish in the top five. But after being put in by Middlesex on a pitch where the odd ball lifted or cut back, they stuttered to a score well below par. Trevor Ward was the one batsman who looked capable of mastering the Middlesex pace bowlers and was the only one to pass a half-century. His innings ended the first ball after lunch and, following Matthew Fleming's dismissal for 30, Steve Marsh was out to a stunning catch by John Emburey. Mark Ealham and Richard Ellison put on 69 but uncharacteristically it took 29 overs and one-and-three-quarter hours. Dean Headley, who joined Kent from Middlesex in 1993, took 4 of the first 5 wickets. Later in the innings he accounted for Richard Ellison to give him a first-innings return of 5 for 100. One-time Kent wicketkeeper Paul Farbrace held 4 catches.

Early in the Middlesex innings Alan Igglesden took his fiftieth wicket of the season when he had Jason Pooley caught by Marsh. With nightwatchman Farbrace not troubling the scorers, Middlesex were 28 for 2 at the close. Disaster struck first thing the following morning with Mike Roseberry and Paul Weekes going cheaply, leaving Middlesex at 39 for 4. Emburey was dismissed before lunch, bringing captain Mike Gatting in to join Mark Ramprakash, whose rearguard action had brought him only 25 runs in the pre-lunch period. The afternoon session belonged to Gatting. He and Ramprakash had added 115, of which his contribution was 73. Their partnership, which finally reached 219, rescued the innings. When Ramprakash was dismissed just after 6 p.m. he had batted for a little over six hours and faced 275 balls. He scored off only 47 of them. Gatting went on to make his eighth century of the season despite batting with a damaged finger. In contrast with his partner, his hundred came off 188 balls and his 150 from 255. Headley and Phil Tufnell took the innings into the third day with a stand of 51. When the innings closed at noon Middlesex had a substantial lead of 146.

Kent's second-innings attempt to set Middlesex a target on the fourth day did not start that well. With 39 runs on the board Benson was caught off Tufnell's bowling. But from then on it was all Kent, with Trevor Ward recording his first double century and sharing a second-wicket partnership of 226 with Neil Taylor, who

completed his sixth hundred of the season. Ward's innings included 29 fours and a six but, unusually, he played more of an anchor role, with Taylor taking twenty-five minutes less to reach his landmark. But with a little over thirty minutes play remaining he was out. Nevertheless, overnight, with just 2 wickets down, the hosts had a lead of 141 (Ward 140*) and were well on their way to leaving Middlesex a challenging target.

Trevor Ward hits Phil Tufnell to the boundary during his undefeated double hundred [John Turner].

Middlesex won the toss and elected to bowl Umpires: S.B. Hassan and R. Palmer

KENT	1ST INNINGS		2ND INNINGS	
T.R. Ward	c Farbrace b Cowans	51	not out	235
*M.R. Benson	lbw b Headley	8	c Pooley b Tufnell	20
N.R. Taylor	c Farbrace b Headley	17	c sub b Williams	101
G.R. Cowdrey	c Farbrace b Headley	38	c Farbrace b Tufnell	46
M.V. Fleming	b Headley	30	not out	23
†S.A. Marsh	c Emburey b Williams	5		
M.A. Ealham	c Farbrace b Williams	34		
R.M. Ellison	b Headley	33		
R.P. Davis	not out	15		
C. Penn	lbw b Williams	0		
A.P. Igglesden	c Headley b Emburey	11		
Extras	(B 5, LB 4, NB 7)	16	(B 8, LB 8, NB 9)	25
TOTAL	(all out)	258	(for 3 wickets declared)	450

FOW: 1-24, 2-64, 3-108, 4-145, 5-162, 6-162, 7-231, 8-232, 9-232   1-39, 2-265, 3-399

Bowling

	O	M	R	W
Cowans	15	3	42	1
Williams	23	3	52	3
Headley	24	5	100	5
Tufnell	16	6	31	0
Gatting	8	4	13	0
Emburey	6.5	1	11	1

	O	M	R	W
Cowans	22	3	78	0
Williams	22	0	87	1
Headley	19	1	112	0
Tufnell	30	9	70	2
Emburey	21	4	53	0
Weekes	12	1	34	0

MIDDLESEX	1ST INNINGS		2ND INNINGS	
M.A. Roseberry	c Ellison b Penn	18	c Ellison b Ealham	5
J.C. Pooley	c Marsh b Igglesden	11	c Marsh b Ellison	14
†P. Farbrace	lbw b Penn	0	(6) lbw b Ellison	0
M.R. Ramprakash	lbw b Ellison	87	(3) c sub b Ellison	5
P.N. Weekes	c Davis b Ellison	4	(4) c Marsh b Ealham	2
J.E. Emburey	lbw b Ealham	20	(5) c Marsh b Ellison	11
*M.W. Gatting	c Davis b Ealham	174	c Ealham b Penn	9
N.F. Williams	lbw b Penn	1	c Ward b Penn	5
D.W. Headley	b Penn	26	b Penn	14
P.C.R. Tufnell	not out	31	c Marsh b Penn	4
N.G. Cowans	lbw b Penn	5	not out	23
Extras	(B 1, LB 12, NB 14)	27	(LB 1, NB 3)	4
TOTAL	(all out)	404	(all out)	96

FOW: 1-27, 2-28, 3-33, 4-39, 5-87, 6-306, 7-311, 8-342, 9-393   1-19, 2-21, 3-28, 4-28, 5-30, 6-45, 7-53, 8-61, 9-71

Bowling

	O	M	R	W
Igglesden	5.1	1	12	1
Penn	39.5	11	105	5
Ealham	18.5	4	47	2
Ellison	35	9	88	2
Fleming	17	3	65	0
Davis	17	1	74	0

	O	M	R	W
Penn	11	3	44	4
Ellison	18	5	40	4
Ealham	8	3	11	2

Kent won by 208 runs

Kent's declaration came at lunch with Ward and Graham Cowdrey, then Ward and Matthew Fleming, adding 163 in the 33 overs bowled in the morning session. Ward's 235* was to be his career-best score and in the morning session he had added 95 runs. Middlesex were left a target of 305 off 69 overs – not impossible on a wicket still batsman friendly.

Brittle batting had been the downfall of Middlesex on more than one occasion during the season and with Gatting suffering a scalded chest after having a pot of hot tea spilled over him during the interval, there was no one to prop up their innings. But the collapse that overtook them in a disastrous afternoon could not have been foreseen. In a masterly spell of swing bowling, Richard Ellison had an opening burst of 4 for 29 in 10.3 overs. He was well supported by Chris Penn and Mark Ealham. Between them, in the space of 37 overs and in under three hours they had wrapped up the whole Middlesex innings. A truly remarkable turnaround.

KENT v. GLAMORGAN

Date: 16-18, 20 September 1993   **Location:** Canterbury

This is a tale of two great West Indian cricketers. Carl Hooper's record for Kent places him high in the all-time list of great batsman who played for the county. A tall, powerfully built and superbly elegant batsman, he hit the ball extremely hard. His six-hitting performances were legendary. Also, he was a more than useful off-break bowler and a superb slip. This match saw him record the highest innings of his career. Vivian Richards dominated West Indian batting for twenty years. A right-handed batsman with superb timing and immense power, he looked to dominate an attack from the moment he came in. This was his last first-class match.

Glamorgan came to Canterbury hoping to end the season as runners-up in the championship. In the midst of the game, the two teams were to play each other to decide the fate of the Sunday League title.

After a blank first day, Glamorgan looked like being on their way to their first target when, in the opening over, Steve Watkin had David Fulton and Graham Cowdrey back in the pavilion without a run on the board. Carl Hooper then joined Trevor Ward and together they added 229 in 50 overs. Trevor Ward went after the attack from the start, scoring 137 off 157 balls with 3 sixes and 23 fours. Ward was a mainstay of the Kent batting order for a number of years. He was a very attacking batsman who, at his best, would not have disgraced an England side, but somehow he never quite reached the level of consistency to achieve that aim. His relative weakness against spin, somewhat stiff hands and his attacking flair could let him down.

Nigel Llong joined Hooper and was out early on the third day having added 171. Hooper went on to achieve what was, remarkably for a player of his skill, the first double hundred of his career. Ealham scored 50 at a run a ball before acting captain Steve Marsh declared, leaving Hooper 236 not out, an innings that portrayed all his talents with 3 sixes and 21 fours in 397 minutes off 330 balls. Oddly, an innings of 524 for 6 included three ducks.

Carl Hooper. Arguably the greatest of Kent's overseas signings, he hit the highest score of his career in this match. [John Turner]

Glamorgan won the toss and elected to bowl Umpires: D.A. Constant and G.A. Stickley

KENT	1ST INNINGS		2ND INNINGS	
D.P. Fulton	b Watkin	0	b Dale	1
T.R. Ward	c sub b Bastien	137		
G.R. Cowdrey	c Hemp b Watkin	0	st Metson b Croft	9
C.L. Hooper	not out	236		
N.J. Llong	c sub b Lefebvre	62		
M.V. Fleming	c Metson b Lefebvre	0	(2) not out	81
*†S.A. Marsh	c Croft b Bastien	21		
M.A. Ealham	not out	50		
D.W. Headley			(4) not out	4
M.M. Patel				
A.P. Igglesden				
Extras	(LB 13, NB 4, W 1)	18		0
TOTAL	(for 6 wickets declared)	524	(for 2 wickets declared)	95

FOW: 1-0, 2-0, 3-229, 4-400, 5-402, 6-447   1-23, 2-78

Bowling

	O	M	R	W
Watkin	26.3	2	126	2
Bastien	30	5	115	2
Lefebvre	35	3	106	2
Croft	18	1	91	0
Dale	8	0	73	0

	O	M	R	W
Bastien	4	1	30	0
Dale	10	1	43	1
Croft	4	1	15	1
Richards	2	0	7	0

GLAMORGAN	1ST INNINGS		2ND INNINGS	
A. Dale	c Ward b Igglesden	0	b Igglesden	2
*H. Morris	b Headley	1	c Marsh b Headley	0
P.A. Cottey	b Headley	79	(4) c Headley b Patel	53
I.V.A. Richards	c Marsh b Ealham	17	(5) c Fulton b Hooper	83
D.L. Hemp	c & b Ealham	13	(6) b Patel	12
R.D.B. Croft	c Headley b Ealham	0	(7) c Marsh b Headley	0
†C.P. Metson	c Ward b Headley	5	(3) lbw b Headley	14
R.P. Lefebvre	c Llong b Patel	4	(9) b Igglesden	49
S.L. Watkin	c Headley b Igglesden	13	(10) c Fleming b Igglesden	9
S. Bastien	not out	5	(11) not out	3
M.P. Maynard	absent injured		(8) c Marsh b Headley	0
Extras	(LB 1, NB 6)	7	(B 6, LB 6, NB 2)	14
TOTAL	(all out)	144	(all out)	239

FOW: 1-0, 2-6, 3-66, 4-84, 5-88, 6-119, 7-126, 8-126, 9-144

1-4, 2-4, 3-25, 4-131, 5-162, 6-162, 7-162, 8-186, 9-212

Bowling

	O	M	R	W
Igglesden	9	2	27	2
Headley	15	6	29	3
Fleming	10	1	41	0
Ealham	9	1	31	3
Patel	3	0	15	1

	O	M	R	W
Igglesden	12.2	3	45	3
Headley	16	2	97	4
Hooper	6	0	26	1
Ealham	2	0	16	0
Patel	8	1	43	2

Kent won by 236 runs

With Matthew Maynard unable to bat because of neck injury, Glamorgan collapsed against the Kent seamers, with only Tony Cottey offering any resistance. Despite leading by 380 runs, Marsh did not enforce the follow-on, the argument being to rest the bowlers. Matthew Fleming opened the innings and in cavalier style scored 81 out of 95 in 20 overs before Kent declared again. A little matter of 476 in 107 overs was Glamorgan's target, but that looked a long way off when the visitors were 7 for 2 at the close.

Kent's dominance over their opponents did not extend to the critical Sunday League match that now intervened. Before a crowd of 12,000, Glamorgan won the title with a comfortable 6-wicket win over Kent, Richards (46*) seeing them through.

The crowd was somewhat smaller on the Monday as Glamorgan slid to an inevitable defeat. But the clear highlight of the proceedings was Viv Richards who, in his final first-class innings in his 507th match, raced to 83 in 61 balls with 2 sixes and 14 fours before being out caught on the long-on boundary going for a third six off Hooper. Glamorgan were denied that runners-up position and had to settle for third place.

KENT v. GLAMORGAN

Date: 24-27 May 1995   **Location:** Tunbridge Wells

Matches that go to the last few balls with all options on the result open are relatively common in these days of limited-overs matches. Instances in first-class cricket are much rarer. This match swung from side to side during its progress to an extent that three balls from the end any of the four outcomes was still possible.

Trevor Ward's record against the Welsh county is unmatched by any Kent batsmen; 6 centuries in 7 previous matches including twice a hundred in each innings. It looked like a seventh when, after Kent had won the toss, Ward was again crashing Glamorgan bowlers to the boundary. Along the way he lost Benson, caught at cover-point, Taylor, retired hurt with a broken knuckle trying to fend off a rising ball from Darren Thomas, and Walker caught behind soon after. But 2 runs short of that seventh hundred, he misjudged the agility of Thomas at wide mid-on. Soon after that, rain brought a premature end to the first day's play.

The second day belonged to Aravinda de Silva. Although he stayed only one season with Kent as a replacement for Carl Hooper, there have been few more popular overseas cricketers to play for the county. Having made a somewhat subdued start to the season, as the summer progressed and the temperature rose, so did his extravagant strokeplay thrill the crowds. He was particularly strong on the leg side, his placement perfect. So it was on this flat pitch, with a bowling attack seeming to lack penetration. Together with Kent's home-produced star Mark Ealham, the two put on 151 in 49 overs, de Silva's hundred, his second of the season, including 23 fours. His second fifty came off 45 balls. At one stage Kent were 314 for 3, with 500 in their sights. But no, the last 5 wickets were lost for 27 and Glamorgan, by the close, had reached 155 without loss, well on the way to at least matching their opponents' total.

Hugh Morris and Adrian Dale took their opening partnership to 238, a record against Kent on the Nevill Ground, but thereafter the Glamorgan innings, like Kent's, fell away. However, tied down by spinner Neil Kendrick, Kent slid to 133 for 5 with all the major batsmen out and Taylor uncertain to bat. Glamorgan's victory chase on the still-excellent pitch looked to be well within their range.

On the final day, another fifty from Ealham, supported down the order by McCague and Headley, allowed Benson to declare, setting a target of 271 in what ultimately proved to be 50 overs. The Glamorgan innings centred on Matthew Maynard, not unknown in Kent having appeared in the county second XI some years before, and Tony Cottey. Maynard scored 73 off 68 balls, taking a struggling Kent attack apart. One drive off Igglesden ended in the stand at long-on. Cottey batted with similar brilliance at the other

end and, as long as he was in, Glamorgan looked well set for victory. After Maynard's departure, Cottey was joined by their overseas player Hamish Anthony who, swinging the bat freely, added another 53. Then, crucially, Anthony was run out, unfortunately from a ball that rebounded off the umpire. Nevertheless, Glamorgan came to the last over, with Cottey and Thomas

Aravinda de Silva at Tunbridge Wells during his memorable single season with Kent. [John Turner]

Kent won the toss and elected to bat — Umpires: D.J. Constant and A.A. Jones

KENT	1ST INNINGS		2ND INNINGS	
T.R. Ward	run out	98	b Kendrick	31
*M.R. Benson	c Croft b Dale	14	c Cottey b Croft	31
N.R. Taylor	retired hurt	13		
P.A. de Silva	lbw b Anthony	135	c Anthony b Kendrick	5
M.J. Walker	c Metson b Anthony	6	c Hemp b Kendrick	24
M.A. Ealham	lbw b Watkin	58	(3) c Metson b Thomas	72
†S.A. Marsh	c Maynard b Watkin	13	c Hemp b Croft	24
M.M. Patel	not out	21	(6) c Maynard b Anthony	0
M.J. McCague	c & b Anthony	1	(8) c Watkin b Kendrick	23
D.W. Headley	c sub b Anthony	2	(9) not out	29
A.P. Igglesden	c Cottey b Anthony	2	(10) not out	5
Extras	(LB 1, NB 4, W 1)	6	(B 3, LB 4, NB 2)	9
TOTAL	(all out)	369	(for 8 wickets declared)	253

FOW: 1-50, 2-148, 3-163, 4-314, 5-342, 6-350, 7-351, 8-361, 9-369 — 1-57, 2-85, 3-99, 4-130, 5-133, 6-194, 7-194, 8-231

Bowling

	O	M	R	W
Watkin	30	5	98	2
Anthony	24.1	6	70	5
Thomas	13	0	61	0
Dale	10	4	31	1
Kendrick	13	2	37	0
Hemp	2	1	8	0

	O	M	R	W
Watkin	15	2	40	0
Anthony	16	6	36	1
Thomas	12.4	0	53	1
Kendrick	37	17	70	4
Croft	23	7	47	2

GLAMORGAN	1ST INNINGS		2ND INNINGS	
A. Dale	c Morris b McCague	133	c Ward b Patel	32
*H. Morris	lbw b Patel	114	c Marsh b Headley	3
D.L. Hemp	c Headley b Igglesden	9	lbw b Patel	20
M.P. Maynard	b Igglesden	1	b Patel	73
P.A. Cottey	not out	37	c Headley b Patel	85
R.D.B. Croft	b de Silva	15	(7) c & b Patel	7
S.D. Thomas	b McCague	0	(8) not out	7
N.M. Kendrick	c Ward b Patel	2		
H.A.G. Anthony	c sub b Patel	0	(6) run out	23
†C.P. Metson	not out	14	(9) run out	0
S.L. Watkin				
Extras	(B 5, LB 17, NB 4, W 1)	27	(B 4, LB 11, NB 4)	19
TOTAL	(for 8 wickets declared)	352	(for 8 wickets)	269

FOW: 1-238, 2-275, 3-275, 4-276, 5-304, 6-308, 7-325, 8-325 — 1-4, 2-42, 3-81, 4-170, 5-223, 6-242, 7-269, 8-269

Bowling

	O	M	R	W
McCague	20	2	64	2
Igglesden	16	2	67	2
Headley	21.3	4	85	0
Ealham	5	1	15	0
Patel	37	9	94	3
de Silva	4	1	5	1

	O	M	R	W
McCague	16	1	83	0
Headley	9	0	44	1
Patel	21	2	99	5
de Silva	1	0	6	0
Igglesden	3	0	22	0

Match Drawn

at the crease to face Min Patel, needing only 5, the bowler having conceded 14 from his previous 6 balls. Three runs were scored but, with 3 balls remaining, Cottey was caught on the boundary off a mistimed pull. Thomas failed to score off the penultimate ball and, with 2 still needed, Colin Metson was run out trying to take a bye to the wicketkeeper, Steve Marsh. Match drawn. Min Patel picked up 5 wickets, reward for a long and generally accurate spell.

1995 ended up a bleak season for Kent. They finished bottom in the County Championship for the first time in 100 years. Winning the Sunday League almost by default through the weather was only a minor consolation. But Aravinda de Silva remained the one highlight. He scored 1,781 runs at 59.37, finishing 800 runs and an average of fifteen clear of any other Kent batsman. Two double hundreds, two Kent record partnerships, including the highest for any wicket, and a memorable Lord's Benson & Hedges final innings, albeit in what was a lost cause, were the best of many highlights.

KENT v. SOMERSET

Date: 15-17, 19 August 1996   **Location:** Canterbury

A little piece of cricket history was made on the St Lawrence ground during what will always be known as Matthew Walker's match. After showing outstanding promise as a youngster, representing England at Under-19 level and captaining the side in 1992 and 1993, it took some while for him to make his mark in the first-class game. But when he did, it happened emphatically. Walker's appearances up to now had numbered 17 and this was only his third match of the season. He had made one century against Surrey at The Oval in the final match of the 1994 season.

An individual batting record for Kent that had stood for seventy-three years, the highest score by a Kent batsman at Canterbury set by the great Frank Woolley against Middlesex in 1923, became Matthew Walker's property in this match. Remarkable also is that, having opened both innings, he was on the field for the whole of the game. This was Kent's best ever score on the St Lawrence ground; indeed only on two previous occasions had the Hop County exceeded their score in this match of 616. Both times it was against Essex.

Walker batted through the three sessions of the first day and through the morning session into the afternoon session of the day following. His innings lasted nine hours and twenty-five minutes. It was the longest by a Kent batsman. He faced 439 balls and hit 41 fours. At the end of the first day his score was 176 out of a total of 413 for 4. There were century stands with Trevor Ward, Carl Hooper and Dean Headley, the last, for the eighth wicket, an undefeated 137. Dean Headley's 63* was at that time his career-best score. Walker's 275* was the fourth highest by a Kent batsman and the best by a left-hander, a remarkable achievement by the then-uncapped batsman. When Kent's acting captain Trevor Ward called a halt the runs had been scored at more than 4 an over.

By the close of play on the second day Somerset had responded with some solid but uninspiring batting. They lost 2 early wickets and by the close had reached 119 for 3. But those runs had been scored off 59 overs. They continued in the same vein on day three. A fourth-wicket stand of 172 between Richard Harden and Simon Ecclestone raised hopes among their supporters that they might reach their first target of 467, thus avoiding the follow-on. But at their current rate of scoring it would have taken them well into the final day to reach that score. Once the Harden/Ecclestone partnership was broken the only resistance came from captain Peter Bowler with 48* and, at the close of play, they were still 78 short of avoiding the follow-on with just 2 wickets remaining.

As it happened, the Somerset captain accepted Trevor Ward's suggestion that they declare the innings closed at their overnight total in the hope of securing a positive result. Somerset duly served up 13 overs of rubbish bowling before Kent declared, setting their opponents 320 for victory in 81 overs, a not unreasonable target on what was still an excellent pitch. Matthew Walker's 43*, which included 8 fours, brought his match aggregate to an undefeated 318.

Kent got off to a great start, Dean Headley having Marcus Trescothick caught before he had scored. But with Mark Lathwell leading the way, they began to sense a somewhat unexpected victory. However, when Dean Headley bowled Lathwell and, right on the tea interval, had Australian Shane Lee lbw without addition to the score, the odds were on Kent. A sixth-wicket partnership of 75 between Simon Ecclestone and Keith Parsons held them up but

Matthew Walker leaves the field after his Canterbury record-breaking innings.
[Anthony Roberts]

Kent won the toss and elected to bat   Umpires: A. Clarkson and B. Leadbeater

KENT	1ST INNINGS		2ND INNINGS	
D.P. Fulton	c Turner b Kerr	19	c & b Harden	9
M.J. Walker	not out	275	not out	43
*T.R. Ward	c Turner b Kerr	57	c Turner b Bowler	24
C.L. Hooper	c & b Batty	76	not out	16
N.J. Llong	c Trescothick b Batty	26		
M.V. Fleming	c Harden b Rose	26		
†S.C. Willis	lbw b Rose	1		
M.M. Patel	b Lee	14		
D.W. Headley	not out	63		
M.J. McCague				
T.N. Wren				
Extras	(B 9, LB 14, NB 26)	49		0
TOTAL	(for 7 wickets declared)	616	(for 2 wickets declared)	92

FOW: 1-57, 3-158, 3-313, 4-361, 5-424, 6-436, 7-479   1-18, 2-61

Bowling

	O	M	R	W
Rose	27	5	92	2
Lee	35	3	159	1
Kerr	27	3	143	2
Batty	41.3	11	122	2
Parsons	12	2	40	0
Trescothick	9	1	37	0

	O	M	R	W
Harden	7	0	39	1
Bowler	6	0	53	1

SOMERSET	1ST INNINGS		2ND INNINGS	
M.N. Lathwell	c Fulton b Headley	43	b Headley	81
M.E. Trescothick	lbw b Headley	8	c Llong b Headley	0
K.A. Parsons	c Willis b Headley	2	(5) c Ward b McCague	30
R.J. Harden	c McCague b Llong	136	c Fulton b Llong	29
S.C. Ecclestone	lbw b Wren	94	(7) c Headley b Patel	56
*P.D. Bowler	not out	48	(3) c Fulton b Hooper	32
S. Lee	c Patel b Hooper	1	(6) lbw b Headley	0
†R.J. Turner	c Willis b Hooper	11	lbw b McCague	1
G.D. Rose	b McCague	6	b McCague	7
J.I.D. Kerr	not out	1	b McCague	0
J.D. Batty			not out	7
Extras	(B 10, LB 10, NB 8, W 11)	39	(B 4, LB 8, NB 2)	14
TOTAL	(for 8 wickets declared)	389	(all out)	257

FOW: 1-27, 2-28, 3-90, 4-262, 5-345, 6-350, 7-375, 8-388   1-1, 2-85, 3-143, 4-154, 5-154, 6-229, 7-235, 8-243, 9-244

Bowling

	O	M	R	W
McCague	23	6	69	1
Headley	29	10	60	3
Wren	20	7	53	1
Patel	43	18	94	0
Hooper	31	10	49	2
Fleming	4	1	12	0
Llong	15	5	32	1

	O	M	R	W
Headley	13	4	39	3
McCague	10.3	3	21	4
Wren	7	1	29	0
Patel	29	8	81	1
Hooper	15	7	38	1
Llong	6	1	37	1

Kent won by 62 runs

when fast bowler Martin McCague had Parsons caught by Trevor Ward and almost immediately removed wicketkeeper Rob Turner, the advantage had moved to the home county. This opinion was reinforced when left-arm spinner Min Patel had Ecclestone caught. But the last three Somerset batsmen showed some stubborn resistance and it was only in the dying moments of the match that the victory was Kent's. McCague had secured Kent's victory with a final burst of 4 wickets for 13 runs in 5.3 overs.

In the annals of Kent cricket this will go down as Walker's match. But, for the left-hander, what immediately followed was something of an anticlimax. Five years were to pass before he reached three figures again in the championship. Only then, somewhat belatedly, did he establish himself as a permanent member of the Kent side. One other point of interest was that E.W. Swanton, whose great hero was Frank Woolley, fearful that Kent immortal's famous record would be consigned to history, is reputed to have tried to persuade the Kent captain to declare the innings closed before Walker reached that mark. If that was true, he did not succeed.

KENT v. HAMPSHIRE

Date: 12-14, 16 September 1996   **Location:** Canterbury

For a period in the mid-to-late 1990s, Kent's strike bowling centred on Dean Headley and Martin McCague. Headley, the son and grandson of West Indian Test cricketers, was a right-arm fast-medium, often fast bowler, with outstanding potential. McCague, of Northern Irish birth but Australian upbringing, a product of that country's famous Academy, was a powerfully built fast bowler who was capable of devastating spells on the flattest of wickets. As a combination, the prospect was appetising but too often one or other or both were injured, so the number of times they were in harness together was comparatively rather few.

For both men, 1996 was to be their peak season, although even then Headley missed the early part of the year through a hip injury. However, McCague did remain fit and bowled throughout with enormous enthusiasm and no little hostility. But it was Headley who caught the eye with an incredible run of bowling achievements, which began at Derby in late July when, at the start of Derbyshire's second innings, he took a hat-trick, two dismissals with the unusual assistance of David Fulton as stand-in wicketkeeper. In the very next match, against Worcestershire in Canterbury Week, he repeated the dose as the visitors moved towards setting Kent a very challenging target that they fell well short of. It was only the fourth time hat-tricks had been achieved by the same bowler in successive matches.

Just over a month later, Kent returned to Canterbury with an outside chance of the championship, no mean achievement given their wooden spoon the previous year. But they needed maximum bonus points. That was still on after the first day, when Kent thumped a weak Hampshire attack to reach 376 for 4. Three batsmen passed the half-century mark, beginning with Ward and Hooper, who put on 137 in less than two hours with the West Indian taking the lead despite a thumb injury and

Martin McCague took the second hat-trick in the match.

Kent won the toss and elected to bat   Umpires: R. Julian and G. Sharp

KENT	1ST INNINGS		2ND INNINGS	
D.P. Fulton	c Kendall b Stephenson	15	c Kendall b Mascarenhas	8
M.J. Walker	lbw b Mascarenhas	30	lbw b Renshaw	6
T.R. Ward	c & b Maru	79	b Bovill	44
C.L. Hooper	c Maru b Mascarenhas	84	b Stephenson	14
N.J. Llong	c Kendall b Stephenson	130	c & b Stephenson	3
M.A. Ealham	c White b Mascarenhas	74	c Kendall b Mascarenhas	22
M.V. Fleming	c Aymes b Stephenson	7	c Kendall b Mascarenhas	7
*†S.A. Marsh	lbw b Stephenson	1	c Maru b Renshaw	55
D.W. Headley	c Aymes b Mascarenhas	0	(11) not out	1
M.M. Patel	b Stephenson	9	(9) lbw b Renshaw	32
M.J. McCague	not out	4	(10) lbw b Renshaw	5
Extras	(LB 5, NB 6, W 1)	12	(B 1, LB 7, NB 6)	14
TOTAL	(all out)	445	(all out)	211

FOW: 1-37, 2-50, 3-187, 4-249, 5-422, 6-422, 7-424, 8-425, 9-431   1-12, 2-30, 3-74, 4-74, 5-77, 6-91, 7-125, 8-175, 9-210

Bowling

	O	M	R	W
Mascarenhas	28	7	101	4
Renshaw	26	7	94	0
Bovill	24	7	91	0
Stephenson	36	8	104	5
Maru	12	3	29	1
Whitaker	4	1	21	0

	O	M	R	W
Mascarenhas	16	4	46	3
Renshaw	14.5	0	75	4
Stephenson	16	2	49	2
Bovill	11	0	33	1

HAMPSHIRE	1ST INNINGS		2ND INNINGS	
G.W. White	c Patel b McCague	6	c Hooper b Fleming	66
J.S. Laney	c Marsh b Ealham	105	lbw b McCague	14
P.R. Whitaker	c Hooper b Ealham	18	b McCague	53
W.S. Kendall	lbw b Headley	34	(5) c Hooper b McCague	3
R.A. Smith	b Ealham	60	(4) c Marsh b McCague	1
*J.P. Stephenson	c Ealham b Headley	28	absent hurt	
†A.N. Aymes	hit wicket b Headley	52	(6) c Patel b McCague	0
A.D. Mascarenhas	b Ealham	14	(7) lbw b McCague	0
R.J. Maru	not out	10	(8) b Fleming	1
J.N.B. Bovill	lbw b Headley	0	(9) b Fleming	0
S.J. Renshaw	lbw b Headley	0	(10) not out	0
Extras	(LB 29, NB 2)	31	(B 6, LB 6)	12
TOTAL	(all out)	358	(all out)	150

FOW: 1-10, 2-74, 3-155, 4-226, 5-249, 6-338, 7-338, 8-358, 9-358   1-25, 2-143, 3-145, 4-149, 5-149, 6-149, 7-149, 8-149, 9-150

Bowling

	O	M	R	W
McCague	32	6	99	1
Headley	32.3	6	83	5
Ealham	33	11	73	4
Patel	11	1	22	0
Hooper	3	1	16	0
Fleming	7	0	36	0

	O	M	R	W
McCague	17	4	51	6
Headley	10	1	29	0
Ealham	11	1	41	0
Patel	4	0	10	0
Hooper	1	0	1	0
Fleming	4.2	2	6	3

Kent won by 148 runs

hitting 14 fours and 2 sixes in his 84. Subsequently the baton was taken up by Nigel Llong, who rode his luck by being dropped three times and reached his second hundred of the season, hammering his seventeenth boundary in a three-hour stay. With Mark Ealham, the two had put on 127 by the close.

Nigel Llong was an unlucky cricketer. A very solid right-hand bat, a superb all-round fielder and a useful off-break bowler, he had fewer opportunities in the first team than he deserved. He scored six centuries in his career, of which this was to prove to be the highest, and had a reasonable batting average of 31. Since his release by Kent in 1999 he has become an increasingly respected first-class umpire.

The promise for Kent of day one did not continue on day two. The Llong-Ealham partnership was extended to 173, whereupon the last 6 wickets went down in 9 overs for 23 runs. On a docile pitch, Kent, despite some hostile bowling by McCague and Headley, made limited progress against an obstinate

Hampshire batting order. Jason Laney made a four-and-a-half-hour hundred, while Robin Smith, fighting a heavy cold, made 60 before being bowled off the last ball of the day.

With the need for maximum bowling points essential, Kent achieved their aim in the most dramatic way possible. One over away from the cut-off for points, Headley first enticed John Stephenson to lift him to third man and then James Bovill and Simon Renshaw were summarily dismissed leg before in the next two balls. With his third hat-trick of the season, Headley emulated the feats of Charles Parker of Gloucestershire in 1924 and J.S. Rao in India in 1963/64, the latter on debut and then twice in the next match. More importantly, Kent had a lead of 87, an advantage they did their best to fritter away with a poor second innings, only retrieved by a late-order 55 from Steve Marsh. All out at the close of play, Kent set Hampshire an eminently achievable 299.

At 1.56 p.m. on the last day, Hampshire were 143 for 1. It seemed only a matter of time before victory was theirs. At 2.38 p.m., Kent had won the match by an impressive 148 runs. Giles White and Paul Whitaker seemed to be batting comfortably, both passing 50, but then McCague produced a burst of rare speed that first sent Whitaker's off stump cartwheeling. Robin Smith was greeted with two very hostile bouncers from the Anglo-Australian, who then induced a low edge to Steve Marsh. Then, in one over, McCague had Will Kendall caught low at second slip by Carl Hooper, Adrian Aymes snicked the next ball to Min Patel and with the next Dimitri Mascarenhas was out leg before. A second hat-trick was thus achieved by a Kent bowler in the same game – a unique feat for Kent. Perhaps more remarkable was the fact that in 149 years of cricket at the St Lawrence Ground there had only been two previous Kent hat-tricks. In not much more than a month, there had been another three.

Hampshire were now 149 for 6 when the ever-combative Matthew Fleming got in on the act with 3 wickets for 0 in 8 balls. With Stephenson unable to bat because of a damaged wrist, Hampshire had lost their last 8 wickets for 7 runs. An ecstatic E.W. Swanton commented that in seventy years of watching first-class cricket, he could 'recall nothing quite like the events at the St Lawrence Ground'. McCague finished with 6 for 51, including 5 for 3 in 17 balls.

The win with maximum points kept Kent in the running for the championship. But what chance they had was thrown away in a dismal performance in their next and final match at Bristol, where they were comprehensively beaten in two-and-a-half days.

The success of the Kent opening attack had the pundits contemplating England call-ups. McCague had already played in 3 Tests a few years before with very disappointing results. But in 1997 an unfortunate experience at Taunton, when he was removed from the attack for seemingly bowling two many bouncers and a beamer seriously dented his confidence and, with more injuries, he was never really the same bowler again. Headley did get picked for England and had major success on the otherwise disappointing tour to Australia in 1998/99, where he took 19 wickets in the Tests and topped the averages. This included a spell of 5 for 9 that turned the Melbourne Test in England's favour. Almost established as a regular England bowler, he then suffered a career-ending back injury in South Africa the following winter.

Opposite:
Dean Headley is joined by David Fulton and Martin McCague to celebrate his third hat-trick of the season [Anthony Roberts].

KENT v. LEICESTERSHIRE

Date: 27-29 July 2001   **Location:** Grace Road, Leicester

There is little that can be more thrilling or absorbing than a game of first-class cricket that goes to the final over of four days with one side requiring 3 wickets and their opponents 16 runs to win the match, and that at the end of a chase in which the victorious side had to score in excess of 400 to win.

This was the situation at the end of a match in which almost 1,600 runs were scored off 400 overs, in which seven players recorded centuries and in which one player on each side had already enjoyed a career with his opponents of the day. Kent's visit to Grace Road brought together the pugnacious Trevor Ward, who had left the Hop County for the East Midlands the previous year, and wicketkeeper Paul Nixon had travelled in the opposite direction in the same year. Both were to play a significant part in the match.

On a good wicket Leicestershire won the toss and not surprisingly elected to bat. Martin Saggers struck with the final ball of his first over, having Ian Sutcliffe lbw and in his fifth he had Trevor Ward taken by Andrew Symonds. Kent then had to wait another 150 runs before a further breakthrough when

occasional bowler Matthew Walker took a fine low return catch from Ben Smith with his third ball. Ben Smith's hundred had come in three hours and twenty-five minutes with 18 fours. It was his third consecutive century. Darren Maddy, the dangerous Shahid Afridi and Vince Wells all struggled against the pace of Ben Trott and Saggers, and the three middle-order batsmen fell while only 29 runs were added to the score. Meanwhile Aftab Habib, one of England's forgotten men who had suffered a family bereavement and consequent loss of form early in the season, happily ploughed on until being bowled by eighteen-year-old debutant James Tredwell, who had only arrived at the ground at 3.45 p.m. He had been at Arundel preparing to play for England Under-19s when he got the call to replace the injured Min Patel. Within fifteen minutes of taking the field he was bowling and in his third over he dismissed the former England batsman. Habib's innings lasted almost five-and-a-half hours. It included 21 fours and a six. Then the last four wickets added 154 runs with the home side gaining maximum batting points early on day two. Their total was scored in just short of even time.

Martin Saggers took 9 wickets in the match.

KENT v. LEICESTERSHIRE

Leicestershire won the toss and elected to bat Umpires: J.W. Holder and A.A. Jones

LEICESTERSHIRE	1ST INNINGS		2ND INNINGS	
T.R. Ward	c Symonds b Saggers	28	c Trott b Saggers	110
I.J. Sutcliffe	lbw b Saggers	4	c Ealham b Trott	5
B.F. Smith	c & b Walker	111	c Walker b Saggers	5
A. Habib	b Tredwell	153	c Nixon b Saggers	5
D.L. Maddy	c Fulton b Saggers	5	lbw b Ealham	111
Shahid Afridi	c Nixon b Trott	5	c Symonds b Tredwell	42
*V.J. Wells	c & b Trott	1	lbw b Trott	0
†N.D. Burns	c Smith b Saggers	60	not out	64
J. Ormond	b Saggers	42	not out	10
D.E. Malcolm	c Walker b Saggers	8		
M.J.A. Whiley	not out	1		
Extras	(B 6, LB 1)	7	(B 4, LB 3, NB 4, W 2)	13
TOTAL	(all out)	425	(for 7 wickets declared)	365

FOW: 1-10, 2-47, 3-198, 4-242, 5-267, 6-271, 7-343, 8-396, 9-411 1-34, 2-44, 3-54, 4-183, 5-236, 6-238, 7-336

Bowling

	O	M	R	W
Trott	24	4	99	2
Saggers	28.1	5	92	6
Ealham	17	5	53	0
Fleming	18	2	66	0
Symonds	19	2	61	0
Walker	3	0	9	1
Tredwell	8	2	38	1

	O	M	R	W
Saggers	19	3	85	3
Trott	17	0	64	2
Ealham	23	9	52	1
Tredwell	18	3	85	1
Fleming	11	1	39	0
Symonds	6	1	23	0
Walker	3	0	8	0
Fulton	1	0	2	0

KENT	1ST INNINGS		2ND INNINGS	
D.P. Fulton	b Malcolm	21	c Maddy b Ormond	22
R.W.T. Key	c Burns b Ormond	5	b Ormond	36
E.T. Smith	c Afridi b Ormond	19	run out	107
A. Symonds	c Ormond b Afridi	48	b Maddy	125
M.J. Walker	not out	120	c Burns b Ormond	12
M.A. Ealham	c Smith b Wells	5	(7) lbw b Maddy	14
†P.A. Nixon	lbw b Whiley	31	(8) not out	29
*M.V. Fleming	b Maddy	59	(6) c Afridi b Maddy	15
J.C. Tredwell	lbw b Sutcliffe	10		
M.J. Saggers	c Wells b Ormond	2	(9) not out	3
B.J. Trott	c & b Ormond	13		
Extras	(B 8, LB 14, NB 22, W 8, P 5)	57	(B 21, LB 9, NB 4, W 6)	40
TOTAL	(all out)	390	(for 7 wickets)	403

FOW: 1-18, 2-42, 3-80, 4-126, 5-153, 6-243, 7-334, 8-357, 9-362 1-62, 2-71, 3-306, 4-329, 5-336, 6-357, 7-380

Bowling

	O	M	R	W
Malcolm	27	6	82	1
Ormond	26.1	6	90	4
Afridi	10	2	48	1
Whiley	16	3	87	1
Wells	7	2	21	1
Maddy	13	3	28	1
Sutcliffe	2	0	7	1

	O	M	R	W
Ormond	31	7	114	3
Malcolm	10	1	59	0
Wells	2	0	2	0
Whiley	7	1	27	0
Maddy	22	1	118	3
Afridi	12	1	53	0

Kent won by 3 wickets

Kent's reply began hesitantly against the hostile bowling of Devon Malcolm, whose move to Leicestershire after three unproductive seasons with Northamptonshire had been greeted with some scepticism around the counties, and James Ormond. With 5 wickets down and a further 120 runs required to save the follow-on, prospects were not good. But a fighting undefeated innings by the left-handed Walker, ably and aggressively supported by captain Matthew Fleming, whose 59 included eleven boundaries, eased the situation. By the close of play the first target had been comfortably passed with Walker 107*. Kent added a further 56 runs the following morning and their total was boosted by

KENT v. LEICESTERSHIRE

Andrew Symonds. His 125 ensured Kent reached their high target.

57 extras, which included 22 no balls and a 5-run penalty resulting from the ball making contact with a fielder's discarded helmet.

As so often happens, Kent were to suffer at the hands of one of their former players. Trevor Ward, who had completely lost his form in his final season with his home county, scored his fourth century of the season and was awarded with his Leicestershire cap. Batting for just over four hours, his innings included 17 fours and a six. However, stunning catches by Ealham and Walker early in the innings had put Leicestershire somewhat on the defensive, but Ward's fourth-wicket stand of 129 with Darren Maddy redeemed the situation. His dismissal brought in the Pakistani all-rounder Shahid Afridi, who launched a vicious assault on the Kent attack, hitting 5 fours and 3 sixes in his 42 runs, scored off only 22 balls. He eventually holed out to Tredwell, giving the debutant a prized second wicket.

Leicestershire went into the final day 340 ahead and with 4 wickets in hand. They continued their innings for a further 10 overs, presumably with the intention of batting Kent out of the game and maybe to run through the Kent batting on a wicket beginning to show some signs of wear. The visitors were left a target of 401 off a minimum of 84 overs. Should they achieve the target it would be only the second time that they had scored over 400 to win a match. Australian one-day star Andrew Symonds, who had arrived mid-season as Kent's overseas player, joined Ed Smith after Kent had lost both openers shortly after lunch. In 47 overs they put on 235 with Symonds scoring at almost a run a ball and Smith playing an anchor role. Their partnership put Kent in with a chance but when 3 wickets fell for the addition of 30 runs it began to look as though a draw would be most likely. Ealham and Fleming raised hopes with quick runs, but as often happens they were both dismissed attempting to put the issue beyond doubt. Nixon meanwhile was clearly intent on getting one over on his previous county. He was joined by Martin Saggers, Kent's first-innings bowling hero, with 21 runs still required and only 2 overs to go. The first of those produced just 6 but, vitally, Nixon was to face the final over from Maddy. From each of the first 4 balls he scored 2 runs. Eight required off the final 2 – a draw was still odds on. Off the first, 4 runs, then amazingly a four off the final ball of the match. Nixon kicked the stumps over in jubilation and a slow-paced match had built to a tumultuous conclusion.

KENT v. NOTTINGHAMSHIRE

Date: 9-11 July 2003   **Location:** Maidstone

When, in the flurry of comings and goings of overseas players in 2003, Kent announced the signing in early June of the Pakistan fast bowler Mohammad Sami it was something of a surprise. Outside of Pakistan Test followers and other aficionados, little was known of him.

Those doubts seemed to be confirmed in his early matches as, amid a mass of no balls, he struggled to find his target. Taken in hand by Ian Brayshaw, Kent's Director of Cricket, suddenly things started to click. A ferocious spell in the Maidstone National League match three days before the Nottinghamshire game accounted for three top-order Glamorgan batsmen and confirmed a Kent win. But in the championship, the county had yet to register a success and the season was nearly half over.

Having won the toss against Nottinghamshire, Kent's innings was one of amazing frenzy to an extent that as early as 3.45 p.m. they were all out for 362, scored at a rate of 6 an over. The innings centred on Ed Smith who, in the middle of a remarkable spell of scoring noughts or hundreds, achieved the latter – a 96-ball hundred raised in the first over after lunch. For much of his career with Kent, Smith had flattered to deceive. A technically very correct batsman, he had never until this point confirmed the high hopes that his impressive start at Cambridge University suggested. The 2003 season found Smith in a more positive persona to the extent that he was selected for England. Smith found a partner in wicketkeeper Geraint Jones, with whom he added the 178 runs, which formed the basis of the total. Nottinghamshire began the reply somewhat more measuredly but suddenly, with the score on 113 for 2, Mohammad Sami, in an over of pure hostility, removed Russell Warren, nightwatchman Andrew Harris and Kevin Pietersen, at the time qualifying by residence for England and scoring many runs, to tilt the match Kent's way.

On the second morning Sami continued the carnage. In the opening half-hour he proceeded to take all the remaining 5 wickets in just 10 balls – all 8 in 38 balls – to give Kent a lead of 194. Somehow the Pakistan fast bowler had extracted something out of a slow, unresponsive pitch. Certainly there was no Nottinghamshire bowler who could do likewise as Kent, not enforcing the follow-on, pounded their attack to an extent that before the close, the visitors were back facing their nemesis with the little matter of a target of 625 before them. Key, having a very disappointing season, finally reached three figures before being out for 140 (239 balls, 1 six, 18 fours). Smith added 233 with Key, reaching his second hundred in a match for the first time (13 fours). Then, for good measure, Symonds thumped his way to an 81-ball hundred. By the close, Sami had already removed Guy Welton and, with the last ball of the day, a near shooter, the dangerous Darren Bicknell.

Nottinghamshire nevertheless fared somewhat better second time around. Captain Jason Gallian dug in and, aided by some good fortune and support from Kevin Pietersen, Chris Cairns and Paul Franks, a fourth day beckoned. No small factor in this was that Sami was off the field for a period with a sprained ankle. When he finally could bowl, it was not from the top end of the ground where he had taken his 10 wickets, but the lower end where a gentle breeze promised to help him gain just enough swing to resume where he had left off the day before. It did. The score of 330 for 5 became 337 all out, all the wickets to Sami. For the second time in the game he had taken the last 5 wickets in 14 balls, as

Mohammad Sami had one memorable record-breaking match for Kent.
[Anthony Roberts]

KENT v. NOTTINGHAMSHIRE

Kent won the toss and elected to bat   Umpires: A. Clarkson and A.A. Jones

KENT	1ST INNINGS		2ND INNINGS	
*D.P. Fulton	c Warren b Harris	6	c Warren b Smith	18
R.W.T. Key	run out	31	st Warren b Vettori	140
E.T. Smith	c Pietersen b Franks	149	c Vettori b Cairns	113
A. Symonds	c Warren b Vettori	8	not out	103
M.J. Walker	c Welton b Vettori	0	not out	11
M.A. Ealham	c Gallian b Vettori	5		
†G.O. Jones	c Gallian b Franks	82		
J.C. Tredwell	b Smith	16		
R.S. Ferley	not out	14		
Mohammad Sami	c Franks b Smith	16		
A. Sheriyar	c Franks b Vettori	0		
Extras	(B 5, LB 3, NB 26, W 1)	35	(B 6, LB 11, NB 14, W 2)	33
TOTAL	(all out)	362	(for 3 wickets declared)	418

FOW: 1-11, 2-98, 3-112, 4-112, 5-121, 6-299, 7-312, 8-336, 9-360   1-22, 2-255, 3-375

Bowling

	O	M	R	W
Smith	13	0	58	2
Harris	9	0	55	1
Franks	10	0	51	2
Logan	6	0	48	0
Vettori	14.3	2	74	4
Pietersen	6	0	39	0
Cairns	3	0	29	0

	O	M	R	W
Smith	12	0	55	1
Harris	14	4	62	0
Cairns	12	2	43	1
Franks	12	1	53	0
Vettori	20	0	124	1
Pietersen	7.3	0	48	0
Gallian	3	0	16	0

NOTTINGHAMSHIRE	1ST INNINGS		2ND INNINGS	
*J.E.R. Gallian	c Jones b Ferley	51	(2) c Tredwell b Sami	106
G.E. Welton	c Symonds b Ferley	17	(1) lbw b Sami	15
D.J. Bicknell	not out	37	b Sami	0
†R.J. Warren	c Jones b Sami	1	lbw b Tredwell	23
A.J. Harris	lbw b Sami	0	(11) b Sami	0
K.P. Pietersen	c Key b Sami	6	(5) c Smith b Symonds	62
C.L. Cairns	b Sami	19	(6) b Ealham	58
P.J. Franks	b Sami	0	(7) b Sami	45
D.L. Vettori	c Jones b Sami	0	(8) c Walker b Sami	0
R.J. Logan	c Tredwell b Sami	4	(9) not out	5
G.J. Smith	b Sami	1	(10) c Jones b Sami	2
Extras	(B 1, LB 9, NB 10)	20	(B 1, LB 11, NB 2, W 7)	21
TOTAL	(all out)	156	(all out)	337

FOW: 1-63, 2-106, 3-113, 4-113, 5-121, 6-146, 7-146, 8-146, 9-150   1-27, 2-29, 3-80, 4-158, 5-249, 6-330, 7-330, 8-331, 9-333

Bowling

	O	M	R	W
Sami	14.1	3	64	8
Sheriyar	6	3	17	0
Ferley	19	6	39	2
Ealham	5	1	17	0
Tredwell	5	2	9	0

	O	M	R	W
Sami	21.2	8	50	7
Sheriyar	13	2	40	0
Ferley	21	6	70	0
Ealham	13	4	39	1
Tredwell	21	5	84	1
Symonds	12	0	42	1

Kent won by 287 runs

fiercesome a piece of sustained hostile bowling as any Kent bowler had ever done. In all he took 15 for 114, the best Kent return since 1939, and the best ever by any bowler in a county match at the Mote.

Kent had signed Muttiah Muralitharan to replace the departing Andrew Symonds. A tasty prospect of the two in an attack together beckoned. The Sri Lankan spinner did bowl Kent out of trouble near the foot of the Division One table, but it was without Sami. His injured ankle ended his season with Kent after just nineteen days. He returned to Kent the following year, coming straight off the plane to take 6 wickets and bowl Kent to a remarkable win in their opening National League game. Then he claimed 10 wickets in the match to defeat Northamptonshire. That was it. His form and seemingly his commitment dipped and he departed for Pakistan almost unnoticed before June was out.

KENT v. WORCESTERSHIRE

Date: 21-24 April 2004   **Location:** Canterbury

It surely cannot often be the case that the month of April, with its not especially friendly cricket weather, produces record batting performances, but the St Lawrence ground witnessed one in this match. If Kent were to win they would have to record their highest ever fourth-innings total.

In a day severely restricted by rain, Worcestershire built a respectable total, although they were aided by a spate of no balls that gave them an additional and unearned 34 runs, David Stiff, Alamgir Sheriyar and Amjad Khan the guilty bowlers. Stephen Peters was the main beneficiary, reaching his fifty off a top-edged no ball and when on 68 being caught off another. Although he added only 8 further runs the damage had been done. Martin Saggers, who had started the season well, got the prized wicket of Graeme Hick, so often the scourge of Kent's bowlers, while captain Ben Smith, having struggled for fifty minutes, carved a catch into the covers. David Pipe, after hitting three fours, edged a seamer to slip and when rain finally ended the day's proceedings, Vikram Solanki had hit 3 fours and a six in his 32*.

If the second day belonged to anyone it was to David Fulton, who scored his first hundred following the dreadful eye injury he had sustained immediately before the beginning of the 2003 season. But before the home crowd was to rejoice in the emotion of that, they had to endure further frustrations. Worcestershire's last 5 wickets added another 189 runs with Solanki and the Australian Andy Bichel adding 122 for the sixth wicket. A typically frustrating 42* by veteran wicketkeeper Steven Rhodes saw the visitors past the 400 mark and 5 bonus points. They had achieved their total at virtually 4 runs an over. Kent's innings got off to a nightmare start with Nadeem Malik, a former England Under-19 regular who had left Nottinghamshire at the end of the previous season, taking the wickets of Robert Key and Ed Smith with successive balls. Fulton and Matthew Walker retrieved the situation, putting on 161 before stumps. However, neither lasted long the following morning, Fulton being dismissed with only 7 runs added to the overnight score and Walker departing soon after. The home crowd was far from impressed, with 8 wickets falling for 91 runs, giving Worcestershire a lead of 112.

Full advantage of this was taken by the visitors. They proceeded to score at a rate expected more from the limited-overs game. Kent made an early breakthrough but were to enjoy no further success until

late afternoon. While Graeme Hick hammered 89 runs in almost even time off just 79 balls and Ben Smith going on where Hick had left off with 78 off 60 balls, South African Steve Moore was quietly moving towards a maiden hundred in only his third match. In contrast to Hick and Smith, his 108* was scored off 168 balls in 213 minutes. In just three-and-a-half hours victory had seemingly been put way out of Kent's reach. When Worcestershire declared, the home county needed 429 to win.

There was to be no repeat of Fulton's heroic first innings for he and Ed Smith, who had a wretched match, both departed before the close. No one would have given Kent a chance at the start of the final day, with their score on 35 for 2. But Key and nightwatchman Martin Saggers added 72 in good time, with Saggers growing in confidence and getting good support from the in-form Matthew Walker. At lunch the total was 166 for 3 but shortly after, and without adding to his total, Saggers was out. He had

David Fulton. His first-innings hundred kept Kent in the game and ensured they had a chance in their record-breaking run chase.

Worcestershire won the toss and elected to bat Umpires: T.E. Jesty and J.F. Steele

WORCESTERSHIRE	1ST INNINGS			2ND INNINGS	
S.D. Peters	b Sheriyar		76	c Walker b Sheriyar	29
S.C. Moore	lbw b Khan		5	not out	108
G.A. Hick	c Tredwell b Saggers		38	c Tredwell b Carberry	89
*B.F. Smith	c Carberry b Khan		8	not out	78
V.S. Solanki	lbw b Stiff		84		
D.J. Pipe	c Tredwell b Sheriyar		12		
A.J. Bichel	c Smith b Tredwell		50		
†S.J. Rhodes	not out		42		
M.S. Mason	c Jones b Sheriyar		16		
S.A. Khalid	c Fulton b Sheriyar		0		
M.N. Malik	c Jones b Sheriyar		7		
Extras	(B 5, LB 13, NB 40, W 5)		63	(B 4, LB 4, NB 4)	12
TOTAL	(all out)		401	(for 2 wickets declared)	316

FOW: 1-6, 2-85, 3-130, 4-183, 5-195, 6-317, 7-331, 8-357, 9-357   1-52, 2-183

Bowling

	O	M	R	W
Saggers	26	9	70	1
Khan	20	2	100	2
Sheriyar	22.3	1	94	5
Stiff	17	3	68	1
Tredwell	16	2	51	1

	O	M	R	W
Saggers	10	3	32	0
Khan	8	1	42	0
Sheriyar	10	1	49	1
Stiff	9	2	46	0
Tredwell	15	1	83	0
Carberry	8	0	56	1

KENT	1ST INNINGS			2ND INNINGS	
*D.P. Fulton	c Hick b Mason		107	b Mason	16
R.W.T. Key	c Smith b Malik		13	lbw b Malik	46
E.T. Smith	c Solanki b Malik		0	lbw b Mason	6
M.J. Walker	lbw b Malik		70	(5) not out	151
M.A. Carberry	c Peters b Mason		10	(6) b Malik	112
†G.O. Jones	c Rhodes b Mason		0	(7) not out	20
J.C. Tredwell	not out		51		
A. Khan	lbw b Malik		1		
M.J. Saggers	lbw b Malik		1	(4) lbw b Mason	64
D.A. Stiff	b Bichel		4		
A. Sheriyar	c Khalid b Mason		5		
Extras	(B 6, LB 9, NB 10, W 2)		27	(B 5, LB 5, NB 4)	14
TOTAL	(all out)		289	(for 5 wickets)	429

FOW: 1-30, 2-30, 3-198, 4-221, 5-225, 6-227, 7-239, 8-249, 9-254   1-17, 2-33, 3-105, 4-170, 5-406

Bowling

	O	M	R	W
Bichel	24	5	74	1
Mason	23.3	8	55	4
Malik	20	3	88	5
Khalid	14	4	42	0
Hick	3	0	15	0

	O	M	R	W
Bichel	21	2	101	0
Mason	24	6	86	3
Malik	19	3	93	2
Khalid	29.3	7	88	0
Solanki	16	1	51	0

Kent won by 5 wickets

recorded his highest first-class score, but Kent were still a long, long way from even survival, let alone a most unlikely victory. Michael Carberry, who was in his second season with the county, had scored a century in the previous match. He set out showing the determination for a repeat performance. His first three scoring shots were boundaries. By tea Kent were 289 for 4 with Carberry 45* and Walker having just completed his century. Victory began to look a possibility but much would depend on the two not-out batsman remaining at the crease to see it achieved. However, that was not to be. With 23 runs still needed Carberry was Malik's second victim of the innings. His 112 had come off 157 balls and he had batted for three-and-a-half hours. But there were to be no alarms in the final stages. Geraint Jones scored 20 of the runs required and what should have been an impossible task was instead a memorable and history-making victory, due more than anything to the self-belief of Matthew Walker and Michael Carberry.

Quite remarkable was that this was also Kent's first victory over Worcestershire at Canterbury since 1914 and their first home success against them on any Kent ground since 1975.

KENT v. SURREY

Date: 20-23 July 2005   **Location:** Guildford

A match where some of the play was referred to as 'dire' is not an obvious justification for inclusion in this volume. But the game's final session conjured up one of Kent's more improbable victories.

Kent and Surrey were vying for the top of the championship. The game was played on the flattest of pitches with an outfield baked yellow by weeks of dry weather. Thus, when Surrey won the toss, Kent were given a long hard day in the field. The main point of interest was Graham Thorpe's 95, made with more than a passing glance to the Test selectors' contentious decision not to include him in the first Ashes Test. Sharing in partnerships of 133 and 98 with Mark Ramprakash and Alistair Brown, Thorpe, frustrated by lack of strike, was finally out just short of his hundred. Ramprakash also perished in the nineties, while Brown, not chancelessly, finally made that three-figure score. Closing on 394 for 5 with Brown still there, a big score beckoned.

That did not happen. Surrey stuttered a bit on the second day and at 452 for 8, with 500 still not beyond question, stand-in captain Ramprakash declared. A challenging declaration? Possibly, but a more cynical opinion could be to deny rivals Kent an extra bowling bonus point. Kent found the conditions equally agreeable, aided by a none-too-penetrative bowling attack. Key was in no apparent trouble until he was out for 65 while, after a little wobble, Walker found a determined partner in Justin Kemp to take the Kent score within striking distance of Surrey, 44 runs with 6 wickets left, by the close of play.

The South African all-rounder Kemp had been a controversial recruit to the Kent side. Having previously announced that they would only take another overseas player in an emergency, the arrival of Kemp, who had performed well against England in the previous winter, caused some surprise. This was not assuaged when Kemp's noted limited-overs abilities singularly failed to shine as Kent disintegrated in the Twenty20 competition and slid down to new lower depths in Division Two of the totesport League. However, here at last he found his feet and, with some memorable straight driving, moved effortless to a century off 125 balls.

The following day, the Walker-Kemp partnership reached 233 off 53 overs before Azhar Mahmood found some away-swing to clip Kemp's off stump. Walker batted on to be sixth out for 173 with 23 fours and 2 sixes. Kent were finally all out just 7 runs short of their highest total ever against their western neighbours.

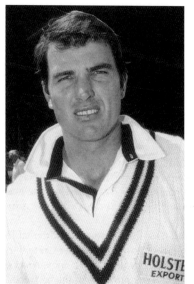

A first innings lead of 120 runs in a bat-dominated encounter did not seem decisive, particularly when Surrey drifted past that initial target with only 1 wicket down. With Ramprakash and Thorpe going well at the close of the third day, it was all heading towards a seemingly inevitable draw.

That conclusion was maintained through much of the final day. Certainly a sparse crowd was hardly enthused as Surrey seemed to bat out time – just six boundaries before lunch. But suddenly, having lost only 3 wickets for 269 in 95 overs, they contrived to lose their last 7 in just 25. Min Patel, having bowled 41 overs without success, found the odd ball turning. So encouraged, Fulton crowded the bat and with some spectacular catching, three bad-pad, the spinner ended the innings with a spell of 4 for 15 in 33 balls. Nevertheless, the post-tea target of 231 off 35 overs (i.e. 6.6 an over) was not straightforward. Fulton and Key opened with a stand of 83 in 14 overs then wickets fell steadily. Hall clubbed a six and 2 fours in his 17

Justin Kemp. His two hard-hitting innings saw Kent through to an unexpected victory.

Surrey won the toss and elected to bat   Umpires: R.A. Kettleborough and B. Leadbeater

SURREY	1ST INNINGS		2ND INNINGS	
†J.N. Batty	c Walker b Patel	50	c Walker b Hall	55
R.S. Clinton	c Kemp b Cook	0	c Fulton b Khan	45
*M.R. Ramprakash	c O'Brien b Cook	97	c O'Brien b Cook	62
G.P. Thorpe	b Patel	95	c Stevens b van Jaarsveld	47
A.D. Brown	c O'Brien b Khan	107	b Walker	34
R. Clarke	b Stevens	18	b Patel	7
Azhar Mahmood	lbw b Hall	41	c Fulton b Patel	25
I.D.K. Salisbury	c O'Brien b Patel	15	c van Jaarsveld b Patel	20
J. Ormond	not out	2	not out	2
N.D. Doshi	not out	0	c Stevens b Hall	4
Mohammad Akram	c van Jaarsveld b Patel	0		
Extras	(B 7, LB 1, NB 16, W 3)	27	(B 25, LB 11, NB 12, W 1)	49
TOTAL	(for 8 wickets declared)	452	(all out)	350

FOW: 1-4, 2-105, 3-238, 4-336, 5-382, 6-400, 7-449, 8-451   1-107, 2-142, 3-240, 4-269, 5-292, 6-301, 7-331, 8-344, 9-349

Bowling

	O	M	R	W
Khan	21	4	92	1
Cook	17	3	78	2
Hall	21.4	4	73	1
Kemp	17	0	60	0
Patel	30	6	96	3
Stevens	11	0	40	1
Key	1	0	5	0

	O	M	R	W
Khan	20	2	86	1
Cook	15	3	37	1
Patel	47.2	8	110	4
Hall	15	5	22	2
Kemp	3	0	16	0
Walker	4	1	6	1
Stevens	13	0	25	0
van Jaarsveld	2	0	12	1

KENT	1ST INNINGS		2ND INNINGS	
*D.P. Fulton	c Brown b Azhar	39	c Clinton b Salisbury	31
R.W.T. Key	b Doshi	65	lbw b Akram	47
M. van Jaarsveld	c Batty b Ormond	36	c Ramprakash b Doshi	25
M.J. Walker	c Doshi b Akram	173	lbw b Akram	18
D.I. Stevens	lbw b Azhar	0	c Clinton b Doshi	4
J.M. Kemp	b Azhar	124	not out	47
A.J. Hall	c Batty b Doshi	24	c Brown b Azhar	17
†N.J. O'Brien	lbw b Salisbury	46	not out	23
M.M. Patel	st Batty b Doshi	27		
S.J. Cook	c Batty b Salisbury	13		
A. Khan	not out	1		
Extras	(B 4, LB 6, NB 14)	24	(B 2, LB 9, NB 8, W 1)	20
TOTAL	(all out)	572	(for 6 wickets)	232

FOW: 1-58, 2-122, 3-201, 4-202, 5-435, 6-483, 7-495, 8-523, 9-571   1-83, 2-87, 3-121, 4-126, 5-140, 6-175

Bowling

	O	M	R	W
Akram	24	2	114	1
Ormond	28	1	109	1
Azhar	24	2	104	3
Clarke	9	0	53	0
Doshi	30	3	111	3
Salisbury	14.5	0	71	2

	O	M	R	W
Ormond	9	0	68	0
Azhar	8.1	0	49	1
Doshi	7	0	58	2
Salisbury	4	0	25	1
Akram	6	0	30	2

Kent won by 4 wickets

from 16 balls, but at 175 for 6 with just 6 overs remaining, victory still seemed unlikely. But Kemp came again and, unperturbed by nine fielders on the boundary, hit three enormous sixes into the adjacent Woodbridge Road. Supported by wicketkeeper Niall O'Brien, the pair took 17 off the penultimate over bowled by Ormond, including a final six by Kemp out of the ground, leaving O'Brien to end the game with a four off the first ball of the last over.

Kent's championship hopes were rekindled as the 21 points took them back to the top of the table. Although they had remained in contention for much of the season, they fell away badly after Canterbury Week. As for Surrey, this totally unexpected defeat heralded a slump that brought not a single success until the last match of the season, when it was too late, and they slid into Division Two for the first time.

Other titles published by Tempus

Kent County Cricket Club
WILLIAM A. POWELL

Founded in 1870 through the merging of the Canterbury and Maidstone clubs, the Kent team have enjoyed success in the County Championship as well as various cup competitions, their greatest era beginning in 1967 and lasting through until 1978. With a selection of over 220 images including memorabilia illustrating the team's history since the nineteenth century, this book will appeal to all fans of Kent CCC.

0 7524 1871 8

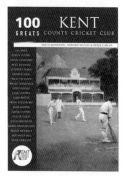

Kent CCC 100 Greats
DAVID ROBERTSON, HOWARD MILTON & DEREK CARLAW

In its long history the county of Kent has had more than its fair share of great cricketers. Men like Nicholas Felix in the mid-nineteenth century led the way, and the likes of Frank Woolley and Colin Blythe followed. This book features illustrations, career statistics and biographies of 100 of the finest, including cricketers from 'The Glory Years' of the 1960s and '70s, such as Colin Cowdrey and Derek Underwood, and some of Kent's best-loved players of the last few years, including Mark Ealham and Matthew Fleming.

0 7524 3454 3

Victory England's Greatest Modern Test Wins
ALAN BONE

With a foreword and commentary from the inimitable Christopher Martin-Jenkins and a wealth of illustration, this book highlights the most memorable occasions on which England has triumphed, be it a consummate thrashing of the opposition or an epic against-all-odds comeback from the brink of defeat. Featuring match reports and scorecards from thirty fine victories including the 2005 Ashes wins at Edgbaston and Trent Bridge, this is a source of great nostalgia and delight for all England cricket fans.

0 7524 3415 2

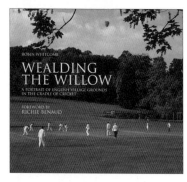

Wealding the Willow
ROBIN WHITCOMB

The Weald area of South East England has been known as 'the cradle of cricket', being the place where the game first started, and in many communities there the cricket ground is still, along with the church and the local pub, at the very centre of village life. With a foreword by the much-loved cricket commentator Richie Benaud, this is a beautifully illustrated record of the great game and the places where it all began.

0 7524 3457 8

If you are interested in purchasing other books published by Tempus, or in case you have difficulty finding any Tempus books in your local bookshop, you can also place orders directly through our website

www.tempus-publishing.com